3R

EUREKA!

Success in Science

Carol Chapman
Rob Musker
Daniel Nicholson
Moira Sheehan

Heinemann

Introduction

Welcome to Eureka! Success in Science

This is the third of three books designed to help you learn all the science ideas you need during Key Stage 3. We hope you'll enjoy the books as well as learning a lot from them.

These two pages will help you get the most out of the book so it's worth spending a couple of minutes reading them!

This book has six units which each cover a different topic. The units have three types of pages:

Setting the scene

Each unit starts with a double-page spread which reminds you of what you know already about the topic. They tell you other interesting things, such as the place of science in everyday life and the history of some science inventions and ideas.

Learn about

- Energy

Most of the double-page spreads in a unit introduce and explain new ideas about the topic. They start with a list of these so that you can see what you are going to learn about.

Think about

- Fair tests

Each unit has a double-page spread called Think about. You will work in pairs or small groups and discuss your answers to the questions. These pages will help you understand how scientists work and how ideas about science develop.

On the pages there are these symbols:

Identical twins

These blue boxes in the text revise relevant ideas that you have already met in *Eureka! 1* and *Eureka! 2*.

a Make a list of foods that give you a lot of energy.

Quick questions scattered through the pages help you check your knowledge and understanding of the ideas as you go along.

Questions

The questions at the end of the spread help you check you understand all the important ideas.

When you revise

These blue boxes list the important ideas from the spread to help you learn, write notes and revise.

This shows there is a practical activity which your teacher may give you. These will help you plan and carry out investigations into ideas about science and collect and analyse results and evaluate your work.

This shows there is an ICT activity which your teacher may give you. You will use computers to collect results from datalogging experiments, or work with spreadsheets and databases, or get useful information from CD-ROMS or the Internet.

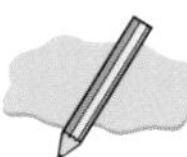

This shows there is a writing activity which your teacher may give you to help you write about the science you learn.

This shows there is a discussion activity which your teacher may give you. You will share your ideas about science with others in a discussion.

This book also has three revision units: biology, chemistry and physics. They will help you revise what you need to know for the national tests. See pages 86–87.

At the back of the book:

All the new scientific words in the text in units 1–6 appear in **bold** type. They are listed with their meanings in the Glossary at the back of the book. Look there to remind yourself what they mean.

There is an index at the very back of the book, where you can find out which pages cover a particular topic.

Activities to check your learning

Your teacher may give you these activities:

Lift-off! When you start a unit, this short exercise reminds you what you already know about a topic.

Unit map You can use this to think about what you already know about a topic. You can also use it to revise a topic before a test or exam.

Quiz You can use the quiz at the end of each unit to see what you are good at and what you might need to revise.

Revision 1 You can use the revision sheets to revise a part of a unit which you aren't so good at.

End of unit test This helps you and your teacher check what you learned during the unit, and measures your progress and success.

Contents

T indicates Think about spread

1.1 Women in white coats?

Perfumes of Babylon

Many people think of scientists as 'men in white coats'. This is an example of stereotyping, or putting people into broad groups which are not always accurate. In fact there have always been women scientists. As early as 1200 BC, Tapputi Belatekallim and her fellow woman researcher Ninu extracted perfumes from plants. They used the same separation techniques such as dissolving and distillation that we use today.

a How do you think the Babylonians extracted the perfume from plants? Suggest a method.

A Babylonian perfume bottle.

The fate of Fang

Fang was a Chinese chemist. She lived at about the time of the first century BC. She thought that she had discovered a way of changing mercury into silver. What she probably did in fact was to use mercury to obtain silver from rocks. Very few metals are found as the metal element. Most metals are found as rocks called ores. The ore is mined from the ground and the useful parts are separated and changed into the pure metal by a chemical reaction. This method of extracting silver using mercury was discovered in the western world in the sixteenth century.

Fang's husband tortured her to find out the secret of her discovery. She did not tell him and finally killed herself after going insane. Her insanity was probably caused by mercury poisoning!

b Explain why modern scientists do not accept Fang's idea about where the silver came from.

A more active role

In the first century AD, Maria Hebraea invented the water bath for heating substances gently in experiments. It still has the French name *bain-marie* named after her. Maria also discovered the formula for hydrochloric acid.

In western society, it has not always been easy for women to follow their interests in chemistry for cultural or religious reasons. A lot of early scientific research happened in monasteries. The university system had its roots in the religious orders and excluded women. Even Queen Elizabeth I insisted on banning women from universities.

In the eighteenth and nineteenth centuries many women chemists helped their famous husbands, but did not get the recognition they deserved. In the eighteenth century, Antoine Lavoisier's wife helped him with his work. By the twentieth century, the universities were open to women and the First World War gave women many opportunities because the men were called to the battle front.

Maria Hebraea.

Marie Curie

The first woman to be awarded a Nobel prize for chemistry was Marie Curie. Marie Sklodowska was born in Poland. In 1891, she travelled from Poland across Germany to France to study at the Sorbonne University in France. At that time, women were not allowed into Polish universities.

Marie gained a good degree in physics and maths and continued with her studies in Paris. It was there that she met Pierre Curie, who was in charge of a laboratory. Pierre was too shy to talk to Marie at first, and he sent her copies of his work on magnetism. Marie continued her scientific work and was the first woman in Europe to become a doctor of physics. Eventually Marie and Pierre were married.

Marie had heard about a chemical element called uranium which is found in an ore called pitchblende. Uranium was unusual because if you put it on a photographic film, it produced an image of itself. No one understood why.

She discovered another element that behaved the same way, and called it polonium after her home, Poland. Marie did not stop there, and after four long years she extracted another similar element, which she named radium. We now describe these elements as radioactive. Marie needed a massive amount of rock to extract just a few grains of radium. When Marie and Pierre went back to the laboratory at night, they found that this new element glowed in the dark!

In 1906, Pierre was killed in a road accident when he was hit by a horse and carriage. Marie carried on with her work in science. During the First World War, Marie set up X-ray units in the hospital battlefields. Vans with X-ray machines in them were called the 'petites Curies'. Marie was awarded a Nobel prize in 1911 for the discovery of the elements polonium and radium.

Ironically, it was only after Marie's death in 1934 that scientists realised that the radiation from the elements she had discovered caused the leukaemia that killed her. Today we use radium to treat cancer. Marie Curie's daughter Irene followed in her mother's footsteps and also gained a Nobel prize for chemistry in 1935.

c i Why did Marie Curie travel from Poland to France?

ii Suggest reasons why Marie Curie's discovery of the elements polonium and radium was worthy of a Nobel prize.

Dorothy Hodgkin

The only other woman to receive a Nobel prize for chemistry was Dorothy Hodgkin. At school, physics clashed with cookery, so being female, Dorothy had to do cookery. This was the last time that her gender got in the way of her career in science. She studied chemistry at Oxford University. She went on to discover the structures of three important molecules, insulin, penicillin and vitamin B12, using X-rays to study their crystals. In 1964, she was awarded a Nobel prize for her work on vitamin B12.

d How did Dorothy Hodgkin build on Marie Curie's work?

Questions

1. Make a time line to show some of the achievements of women chemists.
2. Imagine you are Marie Curie. Write a letter home to Poland with news of your life in Paris and your work.
3. Describe two ways in which Marie Curie demonstrated her commitment and passion for science.
4. Why do you think Marie Curie had to work so hard to extract a few grains of radium from pitchblende?
5. What unusual property does radium have?
6. Describe a problem that Dorothy Hodgkin experienced in realising her scientific ambition. How do you think she overcame it?

1.2 Everyday changes

Learn about

- Useful and not so useful chemical changes

Chemical reactions

In a chemical reaction, the reactants combine chemically to form new products. There is usually evidence of a chemical change taking place. After a chemical change, you might see:

- a colour change, if the reactants are different colours from the products
- a **precipitate**, if a solid mass 'falls out' of the solution
- a gas given off, such as carbon dioxide or hydrogen
- a temperature rise or fall, if thermal energy is released or taken in.

A precipitate appears when sodium iodide reacts with lead nitrate dissolved in water.

Some chemical reactions are useful, like the ones that happen when substances from oil are made into plastics and even cosmetics. Other reactions such as the corrosion of metals are not useful.

Contamination checks

A chemist might use a precipitation reaction to monitor the contamination of water courses (rivers and streams).

If the water is sampled near an estuary, the river water might have a high salinity (sodium chloride content). If silver nitrate solution is added to the water sample, the silver nitrate reacts with the sodium chloride to produce a white precipitate of silver chloride.

silver nitrate	+	sodium chloride	→	sodium nitrate	+	silver chloride
clear solution		*clear solution*		*clear solution*		*white precipitate*

This test is very sensitive. The silver nitrate solution must be made with distilled water rather than tap water, otherwise the slightest trace of sodium chloride present in the water will make the silver nitrate white before the test.

a How do we know that the silver nitrate test is very sensitive?

Yoghurt and yeast

Respiration in microbes is a useful chemical reaction. Yoghurt is made by adding a particular culture of bacteria to milk. The bacteria use a sugar called lactose in the milk for respiration. They produce lactic acid which gives yoghurt its sour taste. The lactic acid prevents unwanted bacteria from growing in the milk and making it go 'off'.

Yeast is a microorganism that is used in brewing and baking. It respires and changes sugar to ethanol (alcohol) and carbon dioxide in a reaction called fermentation. In brewing, the useful product is alcohol. In bread-making, the carbon dioxide is useful because it makes the bread rise.

Cars and chemical reactions

Cars are manufactured using lots of different materials and chemical reactions.

- The plastic for the dashboards has been formed from oil.
- The glass for the windscreen is made from sand.
- The steel for the body contains iron that has been extracted from iron ore.

b Give two examples of chemical reactions being used to make materials for a car. Describe the raw materials and the products.

Rusting

In cars, some of the chemical reactions that take place are useful and some are not useful. Most cars are made of steel. Eventually the steel rusts, because it is a mixture of iron and other elements. Rusting is a chemical reaction. The iron combines with oxygen to form iron oxide, which is rust.

Combustion

When petrol burns in a car engine, the useful chemical reaction is combustion. Petrol is a mixture of hydrocarbons and when it burns in a good supply of oxygen, energy is released. Some of the energy stored in the petrol is transferred to the pistons, which move up and down. The engine transfers this kinetic energy to the wheels of the car.

hydrocarbons + oxygen → carbon dioxide + water

Carbon dioxide in the atmosphere is not toxic, but increased levels add to the greenhouse effect and global warming. Carbon dioxide in the atmosphere is used by growing forests for photosynthesis.

C Which reaction uses up the carbon dioxide produced in combustion reactions? Explain why is it a useful reaction.

Combustion in car engines is not completely efficient. A lack of oxygen getting to the fuel leads to **incomplete combustion**, which produces poisonous **carbon monoxide**:

hydrocarbons + oxygen → carbon monoxide + water

Carbon monoxide and carbon dioxide are part of the waste gases or **emissions** from a car exhaust. The emissions also contain unburned hydrocarbons and carbon particles that come from incomplete combustion. Inside the hot engine, nitrogen in the air reacts with oxygen to form oxides of nitrogen. If nitrogen oxides and hydrocarbons get into the air and the sun shines on them, a haze is formed called a **photochemical smog**. It stings the eyes and aggravates asthma. Chemical reactions take place in the smog producing **ozone**, a toxic form of oxygen. Ozone causes breathing problems and harms plants.

Photochemical smog in Los Angeles.

Catalytic converters

All new cars are fitted with a three-way catalytic converter. This is a device that contains two expensive metals, platinum and rhodium. Three useful reactions happen in a catalytic converter:

- the oxidation of unburned hydrocarbons to carbon dioxide and water
- the conversion of carbon monoxide to carbon dioxide
- nitrogen oxides lose oxygen and become nitrogen.

Questions

1. a Explain why rusting is not a useful chemical reaction.
   b How are car bodies protected from rust?
2. Write a paragraph about useful reactions in the food industry. Include these words: bacteria, yeast, fermentation, respiration.
3. Where might precipitation be a useful reaction?
4. Write down some suggestions to encourage people to use their cars less and walk to work.
5. A gas responsible for global warming is not removed from exhaust emissions by a catalytic converter. Which gas is this? How can we solve this problem?
6. Write a news item to explain to the people of Los Angeles how smog is formed.

When you revise

Virtually all of the materials around us are made by chemical reactions.

Some chemical reactions are useful and some are not. Rusting is not useful, but combustion is often useful to us.

1.3 Acids on test

Learn about

- Useful and not so useful reactions of acids

Acids

An acid is a solution of a particular kind of solid or gas in water. Some acids are found in foods and give them a sour taste. Other acids may be corrosive, toxic, harmful or irritant. You can use an indicator to find out whether a solution is acidic. Indicators give different colours with acidic, alkaline and neutral solutions. An acid reacts with a base to form a salt and water.

Useful acids

Fact file

Extinguishing fires

A simple acid and carbonate reaction is used in red fire extinguishers. Inside the fire extinguisher there is a concentrated sodium carbonate solution, a foaming agent and a glass bottle of concentrated sulfuric acid. Squeezing the trigger on the fire extinguisher breaks the glass bottle. The acid reacts with the carbonate to produce carbon dioxide gas, which forces the water out. The foaming solution of carbon dioxide in water puts out the fire.

The word equation for this reaction is:

sulfuric acid + sodium carbonate → sodium sulfate + carbon dioxide + water

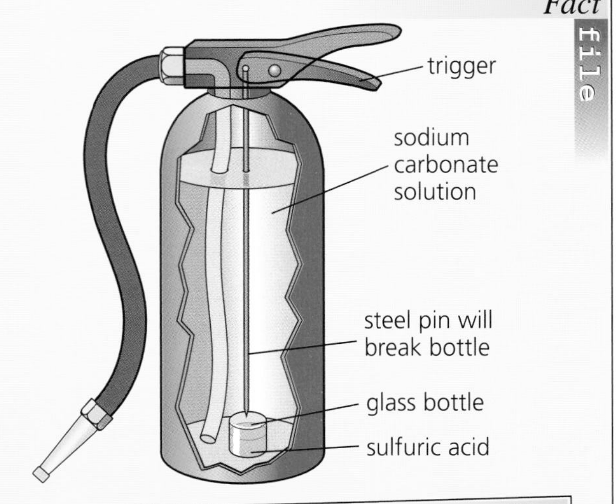

Fact file

Manufacturing industry

Acids are used to manufacture a variety of products including fertilisers. Many fertilisers contain ammonium nitrate or ammonium sulfate. These salts are made by neutralising nitric acid or sulfuric acid. The word equations are:

sulfuric acid + ammonium hydroxide → ammonium sulfate + water

nitric acid + ammonium hydroxide → ammonium nitrate + water

Ammonia and nitrates contain nitrogen atoms, and plants need nitrogen for growth. Ammonium nitrate is a particularly good fertiliser because it contains lots of nitrogen. All nitrates are soluble in water, so they provide nitrogen in a form that plants can take in through their roots.

Fact file

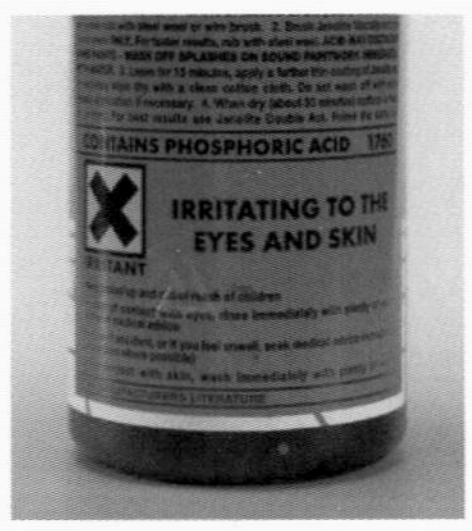

Stopping rust

Phosphoric acid reacts with any rust on the surface of iron or steel objects. This leaves a clean surface that you can protect with zinc, paint or oil.

Fact file

Preserving food

Bacteria cannot survive in conditions of low pH. Vinegar contains ethanoic acid. It is used to pickle food such as onions and red cabbage.

a Describe three useful reactions of acids.

Acids attack

Fact file

Corrosion

Corrosive acids are transported in tankers by road and rail, because they are needed in large amounts for manufacturing industries. If an accident happens and acid is spilled, it will react with metals and other building materials, corroding them. The acid will also corrode any flesh it comes into contact with. Acids should be handled with care. The word equation for the corrosion of zinc is:

sulfuric acid + zinc → zinc sulfate + hydrogen

b What does the hazard warning sign on the back of the tanker mean?

Fact file

Acid rain

Burning fossil fuels creates acid rain. Fossil fuels often contain sulfur as an impurity. The sulfur burns, producing sulfur dioxide. This dissolves in the rain and eventually makes a weak solution of sulfuric acid. Nitrogen dioxide from car exhausts also dissolves in the rain, forming nitric acid. These two acids produce acid rain. Acid rain corrodes buildings, kills fish and damages plants. Power stations spray their waste gases with water and quicklime to dissolve the sulfur dioxide and neutralise the acid produced. This is the reaction:

calcium oxide + sulfuric acid → calcium sulfate + water

c Which two acids are present in acid rain?

Fact file

Acid on the rocks

Rainwater is naturally acidic because some of the carbon dioxide in the air dissolves in the rain to make a weakly acidic solution called carbonic acid. Over millions of years, naturally acidic rainwater and acid rain have slowly dissolved away limestone rocks. Limestone is mainly made of calcium carbonate, so it reacts with the acid. A general word equation for this reaction is:

acid + carbonate → salt + water + carbon dioxide

d Write the word equation for the reaction between sulfuric acid and calcium carbonate.

Monitoring air pollution

Some species of plant and animal are very sensitive to sulfur dioxide poisoning. **Lichens** are made of up two organisms living together, an alga and a fungus. They grow on tree bark and bare rocks. Sulfur dioxide is toxic to some types of lichen and stops them growing in some areas. We can look at the lichens growing in an area to get an idea of the level of sulfur dioxide pollution.

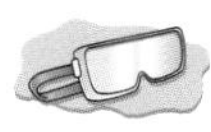

e Why is it useful to be able to monitor sulfur dioxide levels in the air?

Questions

1. Draw a diagram of a red fire extinguisher to show its internal design and describe how it works. Write a word equation for the chemical reaction that takes place when the trigger is squeezed.
2. Which acid: **a** dissolves rust? **b** is used to manufacture ammonium sulfate?
3. Explain how acids preserve food.
4. Which type of chemical reaction is used in the manufacture of fertilisers? Write a word equation for the reaction to produce ammonium nitrate fertiliser.
5. What health and safety precautions do you think should be taken when acids are transported?
6. Some lichens can only live in very clean air with only a trace of sulfur dioxide. Would you expect these lichens to grow on tree trunks in an industrial area? Give a reason for your answer.

When you revise

Reactions of acids are used in fire extinguishers, food preserving and manufacturing industries.

Reactions of acids that are not useful include corrosion and the effects of acid rain.

1.4 It's elementary my dear!

Learn about

- Elements and compounds
- Symbols and formulae

Atoms and molecules

Everything around us is made up of particles. An atom is the smallest particle of an element. An element contains only one type of atom. A molecule is a group of two or more atoms chemically combined together. An oxygen molecule has two oxygen atoms combined together. Compounds are formed by chemical reactions, when atoms of different elements combine together.

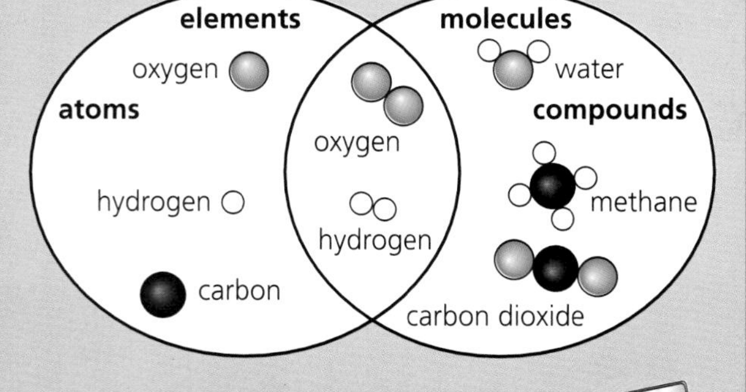

a i Explain the difference between an atom and a molecule.

ii How many molecules are shown in the diagram opposite?

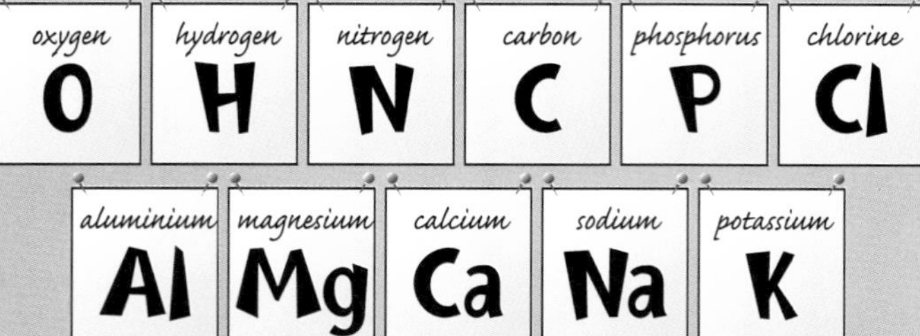

Symbols

We know about 118 elements, and new ones are being discovered all the time. Each element has its own symbol. You can find the symbols on a periodic table. Each symbol is made up of one or two letters. Scientists around the world may speak different languages, but they all use the same symbols. Some symbols are shown opposite.

Compounds in short

If you take elements such as hydrogen and oxygen, you can combine them in different ways to make different compounds. All of the atoms in the reactants end up in the products. The number of each type of atom combining to form a particular compound is always the same. For example, one atom of oxygen combines with two atoms of hydrogen to make one molecule of water. We can draw circles to represent the atoms in the molecule, as shown here:

Or we can write the molecule using the formula H_2O. In the formula, symbols represent the atoms and the numbers tell us how many of each kind of atom there are in the compound. The number '2' is called a subscript number and you cannot change this in the formula for water. If you had a different number of hydrogen or oxygen atoms, the compound would not be water.

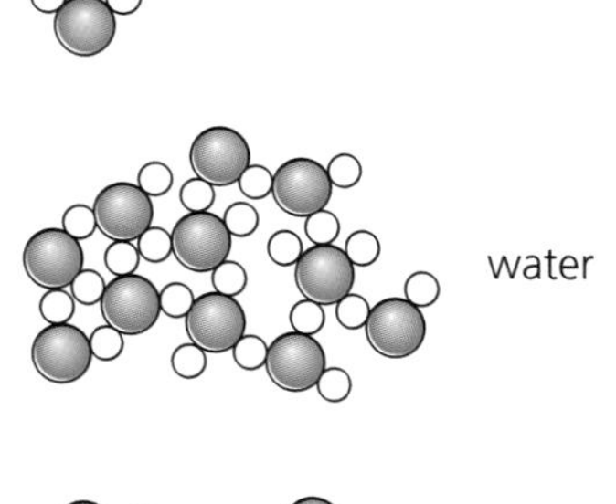

Ratios

In water, there are two hydrogen atoms for every oxygen atom. In the diagram of water molecules, the ratio of hydrogen atoms to oxygen atoms is 2:1, and the formula of water is H_2O.

Look at the diagram of carbon dioxide. In the four carbon dioxide molecules, there are 4 carbon atoms and 8 oxygen atoms. There are twice as many oxygen atoms as carbon atoms. The ratio of carbon atoms to oxygen atoms is 4:8, which can be simplified to 1:2. The formula of carbon dioxide is CO_2.

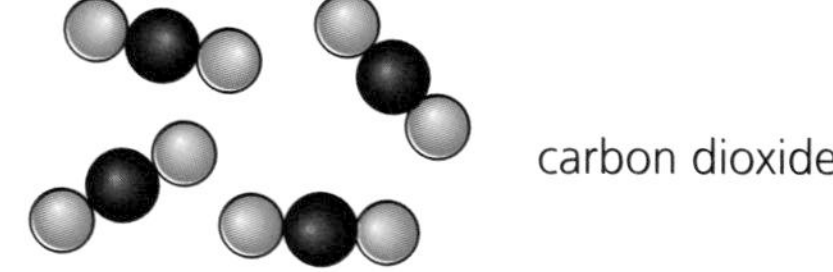

The ratio of the different atoms in a compound is always the same.

b i What is the ratio of carbon atoms to hydrogen atoms in methane?

ii What is the formula of methane?

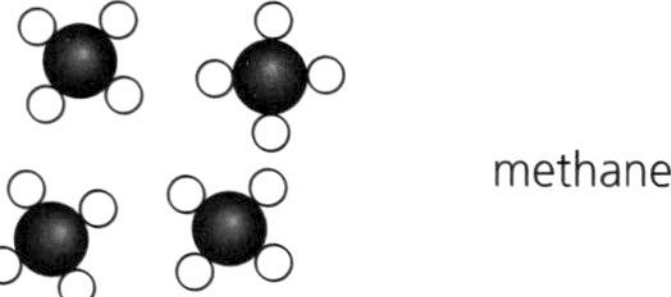

Chemical bonds

Atoms are joined together by forces of attraction called **chemical bonds**. Different atoms can make different numbers of bonds. A hydrogen atom can make only one bond. An oxygen atom can make two bonds. So an oxygen atom can bond with two hydrogen atoms.

Carbon makes four bonds, so it can join with two oxygen atoms.

Chlorine makes one bond. Nitrogen makes three bonds.

water H_2O

carbon dioxide CO_2

c Write the formula for each molecule shown below.

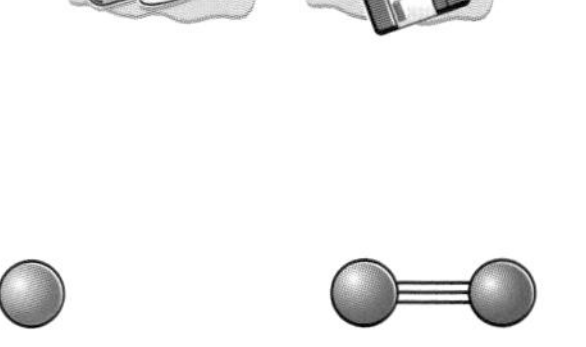

ammonia

hydrogen chloride

oxygen

nitrogen

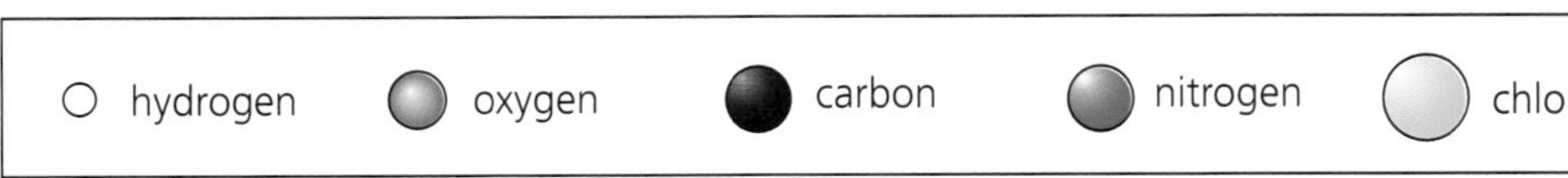

Exceptions to the rule

We have seen that there are rules about how many bonds each type of atom can make. Rules can be helpful, but they do not always work. Instead of making carbon dioxide, carbon and oxygen can combine to form carbon monoxide. The formula for carbon monoxide is CO.

d Find the meaning of the term chemical bond.

Questions

1. Explain how compounds are formed.
2. Explain why these formulae are correct:
   a methane CH_4
   b hydrogen chloride HCl.
3. Give one advantage and one disadvantage of using rules to work out the formulae of compounds.
4. **a** Why is the formula of water always written as H_2O?
   b Hydrogen atoms and oxygen atoms do not only combine to make water. They can combine to make a compound called hydrogen peroxide, which has the formula H_2O_2. Draw a diagram showing how you think this molecule might look.
5. Explain why carbon monoxide is an exception to the rule when it comes to bonding.

When you revise

Everything is made up of particles. Atoms are the smallest particles of an element.

Elements have only one type of atom. Each element has its own symbol.

Molecules have two or more atoms chemically combined.

Compounds are formed by chemical reactions when different atoms combine together. The atoms are joined by **chemical bonds**.

The chemical formula of a compound shows the ratio of different types of atom in the compound.

1.5 Atoms don't change

Learn about

- Conserving mass
- Equations

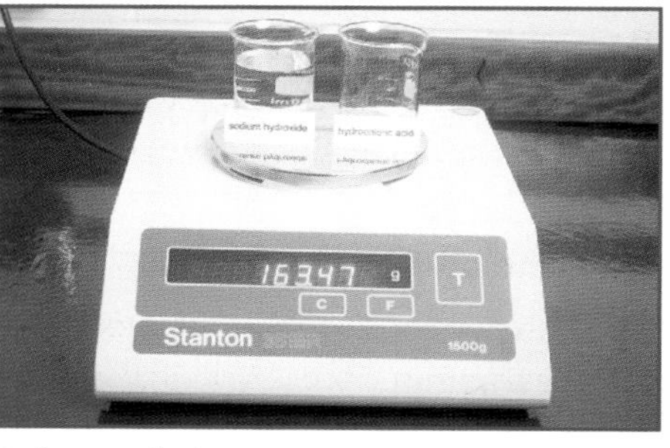

Before and after mixing.

Mass is conserved

Atoms can combine in different ways, and they are rearranged by chemical reactions. The number of atoms in a reaction stays the same, so the mass stays the same. The photos show neutralising hydrochloric acid with sodium hydroxide solution. The products are sodium chloride and water.

a Explain why both balances in the photos show the same reading.

Antoine Lavoisier was the person who first explained the law of conservation of mass. He had experimented with burning copper, tin, mercury, phosphorus and sulfur. He weighed them before and after burning to collect evidence for the conservation of mass.

Burning magnesium

An analytical chemist weighed some magnesium and heated it strongly until it stopped reacting. Magnesium burns in air, reacting with the oxygen to produce magnesium oxide. She did the experiment five times. Here are the results:

Experiment	Mass of magnesium in g	Mass of magnesium oxide in g
1	0.6	0.9
2	1.2	2.1
3	1.4	2.3
4	2.2	3.7
5	3.3	5.5

b Plot a graph of the mass of magnesium oxide against the mass of magnesium.

c Explain the relationship between the mass of magnesium and the mass of magnesium oxide.

d Why does the magnesium oxide weigh more than the magnesium?

e Estimate how much magnesium oxide would be formed from 2.4 g of magnesium.

f What mass of oxygen would react with 2.4 g of magnesium?

Writing equations

Hydrogen is used as rocket fuel. It burns in air and reacts with oxygen to produce water. The word equation for the reaction is:

hydrogen + oxygen → water

The reactants are on the left of the equation and the products are on the right. You can write an equation for the reaction using formulae and symbols. Hydrogen and oxygen atoms both go around in pairs, as molecules. One atom of oxygen combines with two atoms of hydrogen. If we write the formulae for the reactants and products, the reaction looks like this:

$$H_2 + O_2 \rightarrow H_2O$$

This equation does not have the same number of atoms on each side. It is not balanced. But as we know, mass must be conserved and there must be the same number of atoms on both sides.

Balancing equations

A chemical equation shows that the number of each type of atom is the same on both sides. When this is the case, we call it a **balanced equation**, because the number of atoms on one side balances the number on the other side. To write a balanced equation, follow these steps.

1. Write the word equation: hydrogen + oxygen → water
2. Write the chemical equation using the correct symbols and formulae: $H_2 + O_2 \rightarrow H_2O$
3. Draw coloured dots for each atom: $H_2 + O_2 \rightarrow H_2O$
4. Add number(s) in front of the formulae to make the numbers balance: $2H_2 + O_2 \rightarrow 2H_2O$

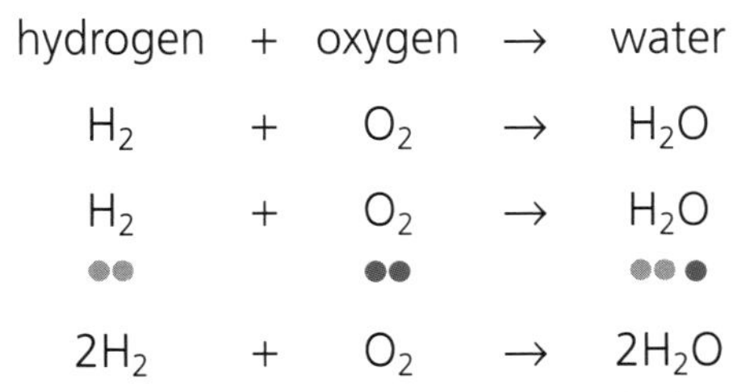

Remember: to make the equation balance, you change the numbers in front of the symbols or formulae. You must not change the subscript numbers in the formulae.

g Write a balanced equation for the combustion of methane, following the steps above.

Calcium carbonate cycle

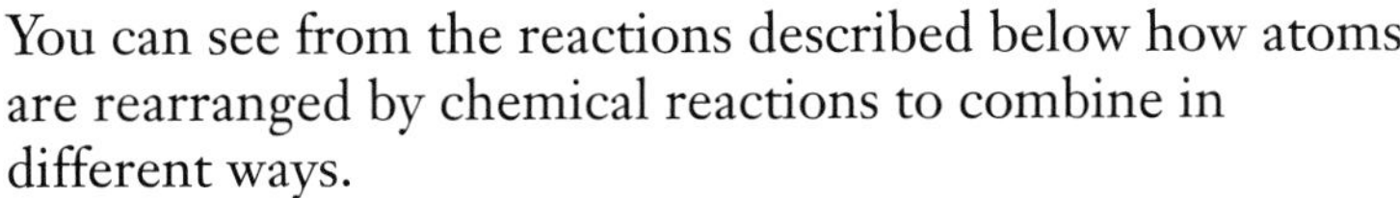

You can see from the reactions described below how atoms are rearranged by chemical reactions to combine in different ways.

- Limestone is mainly made of calcium carbonate. If you heat limestone, it gives off carbon dioxide and calcium oxide is formed, which is called quicklime. This is used to neutralise acidic soils.
- If you then add water to the calcium oxide, calcium hydroxide is formed, which is called slaked lime. This may be mixed with sand to make mortar.
- A solution of slaked lime in water is called limewater. When carbon dioxide gas is bubbled through it, a milky white precipitate forms. This is the test for carbon dioxide.

h What is the name of the precipitate formed in the test for carbon dioxide?

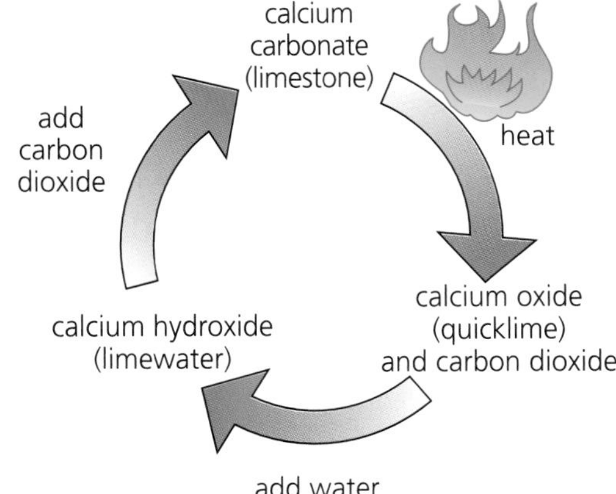

i Write word equations and balanced equations for the three reactions that take place in this cycle.

Questions

1. How could you show by experiment that mass is conserved during a chemical reaction?
2. **a** Does this equation balance? $Mg + HCl \rightarrow MgCl_2 + H_2$
   b Can you make it balance?
3. Sodium reacts with water to give sodium hydroxide and hydrogen. Copy this symbol equation for the reaction, and balance it.
   $Na + H_2O \rightarrow NaOH + H_2$
4. **a** In the calcium carbonate cycle, which compound was broken down and then remade?
   b Make a list of three useful products in the carbonate cycle and say what they are used for.

When you revise

In a chemical reaction, mass is conserved because the total number of atoms stays the same.

In a chemical reaction, the atoms are rearranged and combined in different ways to make new compounds.

Chemical reactions can be shown as **balanced equations**.

1.6 A volcano erupts

Think about

- Formal models

Mount St Helens

a Read the article opposite. When the volcano erupted:

i what evidence suggests that chemical reactions had taken place?

ii what evidence suggests that physical changes were happening?

After sleeping for 123 years, Mount St Helens in Washington State, USA, woke up on 20 March 1980. A huge earthquake rumbled beneath it. Seven days later, the first steam explosion blasted a 250-foot wide crater through the volcano's ice-cap. The volcano ejected an enormous column of ash, steam and gas. Lava oozed out, solidifying into a steep-sided dome.

The inside story

When a volcano erupts, both physical changes and chemical changes take place. Inside the Earth, the rocks are very hot. The deeper you go, the hotter the rocks get. In parts, the temperature is high enough to melt the rocks or to form new compounds.

Molten rock is called **magma**. Magma is a mixture of different elements and compounds. If the magma reaches the surface, it pours out as **lava**. The lava is red-hot but soon cools to form solid rock. A **volcano** is the hole that the magma comes out of.

Sometimes, magma has steam and other gases such as sulfur dioxide and oxides of nitrogen trapped in it under pressure. The pressure builds up gradually. The steam and other gases escape when the magma reaches the surface, causing an explosion. The sulfur dioxide dissolves in water, causing acid rain.

b Think about what all substances are made up of. Use this to explain:

i where you think the steam comes from

ii what is happening when rock melts and lava solidifies.

ash, steam and other gases
volcano
layers of ash and lava
rock layers
magma

Lava flow

Magma contains a variety of elements, including oxygen, silicon, aluminium, iron, magnesium, calcium, sodium, potassium, titanium and manganese. Some lava contains less gas and is rich in silicon. It is thick, flows slowly and the gases do not move easily. The pressure can build up, causing an explosion. Some lava contains a lot of gas and less silicon. It is thin, flows quickly and the gas escapes easily from it.

Sharing ideas

Some students were discussing their ideas about why lava with a lot of silicon it in flows more slowly. Read their ideas.

c Why do you think silicon-rich lava flows more slowly? Give your reasons.

It's all down to the particles. Silicon particles don't slide over one another very easily.

It's nothing to do with particles – no one knows if they exist anyway.

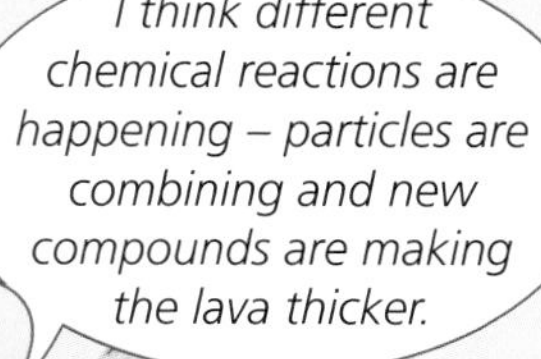

If the lava has more gas particles trapped in it, they will push the other particles apart.

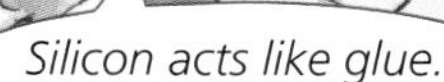

Time to experiment

Their teacher decided to build on some of their ideas about particles. When we use the idea of particles such as molecules and atoms in science, we call this idea a **formal model**. The model helps us to understand what is happening when we cannot see what is going on.

The teacher did two experiments. In the first one, shown opposite, she showed how a large volume of steam can be formed from a very small volume of water in the hot volcano. She began by heating a large beaker of salt solution, which boils at a higher temperature than pure water. She took a $100\,cm^3$ glass syringe with a self-sealing cap on the end and heated it in the beaker. When the large syringe was hot, she injected $0.1\,cm^3$ of water into it using a small hypodermic needle pushed through the self-sealing cap. She pointed out the volume on the large syringe as the water inside boiled and turned into steam. The volume of steam in the syringe was $70\,cm^3$.

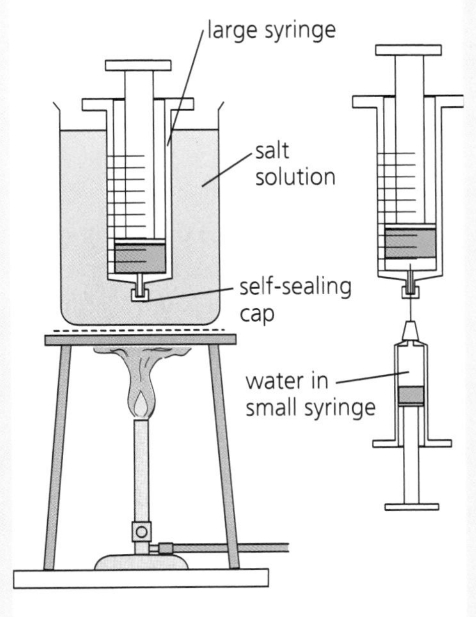

The water molecules in the hot syringe gained thermal energy. This was transferred to kinetic energy, causing them to move faster. At a certain temperature, the molecules vibrate so much that the forces of attraction between them break, and they are free to move far apart and form steam, a gas. In steam, the molecules are moving fast and in all directions. They fill whatever space is available.

d How many times greater was the volume of steam than the original volume of water?

e Explain why you think a volcano produces so much steam. Use the idea of water being made up of particles. Draw diagrams of the particles to help you.

f Why do you think steam and other gases in the magma are under pressure?

For her second experiment, the teacher showed the sparks, colours and flashes you often see when a volcano erupts. She took a piece of iron wool, lit it in a Bunsen burner flame and then plunged it into a jar of oxygen. The iron burned brightly and gave out sparks. Then she burned a small piece of calcium. This time the flame was red. Finally, she burned a tiny piece of sulfur. This time the flame was blue.

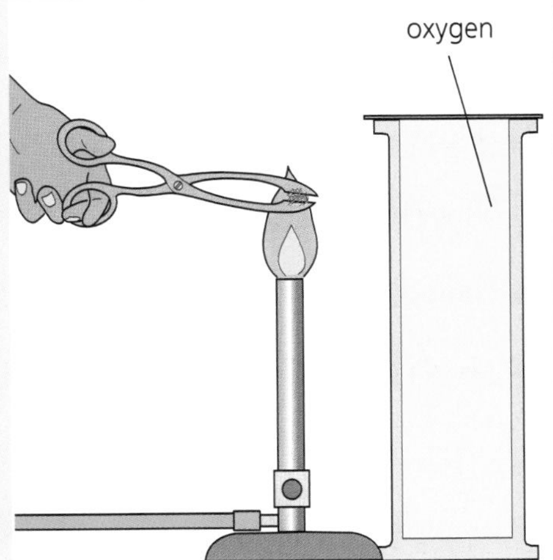

g Explain how new chemicals are produced when a volcano erupts. Use the idea of particles. Draw diagrams if you wish.

Questions

1. Write about what might have happened to a water molecule in the ice-cap on top of Mount St Helens on the day it erupted. Include illustrations.
2. Tom thought he could taste sulfur dioxide in his bottle of volcanic spring water. Could he be right? Where might the sulfur dioxide have come from? How could it have been formed?
3. If you shake a can of fizzy drink and then open it, what happens? How do you think this is like a volcano erupting?
4. Can you think of any other situations that remind you of a volcano? Explain your answer.

That's life

Reproduction

There are millions of different species of plants and animals on the Earth. Within each species, some organisms compete more successfully than others for resources such as food, water and space. These organisms are most likely to reproduce and leave more organisms, which become the next generation. The new organisms are called **offspring**.

Early ideas about reproduction

In ancient times, people believed that organisms were created out of nothing. The Chinese thought that insects were made out of wet bamboo.

In the fourth century BC, Aristotle thought that men's semen made limbs and organs out of women's menstrual blood. He compared this with how the Earth's rivers and continents have been shaped from matter. This kind of comparison or **analogy** helps people to explain ideas using a similar example.

a What analogy did Aristotle use?

In the seventeenth century, Jan Swammerdam believed that human sperm contained miniature humans. He called this mini-human the 'homunculus' and he thought it took in food from the egg. It gradually unfolded and grew into a fetus. Followers of this theory were called 'spermists'. At this time, Antoni van Leeuwenhoek was the first person to look at sperm under a microscope like the ones we use today. Many biologists were still convinced they could see the homunculus under the microscope!

On the other hand, Regnier de Graaf and his followers were called the 'ovists'. They thought that the egg, also called the **ovum**, contained a miniature human, and that the sperm caused it to grow.

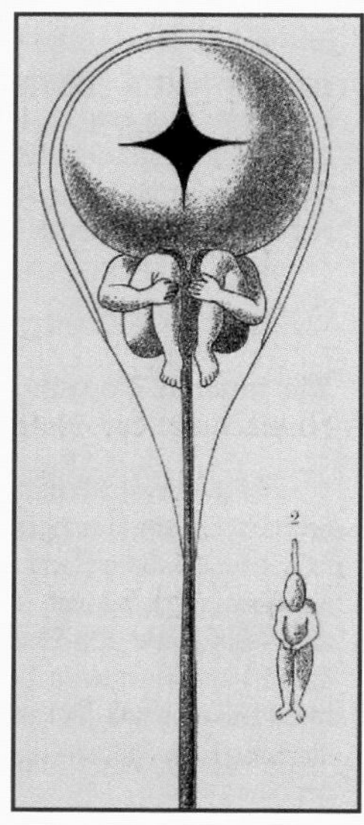

The spermists' model.

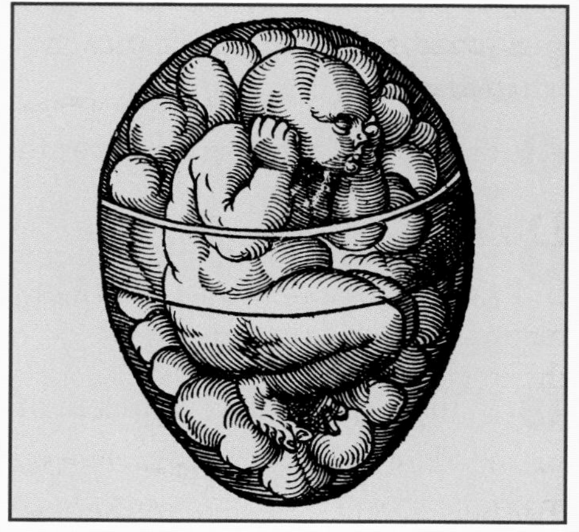

The ovists' model.

Looking for evidence

These beliefs of the spermists and ovists were only ideas. No one could say which idea was the right one, because there was no evidence for either of them.

By the end of the nineteenth century, cells had been discovered and scientists saw fertilisation happening under the microscope. The nuclei of the sperm cell and the ovum cell fused together to make the first cell of the new organism. This was evidence that both parents contributed to the offspring.

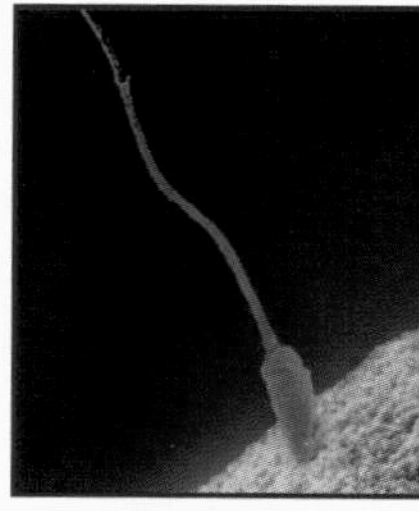

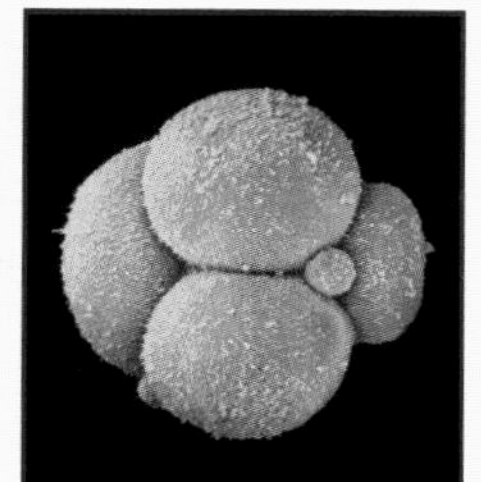

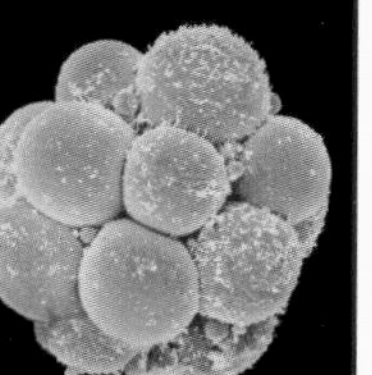

The sperm cell nucleus fuses with the ovum nucleus to form one cell.

The cell divides into 2, 4, 8 cells, and so on, until there is a ball of cells to form the embryo.

Mendel's discovery

In the nineteenth century, an Austrian monk called Gregor Mendel did many plant-breeding experiments. From these he concluded that features are passed on to the offspring as separate particles from both parents. Mendel died in 1884, before microscopists could clearly see the structure of cells and how they divide. His discoveries were not accepted because they did not fit in with the theories people had at that time. At the end of the nineteenth century, Mendel's principles were rediscovered and began to fit in with new ideas about cell structure. In 1909, the Danish biologist Wilhelm Johannsen called Mendel's particles **genes**. Mendel is now known as 'the father of modern genetics'.

b Why were Mendel's discoveries not accepted at first?

Cracking the code

In 1953, Francis Crick and James Watson worked out the structure of the substance that makes up genes. This substance is called **DNA**, and it carries instructions that are passed on through the sperm and the ovum. Their evidence came from many experiments, long hours in the laboratory and a lot of thinking. Now that scientists understand the code, they can explain how offspring inherit their features from their parents.

A DNA molecule has two strands twisted tightly together in a shape called a double helix. If you stretched out all the DNA from a human body, it would reach over a million million metres – to the Moon and back over 800 times!

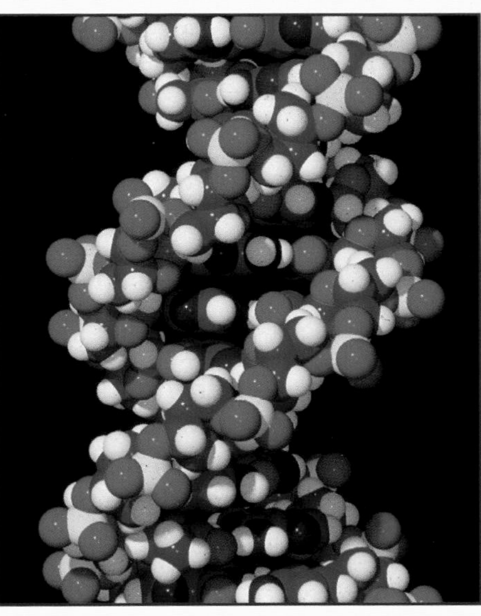

> Back in my rooms I lit the coal fire, knowing there was no chance that the sight of my breath would disappear before I was ready for bed. With my fingers too cold to write legibly I huddled next to the fireplace, daydreaming about how several DNA chains could fold together. Soon, however, I abandoned thinking at the molecular level and turned to the much easier job of reading biochemical papers.

from The Double Helix *by James D. Watson*

c Read the passage from *The Double Helix* by James Watson. After Watson had finished working in the laboratory, what else did he need to do to work out the structure of DNA?

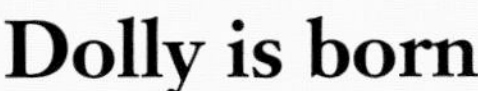

Dolly is born

In 1996, a team of scientists lead by Dr Ian Wilmut took a cell from the mammary gland of an adult sheep and removed the nucleus. They removed the nucleus from a sheep ovum and replaced it with the mammary gland cell nucleus. The ovum grew into an embryo which was transplanted into a surrogate mother sheep, which gave birth to Dolly. Dolly was the first mammal that was cloned from an adult cell. **Clones** are genetically identical organisms – all their genetic information comes from one parent's DNA.

d Scientists might soon be able to clone human beings. Do you think this would be a good idea? What problems would it cause?

Questions

1. Which three resources can affect the successful reproduction of plants and animals?
2. Make a time line to show how theories about reproduction have changed.
3. Describe how the spermists' and the ovists' theories differed. Why was no one able to say whether the theories were right or wrong?
4. How did scientists at the end of the nineteenth century use the evidence from microscopes to create new theories about reproduction?
5. What did Gregor Mendel conclude from his plant-breeding experiments? Do you think his conclusions can be applied to animals?
6. Explain the meaning of the word 'gene' by putting it in a sentence.
7. Why was the discovery of the structure of DNA so important?
8. Describe the consequences of cloning in terms of variation between parents and offspring.
9. Think of five questions you would like to ask a scientist about cloning, and search the Internet to find the answers.

The way we are

Learn about

- Inheritance
- Variation

Why do we look like our parents?

If you look at the members of a family you will see that although they are all different, they often look similar. This is because some of the same features from their parents and grandparents have been **inherited** or passed on to them. A baby inherits some features from its mother and some from its father. The information about these features is carried inside the nucleus of the sperm and the nucleus of the ovum. One successful sperm fertilises the ovum. The sperm and ovum nuclei fuse during fertilisation to form the first cell of the new baby.

The nuclei of both the sperm and the ovum contain genes. Genes are instructions that control the way our features develop. There are genes to control all of our features. For example, there are genes for eye colour, and a gene for whether you can roll your tongue or not. Each baby inherits half its genes from its mother and half from its father.

When a sperm and ovum fuse to form a fetus, there is a completely new combination of genes. That is why the children of two parents are not the same, except for identical twins, although they may have many similarities. Each baby resembles its parents in some ways, but is not exactly like either of them.

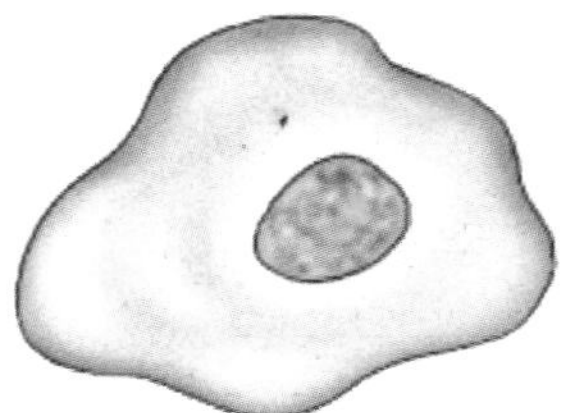

The nucleus of the cell contains thousands of genes.

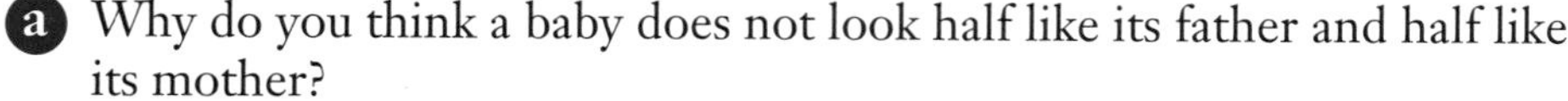

a Why do you think a baby does not look half like its father and half like its mother?

Identical twins

When a sperm fertilises an ovum, the fertilised ovum sometimes splits into two embryos and identical twins are formed. Both twins have come from the same sperm and ovum, so they have the same genes and the same features.

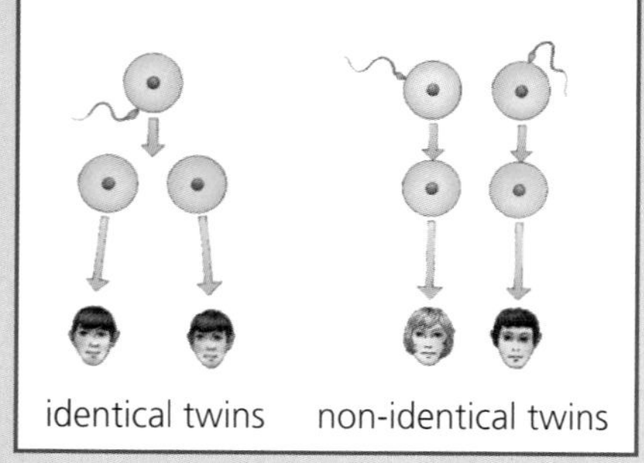

Non-identical twins

If two sperms fertilise two separate ova at the same time, the twins will have different genes and different features. They are non-identical twins.

b Can identical twins be of different sexes?

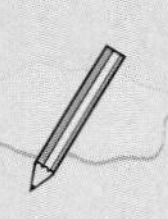

Inherited variation

There are genes to control all of your features.
Your genes decide, for example, whether you will have:

- curly or straight hair
- blue or brown eyes.

Some of these features controlled by your genes are either one thing or another – there is no 'in between'. For example, you can either roll your tongue or not – try it! Graph **A** shows this kind of variation.

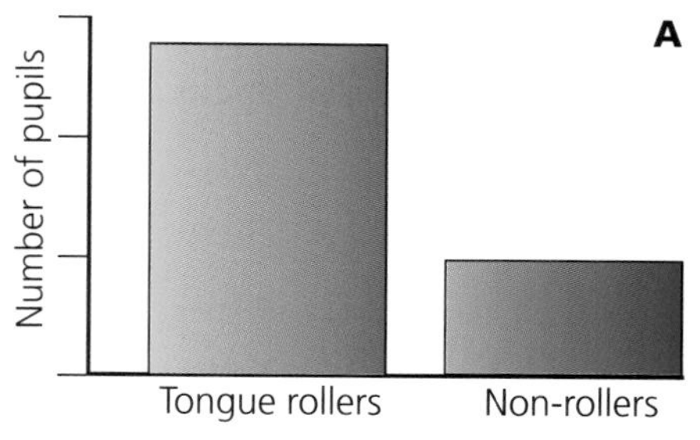

Other features show a range. For example, for height there is a range from very short to very tall with lots of heights in between. Graph **B** shows this.

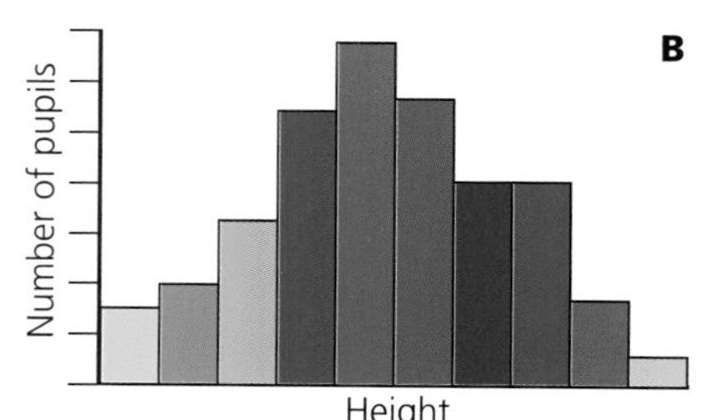

If a baby inherits genes for tallness from both parents, it will probably be tall. If it inherits genes for tallness and genes for shortness, we can't be sure what effect these genes will have on the person's height.

Environmental variation

Identical twins have exactly the same genes, but they sometimes look different when they grow older. Studying identical twins gives us a lot of information about how features are affected by the environment.

For example, a pair of identical twins may both inherit genes for tallness, but one may have a poorer diet than the other. The one with the healthier diet will grow taller. If one twin does not attend school, he or she may not reach the same level of intelligence as the twin who is educated.

The environment can affect plants. Bonsai trees are miniature trees. They have the normal genes for tallness, but are small because they have been grown in small pots.

All these examples show how not just genes but also the environment can cause variation in features. This means some features are a result of both inherited variation and environmental variation.

Family trees

The diagram shows the family tree for the Foster family. The children inherit their hair colour from their parents.

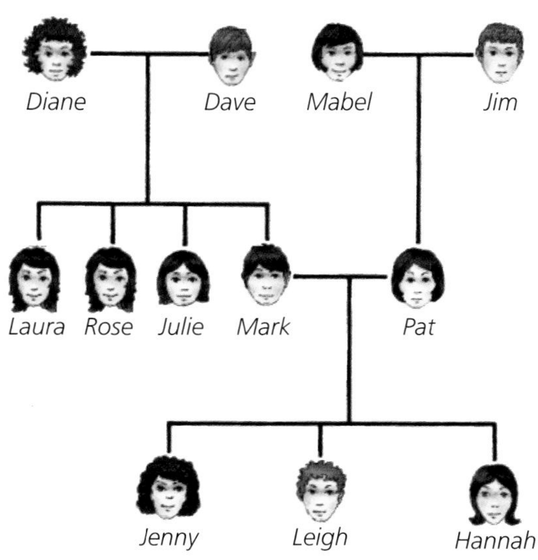

c Examine the family tree. From which people has Leigh inherited genes for red hair?

d Laura and Rose are identical twins. Why have they both got dark hair?

e Suggest two other features that will be the same for Laura and Rose.

f Laura weighs 65 kg and Rose weighs 50 kg. Suggest why their weights are not identical.

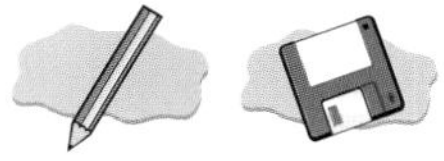

Questions

1. Explain how we inherit our features from our parents.
2. Where in the cell are the genes?
3. Here is a description of a Year 9 girl: 'blue eyes, small stature, olive skin, red hair, intelligent, tongue roller'. Which of these features may have been affected by her environment?
4. Draw diagrams to explain how identical twins and non-identical twins are formed.
5. Scientists often study identical and non-identical twins as they grow up. Suggest some of the ideas they might investigate.
6. Two seeds from the same apple were planted in different areas. One tree had large apples, and the other tree had small apples. Describe two factors that might have caused this variation.

When you revise

A baby **inherits** features from both its parents. These features are controlled by genes.

Identical twins have the same genes because they come from the same sperm and ovum.

Non-identical twins are formed when two sperms fertilise two ova.

Both genes and the environment cause variation between the members of a species.

Finding food

Learn about

- Adaptation
- Competition

Early life

A mammal develops inside its mother's body, and gets all the food it needs from her. Even after it is born, it is fed on milk from her mammary glands. This gives young mammals continuous access to nutrients, and also protection from other animals. Animals that do not look after their young like this have more offspring at a time. Some of them die, but because there were more of them, some are likely to survive.

a Humans usually give birth to one offspring at a time. List the ways in which humans help this offspring to survive.

Day to day

Some animals adapt their behaviour throughout the day to avoid **competing** with other species for food. Crows and starlings visit dustbins during the daytime, and foxes and cats raid them at night. We call animals that are active at night **nocturnal** animals.

Some animals and plants also respond to the length of the day. Poinsettia plants have red leaves and are popular for decorating houses at Christmas. They need at least 12 hours of complete darkness each day to bloom and develop their colourful leaves. This built-in mechanism ensures that they flower at the best time for survival. Commercial growers pull a blackout shade over the crop from 5 p.m. till 8 a.m. Only 5 minutes more light each evening would delay flowering by two weeks!

Day length is also the trigger for egg laying in birds. The days are getting longer in the spring, so this is when birds lay their eggs. The chicks will hatch at the time when it is easiest to find food for them.

b Explain three ways in which animals or plants adapt their behaviour in response to day length.

Surviving the winter

Some animals sleep through the winter when food is scarce to avoid the harsh conditions. This is called **hibernation**. Before hibernating, a dormouse eats so much food that it looks like a round ball. It stores the food as fat. It finds a hole to curl up in and goes to sleep. Its heart rate and breathing slow down. This way the body uses very little energy, so the fat stores last a long time. The increase in temperature at the end of the winter causes the dormouse to wake up – very hungry!

Caterpillars change into a pupa or chrysalis in the winter. This how the butterfly and moth species survive the cold weather. In this state, they take shelter and stop feeding and moving. This saves energy. Inside the pupa, they change into butterflies and moths ready to emerge in the spring.

Seeds from plants can survive the very cold and dry winter conditions. They are **dormant**, which means 'sleeping'. Seeds respire at a very low rate and will only 'wake up' and start to grow when conditions such as temperature and availability of water are just right. This starting to grow is called **germination**.

Migration

Many species of bird spend summer in this country but fly off in the winter to warmer climates where it is easier to find food. This travelling is called **migration**.

Swallows migrate to Africa. The route they take is a straight line which passes over eight countries. They fly in a straight line because this is the shortest route to food, and they need to save energy. Migrating birds use a number of methods to find their way. In the daytime, they recognise landmarks such as mountains and valleys. They sense the position of the Sun in the sky. Some birds appear to have a built-in compass and use the Earth's magnetic field. Not all birds fly south. Canada geese fly north in summer to find a place to moult safely.

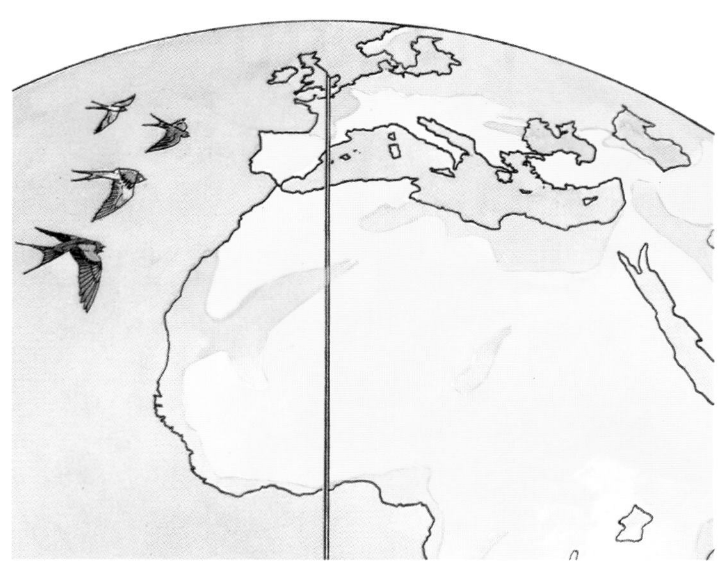

 How do migrating birds navigate?

Competing for food

Some animals compete for food with members of the same species, and also with other species. There is more **competition** when conditions are difficult, for example if it doesn't rain for several months and plants cannot grow, or during very cold or very hot spells. Some animal species depend on a different food source from other species, so they don't compete as much. Plants and animals also compete for water, space and light.

Look at the photos. They show greenflies, a woodlouse and a spider. Each has a different food source.

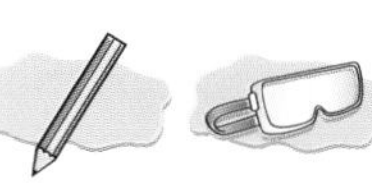

Questions

1. Explain why the offspring of a cat are more likely to survive than the offspring of a fish.
2. In what circumstances do animals compete most for food?
3. Why do some animals hibernate?
4. Find out the names of some animals that hunt their prey at different times of the day. Classify them using these words: dawn, day, dusk, nocturnal.
5. Hens naturally start laying eggs in the spring, when the days get longer. Hens kept for egg production are kept in artificially lit houses, so that day length is controlled. This means they start laying eggs younger.

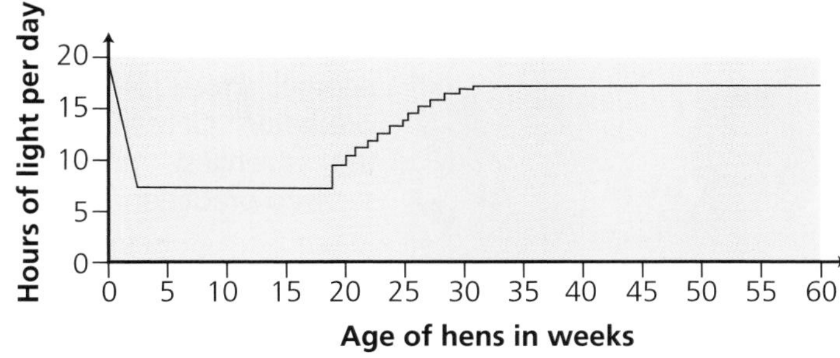

   a Look at the graph. At what age do you think these hens will start to lay?
   b Why does the farmer want the egg-laying period to start earlier?

When you revise

Animals that feed their young have fewer offspring than animals that don't feed them. Being fed by the parents makes the offspring more likely to survive.

There is **competition** between members of the same species and between different species for food, water, space and light.

Organisms adapt their behaviour to reduce competition for food with other species, and to avoid harsh conditions.

Predator eats prey

Learn about

- Competition
- Populations

Competition on Onkar

In any habitat, we find lots of species. The number of organisms of a particular species living in a habitat is called the **population**. Read about a population of gimbuls in *Onkar outback*.

Onkar outback

The moon Onkar orbits the outer planet of a distant galaxy. Conditions on Onkar are very similar to those on Earth. The intelligent life form is the luhans. They resemble humans but their skins are highly sensitive to ultraviolet light. They live in underground cities away from natural light.

On the ground above the cities, the luhans hunt small mammals called gimbuls to eat. The gimbuls feed on grass and the seeds of the red zetta plant in the early hours of the morning before dawn breaks. Most of the ground is covered with thorny hintel bushes. The thorns protect the bushes from being eaten by the gimbuls.

The gimbuls have adaptations that help them to avoid being eaten by their daytime predators, the wooks. They have large yellow eyes at the sides of their heads for good all-round vision. Their fur has green and red patches that camouflage them against the vegetation. They have large, jagged ears. This means they can see and hear the giant wook birds approaching. The gimbuls come out at night and sleep during the day.

The wooks are also adapted for catching their prey. The aggressive wooks have eyes that point forward for targeting their prey as they get ready to pierce them with their pointed beaks and tear them apart with their sharp claws.

A pair of gimbuls nested in a disused overground lift shelter. There was plenty of dry vegetation among the ruins. The gimbuls ate well and reproduced. They were well hidden from the wooks. The number of gimbuls in the shelter grew to a population of 102 after 35 weeks!

Competition

Soon things began to go wrong for the gimbuls in the lift shelter. Death and disease became widespread.

a Why do you think the gimbuls were dying?

There was competition between the gimbuls for the resources they needed, such as food, water and space:

- The food was running out.
- There wasn't enough clean water.
- The shelter was overcrowded and very dirty, so diseases were being passed on.

Even the zetta plants that had not been eaten by the gimbuls were competing for resources, especially for light.

Predation

A wook had started to notice the gimbuls running in and out of the shelter. He was hungry and ready to attack the gimbuls at dusk. Wooks had always eaten a few gimbuls, and the gimbuls now became the main food for the wook. A prey animal that is hunted by another animal for food is the target of **predation**. Only the gimbuls that were the strongest and fastest runners survived predation.

b What do you think happened to the gimbul population in the lift shelter?

c Why do you think only the strongest survived predation?

d What do you think happened to the wook population now that the ailing gimbuls were their main food source?

A change in population

The table shows how the gimbul population in the shelter changed over 40 weeks.

Time in weeks	0	5	10	15	20	25	30	35	40
Number of gimbuls	2	8	19	34	65	93	99	102	102

Plants compete too

Plants also compete with each other for resources such as space to grow, water, minerals and especially for light. In the Onkar outback, the purple grelip plants flower in the spring. In the summer they die down, when the hintel bushes grow their leaf canopy. This shades the grelip plants and they cannot get enough light to make food by photosynthesis.

Look at the table on the left.

e Draw a graph of this data.

f Label your graph to show:

- when the population growth was fast
- when the population growth began to slow down
- when the number of gimbuls being born was equal to the number of gimbuls dying.

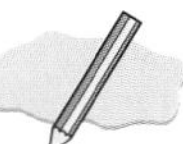

Interdependence

The size of any population depends on competition between the members of that species and also on how many of them are eaten by other species. The different species in a habitat are all **interdependent**. Animals depend on plants for food.

Questions

1. Explain three ways in which competition for resources can affect the size of a population.
2. In the Onkar outback:
   - a Which animals are prey?
   - b Which animals are predators?
   - c How do the gimbuls feed?
   - d Explain how the gimbul's features help it to avoid being eaten by the wook.
   - e Explain how the wook's features help it to hunt the gimbuls.
   - f Why are the gimbuls only hunted by the luhans at night?
3. What factors do you think caused the gimbul population growth to slow down?
4. Continue the story of the Onkar outback to describe what happens to the luhans when the population of gimbuls is affected by competition and predation.
5. Draw a food web for the Onkar outback.
6. In a field of wheat, the weeds compete with the wheat plants. For what resources do you think they compete?
7. In a wood, the bluebells begin to die back in the summer as the tree leaf canopy grows. Why do you think this is?

When you revise

A **population** is the number of individuals of a species living in a habitat.

An animal that is hunted by another animal as prey is the target of **predation**.

Competition, predation and disease all affect the size of a population.

Prey animals have adaptations, such as camouflage that help them to avoid their predators.

Predators are adapted to hunt by having features such as sharp beaks and claws.

Plants may have adaptations such as thorns to help them avoid being eaten.

All down to numbers

Learn about

- Pyramids of numbers

Count them!

seaweed → mussels → crab

Here is a simple food chain. The arrows show the flow of energy. In a day, one crab would eat more than one mussel, and each mussel would eat more than one seaweed plant. If you count the number of crabs, mussels and seaweed plants, you can draw a scale diagram. You can represent the size of the population by a bar, so a bar 1 centimetre long could represent 100 organisms and a bar 2 centimetres long could represent 200 organisms. The diagram would look like a pyramid. It is called a **pyramid of numbers**.

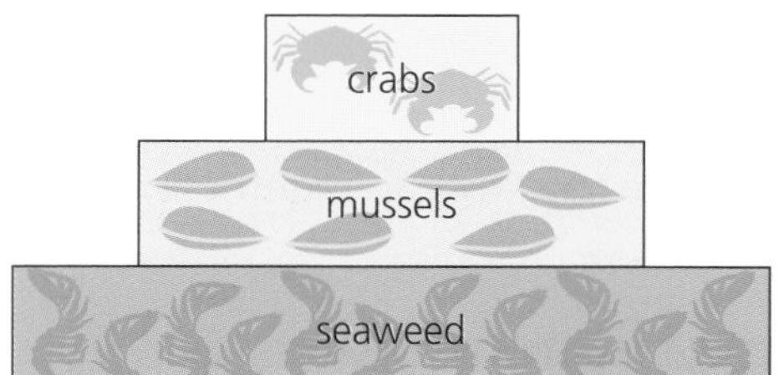

The seaweed plants are the producers, because they produce food by photosynthesis. The herbivores are the first organisms to eat the producers. They are called the primary consumers. The carnivores eat the herbivores. They are the secondary consumers.

However, the diagram for a food chain does not always look this shape. For example, a single oak tree might have more than 10 000 caterpillars on it. A family of bluetits might prey on these, and one owl might eat all of the bluetits. The diagram for this food chain would not be a pyramid shape.

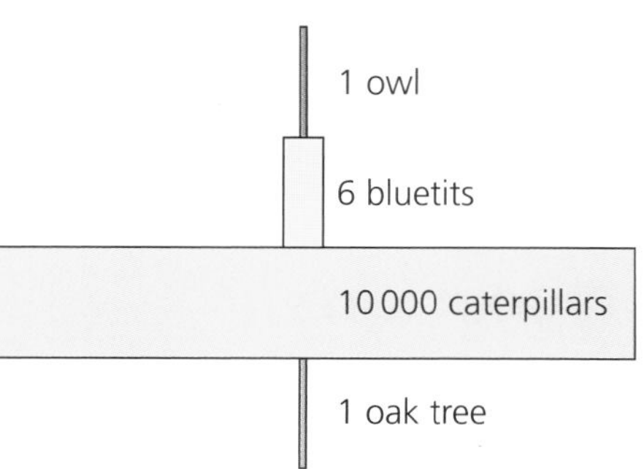

Stored energy

Energy is stored in the biomass of an organism. It is possible to find out how much energy there is at each level of the food chain. The biomass of an organism is the mass without the water. This helps us see how the energy flows through a food chain as one organism eats another.

Look back at the odd-shaped pyramids of numbers for the oak tree. The energy stored in the biomass of the organisms at each level is a more useful thing to look at than the number of organisms. There is only one oak tree, but it has more biomass than all of the caterpillars put together. All the caterpillars have more biomass than the family of bluetits, and the bluetits have more biomass than the owl.

Predator and prey numbers

The snowshoe hare is prey for its predator, the Canadian lynx. The numbers of these animals were studied in Canada between 1845 and 1935. The population numbers were estimated from the numbers of furs that the Hudson Bay Company gained from trappers. The graph shows this data. The number of predators depends on the number of prey.

a Look at the graph. Describe the relationship between the number of lynx and the number of hares.

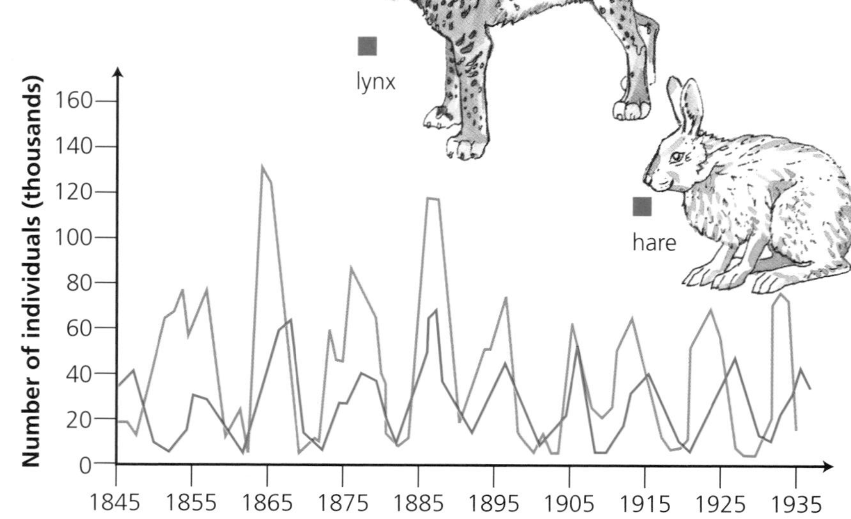

When the population of prey goes up, the population of predators also goes up because they have a better supply of food. The pyramid of numbers keeps its shape, it just gets bigger.

b What happens to the pyramid of numbers when the number of prey goes up?

The bigger population of lynx eventually starts to wipe out the hare population, and both populations then fall for a time.

Pond life

A group of biologists studied the populations of two microscopic pond organisms. They counted the numbers of the predator, hydra, and its prey, daphnia, in the same volume of water each week. Their results are shown in the table.

Time in weeks	1	2	3	4	5	6	7	8
Number of hydra	0	0	1	10	15	9	8	0
Number of daphnia	15	65	90	80	52	20	0	0

c Draw graphs of their results. Plot both sets of data on the same axes.

d What happens to the number of daphnia as the number of hydra goes up?

e Why did the biologists sample the same volume of water each week?

f Why do you think that some samples had no hydra?

Questions

1. Copy the pyramids below. Label them to show which one best represents each of the following food chains.

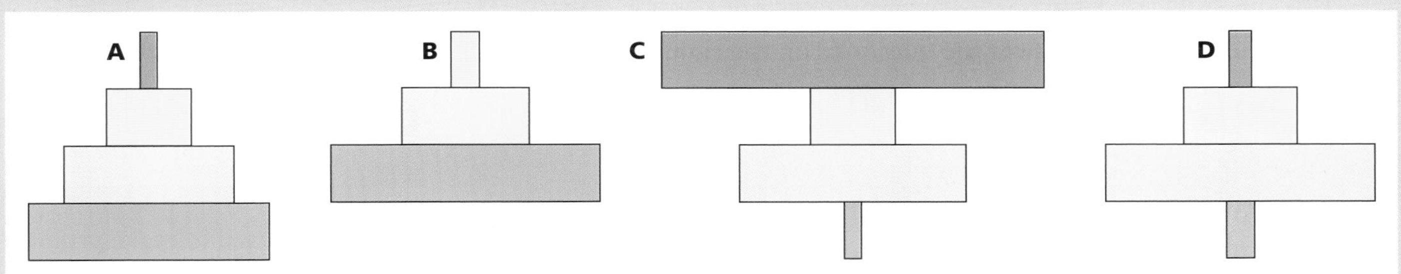

   a grass → rabbits → fox
   b oak tree → caterpillars → robins → owl
   c blackberry bushes → caterpillars → bluetits → owl
   d oak tree → caterpillars → robins → fleas

2. Use a piece of graph paper to draw a pyramid of numbers for 500 grass plants, 10 field mice and one owl. Use the scale: 1 mm bar width represents 2 organisms. Make sure the bars are all the same depth. Label your pyramid.
3. Explain one reason why we can get odd shapes when we try to draw pyramids of numbers for some food chains.
4. a If the mussels on a beach are poisoned by toxic algae, what will happen to the crab population?
   b What changes might you see on local restaurant menus?

When you revise

If we count the number of organisms at each level of a food chain, we can draw a **pyramid of numbers**.

In some food chains, a pyramid of numbers is not pyramid shaped, for example if the producer is a large tree.

If the number of prey in a food chain increases, the number of predators also increases.

2.6 Another pint of milk

Learn about

- Selective breeding

Milk yield in cattle

Like other mammals, the cow produces milk to feed her calves after they are born. This is called **lactation**. The milk gives young mammals a continuous supply of nutrients, and also protects them from disease. The amount of milk a cow produces is called the **milk yield**. Farmers sell milk for a profit, so high milk yield is a **desirable feature** in a cow.

High milk yield is a feature that is inherited from both the bull and the cow. A bull that has genes for high milk yield can be mated with many cows that produce the most milk. New varieties of cattle with higher milk yields are produced. In this way, farmers select the bull and cows that have a feature they want to pass on. This is called **selective breeding**.

Artificial insemination

Instead of mating a bull and a cow at the farm, scientists at a breeding station may choose a bull that can pass on high milk yield and sell its semen to farmers. The farmer puts the semen into the cow's vagina through a long tube. We call this **artificial insemination**.

To collect the bull's semen, the bull may be introduced to a frame that is made to look like a cow, with a cow's hide over it and a rubber vagina inside. The bull tries to have sexual intercourse with it, and the semen is collected in the artificial vagina. The semen is frozen in straws until it is needed.

Collecting semen from a bull. Using artificial insemination, a bull may father lots of calves without ever meeting a cow!

The table shows the statistics for cows bred from Gemidge and Goldfinger, two different bulls. Use it to answer the questions on the right.

Gemidge	Yield compared with the average	Goldfinger	Yield compared with the average
Milk	+902 kg	Milk	+1203 kg
Fat	+23.3 kg	Fat	+30.0 kg
Protein	+29.1 kg	Protein	+31.8 kg
Milking speed	Average	Milking speed	Fast
Temperament	Very good	Temperament	Good

a Which bull do you think passed on genes for the highest milk yield, Gemidge or Goldfinger?

b Milk is used to make products such as cheese and yoghurt. Cheese is made from milk protein. Which bull's semen would you use to produce a cow if you wanted to use its milk to:

i make better cheese?

ii make low-fat yoghurt?

Other features

If you select two parents that each have different desirable features, such as resistance to disease or strong legs, you can try and produce new varieties of cattle with all of these features. The wild ancestors of our domestic cattle were the aurochs. They are now extinct, but there are cave paintings of them. Longhorn cattle are similar to the aurochs. They were once popular as dairy and beef cattle because they could walk a long way to market. Longhorns are now a rare breed, and we must protect them from becoming extinct. When a species becomes **extinct**, it dies out altogether and we lose its useful genes.

c i Why do you think longhorn cattle are less popular as dairy and beef cattle now?

ii Why do you think it is important to protect them?

A loaf of bread

Wheat is grown to make flour. Wild wheat was one of the earliest plants cultivated by humans. Scientists think that wild wheat was the offspring of wild grasses. New varieties of wheat have been produced by selective breeding that give a high yield of grain of good quality. Modern wheat varieties are also resistant to disease.

The wheat flower is normally self pollinated. The pollen cell nucleus from the male part of the flower fertilises the ovule cell nucleus of the same flower. When new varieties are produced:

- The parents are selected for desirable features.
- The parent plants are planted in two rows, one chosen to be the females and one chosen to be the males.
- A chemical is sprayed onto the female parent plants to sterilise the male part of the flower. The male parent plants are not treated.
- The pollen is carried by the wind from the male parent plants to the female parent plants.

The offspring produced will have desirable features from both parents.

Wild wheat.

Modern cultivated wheat.

Genetic engineering

Scientists can now take genes out of one species and put them into another to give them desirable features. This is called **genetic engineering**. It is a modern form of selective breeding. Genes have been inserted into soya beans so that they can make their own pesticides. Human genes have been inserted into sheep cells so that they produce milk with a human protein in it. This can be used to treat people with the lung disease emphysema.

In **genetically modified (GM) food**, genes may be switched off or new genes may be inserted to change the features of the plant. In genetically modified tomatoes, the gene that makes them go soft has been switched off so they stay firm for longer.

Questions

1. Explain what we mean by 'desirable features'. Give an example.
2. List what a farmer can do to selectively breed cattle for high milk yield.
3. Make a list of features in cattle other than milk yield that a farmer might selectively breed for.
4. Explain why selective breeding is as important in plants as it is in animals.
5. When breeding wheat, how does the farmer make sure that some of the wheat flowers are pollinated by pollen from the selected plants?
6. 'Genetic engineering might replace selective breeding.' Suggest a reason for this statement.
7. The British Government does not allow genes to be inserted into human embryos for ethical reasons. Organise a debate on the motion: 'Genetic engineering of humans should be allowed'.

When you revise

Desirable features are features you want to pass on.

We can select parents with desirable features to produce new varieties of animals or plants that have these desirable features. This is called **selective breeding**.

Genetic engineering is taking genes out of one species and putting them in another.

Competition 2.7

Happy families

Think about

- Probability

Boy or girl?

All the information that decides whether a baby is male or female is carried inside the sperm and the ovum. The sperm can have a male Y factor or a female X factor. The ovum can only have an X factor.

If an X factor sperm joins with an X factor ovum to give XX, the baby will be a girl. If a Y factor sperm joins with an X factor ovum to give XY, the baby will be a boy.

a If a couple's first child is a boy, do you think their second child is more likely to be a girl?

Heads or tails?

If you spin a coin, there are two possible outcomes: heads or tails. Each time you spin a coin there is an equal chance of getting heads or tails. If you get two heads in a row, it is called a run of two. Three heads in a row is called a run of three, and so on.

For every baby that is born, there is an equal chance or **probability** of it being a boy or a girl. The possible combinations of X and Y factors are XX and XY. There are two possibilities, just like spinning a coin. If you have five girls in a row, it is like a run of five heads.

b Work with a partner. Try spinning a coin 25 times. Write down whether you get heads or tails each time. Count up how many runs of two, three and four you got.

Any choice?

The torn and faded pages of a Chinese manuscript tell the story of Chan, a rich emperor who desperately wants a son. He is very old fashioned and believes that a son must inherit his wealth. Chan and his wife Jade have five daughters. Chan is hoping for a sixth child – a son. Jade thinks that their family is large enough, and anyway a sixth child might be another girl.

One day, Jade thinks of an intriguing plan to change her husband's mind. She makes three types of card.

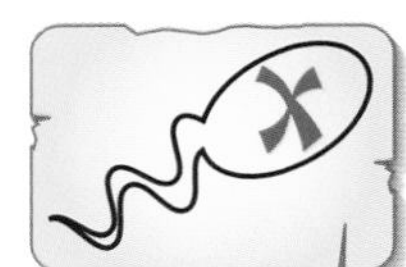

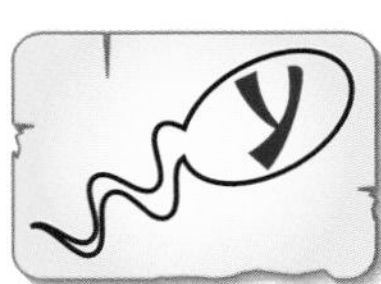

'My dear husband, only you have the power to decide whether our next child will be a boy. Each of your sperm has either the Y factor for a boy or the X factor for a girl. I can only make the X factor.'

Chan is flattered that he should have such power and listens carefully.

'There are 10 male cards. 5 have the Y factor and 5 have the X factor. There are 10 female cards. They all have the X factor. I will shuffle the cards. You must choose one male card and one female card each time.'

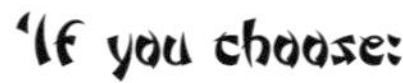

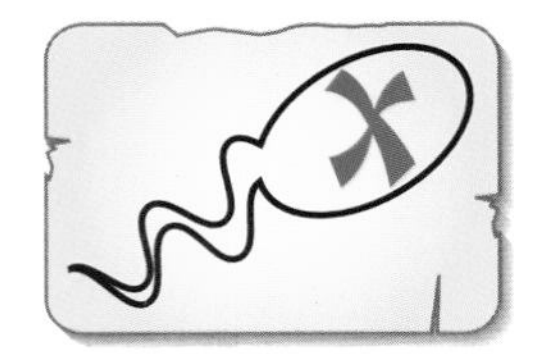

it is the same as having a female child.'

'If you choose:

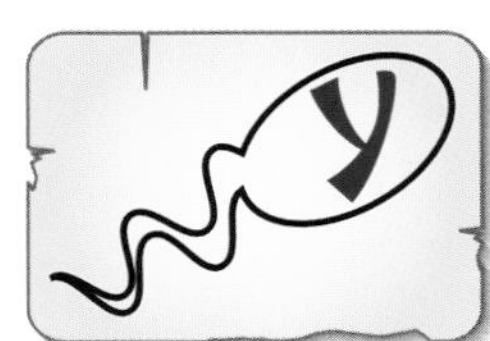

it is the same as having a male child.'

The emperor makes his first choice:

c What is the sex of this 'child'?

The emperor puts back the cards.
He makes four more choices in this way, and each time the combination is female. 'Fascinating! This is just like our family!' Chan exclaims in surprise.

d Do you think this result is surprising? Explain your answer.

The bargain

'Now you must make your sixth choice,' said Jade. 'If your sixth choice is male, I will agree to having another baby, but if your sixth choice is female, our family is complete and all our wealth will be divided between our five daughters.'

e What do you think is the probability of the sixth choice being male?

f Do you think Jade's card game was a good idea? Explain your reasons.

g How many children do you think the emperor and his wife would need to have to be sure they had a boy? Explain how you could show this with the cards.

Family planning in China

Shanghai, China's largest city, has a population density of more than 2000 people per square kilometre. 21 million babies were born in 1997 in China, whereas only 4 million were born in the USA. Because the growing population has caused problems, the country has a family planning policy. Late marriage and late childbirth are advocated and couples normally have only one child. The family planning programme started in the early 1970s and it is estimated that China would have 260 million more people than it has now if the programme had not been adopted.

h Some Chinese people have argued that the limit should be one son, rather than one child, as daughters are not popular there. Supporters of this 'one son' policy say that more than 98% of the families trying to have one son would have six or fewer children. What do you think?

Advertisements in China encourage people to accept a daughter instead of a son.

Questions

Discuss the questions with a partner. Write down the answers.

1. a If a sample of a man's semen contains 300 million sperm, how many of the sperm do you think will have:

i the Y factor? **ii** the X factor?

b A woman produces one ovum each month. How many of them have the X factor?

2. a Estimate the number of ova a woman produces in her lifetime.

b Why do you think that a man produces so many more sperm than a woman produces ova?

3. The Smith family have three children. The oldest one is a boy and the two younger girls are twins. What do you think is the probability of their fourth child being a boy?

4. Explain why the average family does not have equal numbers of boys and girls.

5. A London clinic claims to have developed a new technique for separating out sperm carrying the Y factor. What do you think of this new development?

3.1 Machines and force

Machines

People use machines to do jobs more easily. Some machines let you lift or move things using less force, for example, a pulley system. Other machines let you use more force so that you don't need to move things so far, for example, a pedal bin. The force of the object you are trying to move is called the **load**. If you are trying to lift something, then the load is its weight.

Machines come in many shapes and sizes. We shall look at some examples of simple machines. Other machines combine several simple machines in one more complex one.

The development of simple machines

It is difficult to find out exactly when some simple machines were developed. Machines such as inclined planes, wheels and pulleys have been used for thousands of years.

An **inclined plane** reduces the force needed to lift an object up. But you have to push the object further up the slope compared with lifting it straight up. People doing removals and deliveries use inclined planes to move heavy items in and out of vans and lorries.

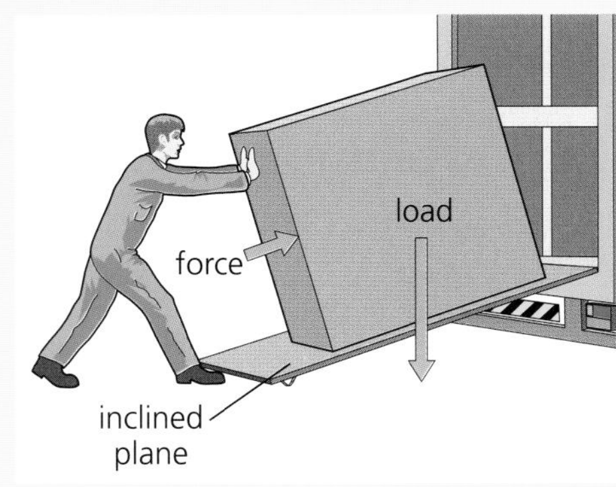

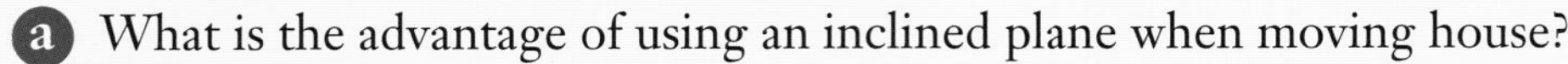

a What is the advantage of using an inclined plane when moving house?

The **wheel and axle** which is found on machines such as this grinding machine is thought to have been developed about 2000 BC. An animal such as a horse turns the wheel on its axle. The horse moves in a bigger circle than the axle, so the force on the axle is bigger than the pushing force of the horse. The wheel moves in a bigger circle than the axle, so by moving the axle a little you move the wheel a lot.

Pulleys were used widely by the Egyptians around 2700 BC for building structures such as the Pyramids. They used a rope and pulleys to lift heavy objects such as stone blocks vertically. In the pulley shown in the diagram, the rope is passed round the two pulleys. Someone pulls down on the free end of rope. You need less force to lift the load, but the rope you pull on has to move further than the load moves.

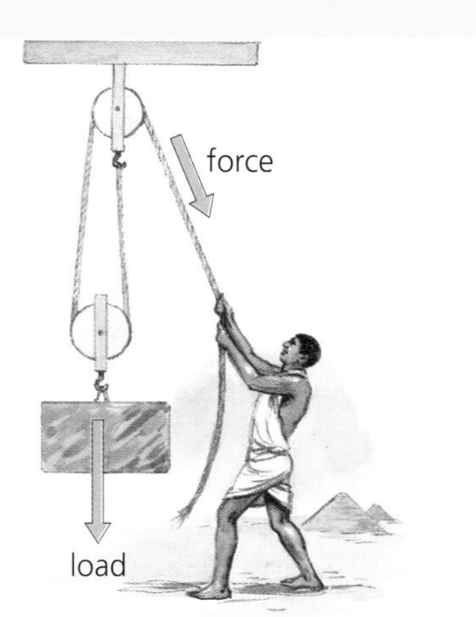

Archimedes invented a screw mechanism in the third century BC to lift water up to irrigate fields. The **Archimedes screw** is a bit like an inclined plane. You turn the screw with a smaller force than you would need to lift the water straight up. The water moves along inside the screw. The turning of the screw lifts the water inside the tube higher and higher until the water is at the surface.

b How do you think people lifted water to irrigate fields before the Archimedes screw was invented?

You have probably seen **gears** on many machines such as bicycles. Gears are made up of several cog wheels with teeth which turn each other. Sometimes a chain is used to link two cog wheels. The force needed to turn the wheels depends on the size and arrangement of the cog wheels. Sometimes you use gears to make the output cog turn faster and more easily than you are turning the input cog. Sometimes the gears make the output cog turn slower and less easily than you are turning the input cog.

Input cog turns fast and easily. Output cog turns slowly.

Input cog turns slowly. Output cog turns fast and easily.

c Look at the two diagrams above. Which would help you go faster and which would help you go slower?

Complex machines

More complex machines such as a petrol engine, a bicycle, a windmill or a combine harvester combine lots of different simple machines for a greater overall result. Bicycles use cogs, chains, gears and levers.

d Find as many simple machines on this bicycle as you can. For each one, name the machine and the part of the bicycle that uses it.

The natural machine

People have developed many different types of machine which copy nature. A windmill mimics the seed dispersal method of the sycamore tree. The catapult also resembles the way many plants disperse their seeds.

e Explain how a catapult is similar to the way some seeds are dispersed.

Questions

1. Explain simply how the following work:

   a an inclined plane **b** a wheel and axle **c** the Archimedes screw.

2. In a gear system, as you move one wheel, it moves the second intermeshed wheel. What do you think happens to the force you use to turn the first wheel and to the speed of the connected wheel if:

   a a small cog wheel with 5 teeth is intermeshed with a larger wheel with 10 teeth?

   b a large cog wheel with 10 teeth is intermeshed with a smaller wheel with 5 teeth?

3. Explain why each of the following is a complex machine:

   a a combine harvester **b** a windmill.

4. Produce a leaflet to help Year 7 pupils find out about simple machines. You could call your leaflet 'Simple machines through time'.

3.2 Where's the pivot?

Learn about

- Pivots and levers

Pivots are everywhere

Forces can make objects move forwards or backwards or stop moving. Forces can also make things turn. Think about a door. It opens around the hinge. A wheel turns around the axle. The **pivot** is the point around which something turns. When you open the door the hinge turns very little but the whole door turns more.

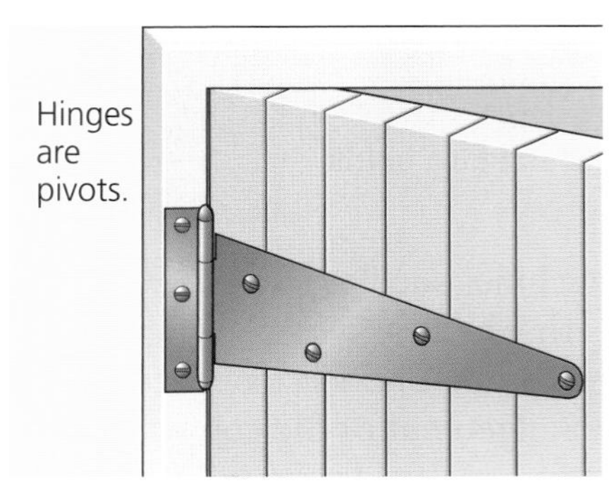

a Look at the diagram above and explain which part works as a pivot.

The joints between your bones also act as pivots.

A wheelbarrow uses a pivot. When you lift a load in a wheelbarrow, the wheel acts as a pivot. The wheelbarrow helps you lift the load up more easily than if you lifted it straight up without the wheelbarrow.

b Draw simple diagrams of the person lifting the sack and then using the wheelbarrow. In each diagram label the pivot, the load and the force the person exerts.

More distance, less effort

Imagine that you are closing a door. First you try to push it very close to the hinge, as shown in the picture. Now imagine you push the door shut at the handle. The further away from the pivot you are, the less force you need to turn the door around the pivot.

You'll remember that when you sit on a seesaw with a friend on the other end, you can exert more force and lift the friend more easily if you sit far away from the pivot than if you sit close to it.

Holly and Cameron both have the same weight. If they both sit at the ends of the seesaw, it is balanced. But if Holly moves towards the pivot, her end of the seesaw moves upwards. It is unbalanced.

c Why does Holly's end move upwards when she is closer to the pivot?

d If Cameron were heavier than Holly, where should he sit to balance her when she sits at the end?

Levers

Levers are machines that work a bit like seesaw. You apply your force at one end of the lever. The lever has a pivot and, as it turns, it pushes against a load.

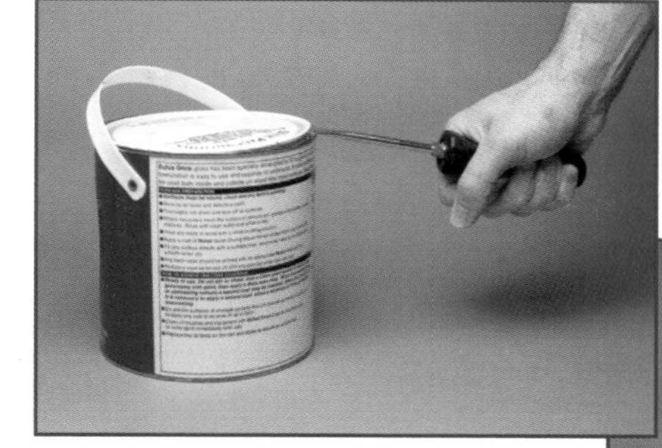

e Look at the photos opposite. For each one, say what is the lever, what is the pivot, and what is the load that the lever pushes against.

For the levers in the photos, the further away you are from the pivot (or the longer the lever), the less force you need to apply.

f The lever on a seesaw is a fixed length.
How can you make it act as if it is longer or shorter? 

Turning effect

Look at the diagram of a force making a screwdriver turn. The force arrow does not point towards the pivot – the force is to one side. Whenever the force on an object is applied to one side of a pivot, the force tries to make the object turn. This is called the **turning effect** of the force.

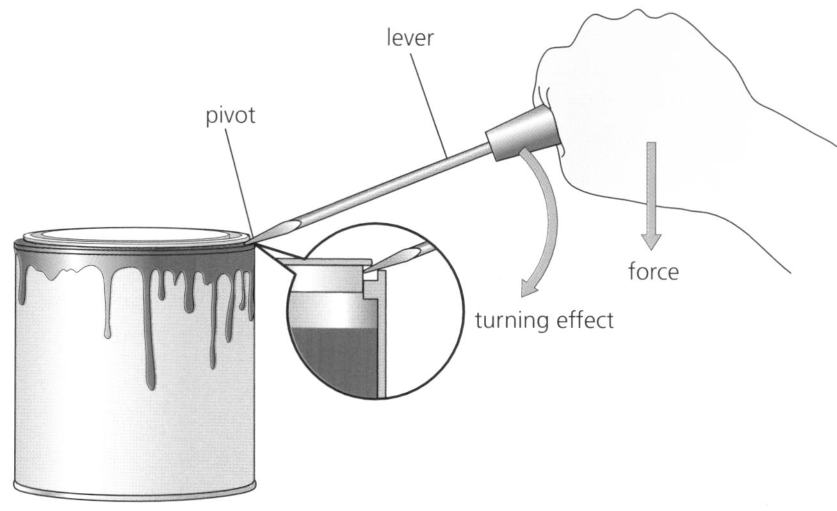

The turning effect of a force depends on the size of the force. It also depends on the distance between the pivot and the force arrow. If the force is applied directly towards the pivot then nothing will turn. This is shown in the diagram of the tap – the forces marked ✗ have no turning effect on the tap.

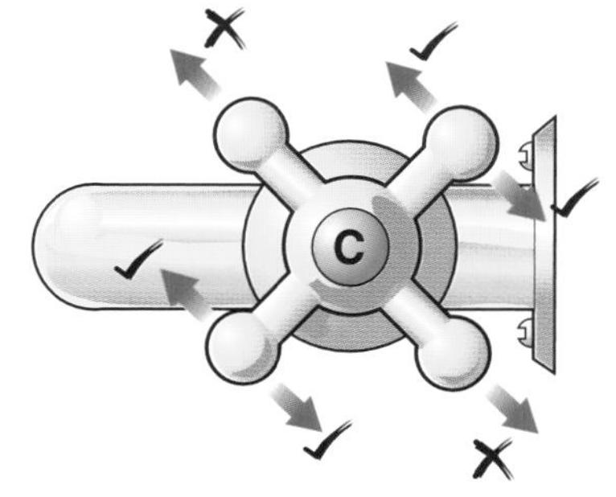

g Look at the photo of a crowbar above. Draw a simple diagram to show the lever, the pivot, the force you apply and the turning effect.

Questions

1. List all the pivots you can think of on a bicycle.
2. Explain why the distance between the pivot and where you exert the force is important.
3. People with arthritis in their hands find it hard to grip things and apply enough force to screw and unscrew things. What could a designer do to help them with this problem?
4. Design a simple activity to explain to primary school children why levers are useful machines. Provide answers for any questions you set.

When you revise

A **pivot** is the point around which an object such as a crowbar turns.

A **lever** turns around a pivot and pushes against a load.

When a force tries to turn an object, the force has a **turning effect**. The turning effect of a force depends on the size of the force and the distance from the pivot to the force arrow.

3.3 Just a moment

Learn about

- Balanced turning effects
- Unbalanced turning effects

Balanced and unbalanced forces

When the forces on an object are balanced, the object will stay still or it will move at a steady speed.

For something to start moving, or to speed up or slow down, the forces on it must be unbalanced. For example, to start moving forwards or to speed up there must be a greater forwards force than the backwards force.

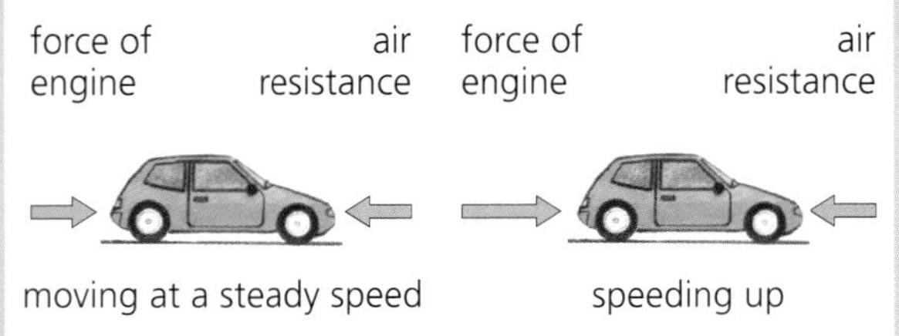

A balancing act

To turn something around a pivot, the turning effects of the forces on the lever must be unbalanced. Cameron pushes the rotating door with a force of 50 N. Mahir pushes it harder in the opposite direction, with a force of 60 N, so the door is turning. There is an **unbalanced turning effect**.

Sometimes the turning effects may be balanced. In this picture Cameron is pushing the rotating door in one direction with a force of 50 N. Holly is pushing against him in the opposite direction also with a force of 50 N. The forces exerted by Cameron and Holly are balanced.

The two forces of Cameron and Holly pushing are balanced around the pivot of the door. Their two forces have a **balanced turning effect** on the door. The door does not turn!

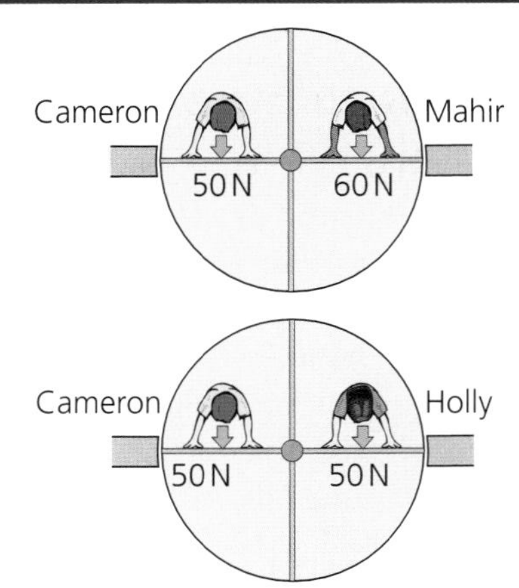

a Look at the two diagrams above of people pushing on the rotating doors. What can you say about the distance from the pivot that they are pushing?

Moments

Cameron's pushing force acts on the door in an anticlockwise direction. Holly's pushing force acts on the door in a clockwise direction. The two forces are the same size and are acting in opposite directions, so they are balanced.

The turning effect of a force around the pivot of the door depends on both the size of the force applied and the distance from the pivot to the force arrow. The distance from the pivot is measured perpendicular to the direction of the force.

The turning effect of a force is also called the **moment** of the force. We measure force in newtons, and distance in metres, so the units for a moment are **newton metres** (Nm). This is summarised in the equation:

moment of a force in Nm = force in N × distance in m

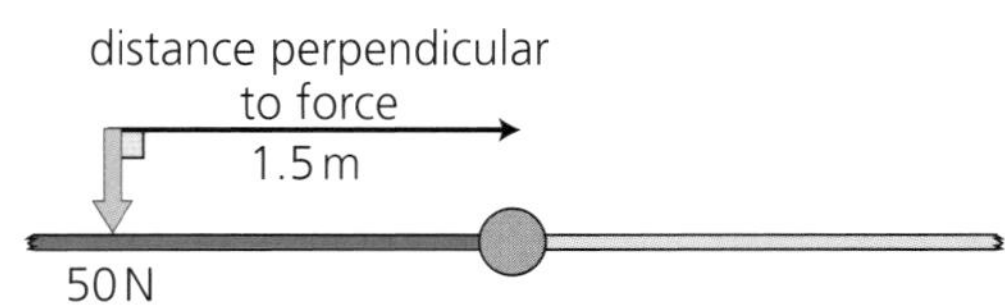

In the diagram of the revolving door, Cameron is exerting a force of 50 N. The force is 1.5 m from the pivot.

moment of Cameron's force = force × distance
= 50 N × 1.5 m = 75 Nm

When Cameron and Holly push the door, the two moments are balanced. Cameron's anticlockwise moment is equal to Holly's clockwise moment. The **principle of moments** says that when the door is not turning:

the sum of the anticlockwise moments = the sum of the clockwise moments

b What is the size of the moment around the pivot when Holly pushes the door?

Balanced moments

On this seesaw Cameron's weight is 500 N and Yeter's weight is 375 N. Cameron is 1.5 m from the pivot and Yeter is 2 m from the pivot. We can put these numbers into the equation to find the moments on each side. Remember that each moment is given by force × distance.

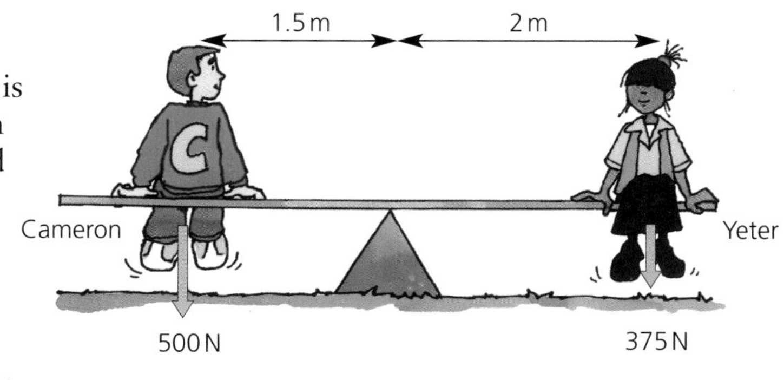

When the seesaw is balanced:

anticlockwise moment	= clockwise moment
force × distance for Cameron	= force × distance for Yeter
500 N × 1.5 m	= 375 N × 2 m
750 Nm	= 750 Nm

As you can see the moments are the same, so they balance. 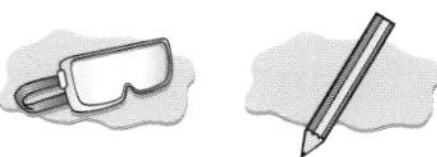

Unbalanced moments

Now Yeter moves towards the pivot of the seesaw, and it tips. We can do the same calculations to see what the moments are now and why they don't balance.

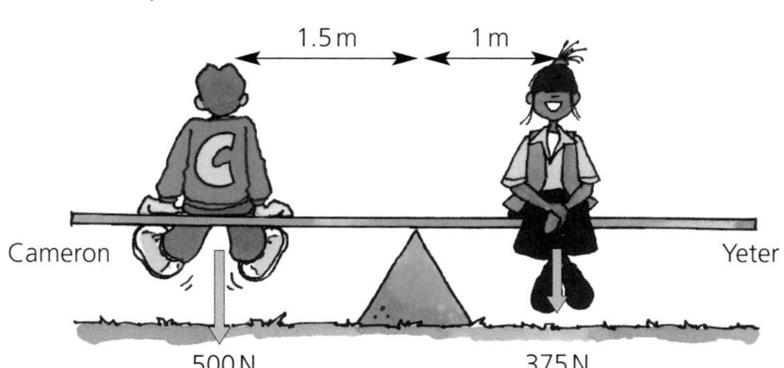

anticlockwise moment	clockwise moment
force × distance	force × distance
500 N × 1.5 m	375 N × 1 m
750 Nm	375 Nm

As you can see the moments are not the same, so they don't balance.

c Which is greater, the clockwise moment or the anticlockwise moment?

d Which way will the seesaw tip?

Questions

1. Explain: **a** what is meant by the moment of a force
   b what happens when the anticlockwise moment is bigger than the clockwise moment.
2. Copy the table and complete it by calculating the missing values.

Example	Force in N	Distance	Moment of force in Nm
A	10	1 m	?
B	?	50 cm	25
C	55	?	38.5

3. **a** Look at the diagram below. Calculate the anticlockwise and clockwise moments.
   b Will the seesaw balance or not?

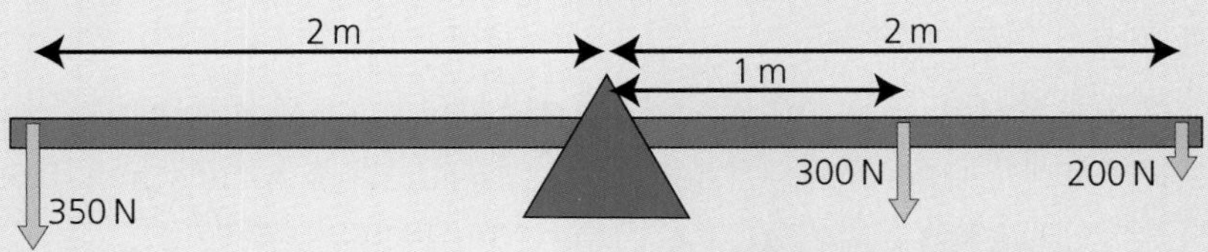

When you revise

The turning effect of a force is called the **moment** of the force.

moment of a force (in Nm) = force (in N) × distance (in m)

When two moments are balanced, an object will not move and the **principle of moments** applies. This is summarised by the equation:

sum of the anticlockwise moments
=
sum of the clockwise moments

Using moments

Learn about

- Application of moments

iMoments in life

As we have seen, a lever turning round a pivot is a simple machine that can be very useful to us in everyday life. We can calculate moments and use the principle of moments to understand how and why everyday machines work.

If we calculate the moments about a pivot, we can see what a difference a lever makes to lifting things. A lever is like a seesaw: there are clockwise and anticlockwise moments. You can see these in the diagram.

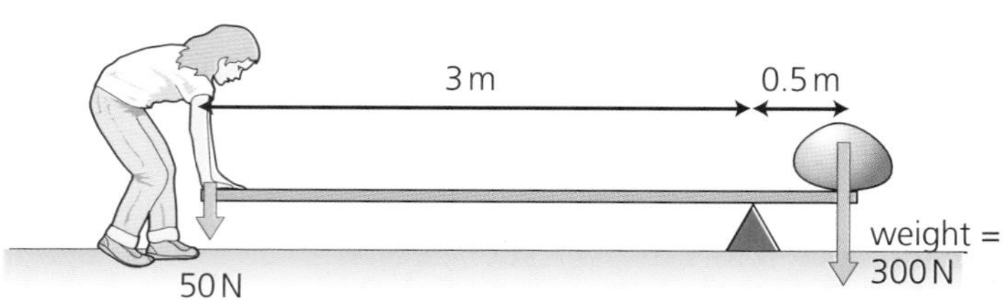

anticlockwise moments	clockwise moments
50 N × 3 m	300 N × 0.5 m
150 Nm	150 Nm

You might think that you are getting something for nothing, because you use less force to lift the load than the load exerts. But this isn't the case. The load moves through a very short distance when you lift it on the end of the lever, while you have to move the end you are pushing on through a much greater distance. So although you need to use less force, you have to move the lever through a greater distance than the load moves.

More moment calculations

When something is balanced, if you don't know one of the values making up a pair of moments then you can calculate it as long as you know the other values. For example, if you know that a rock weighs 600 N, the rock is 1.5 m from the pivot and you can push with a force of 450 N, you can calculate how long a lever you would need to hold the rock up.

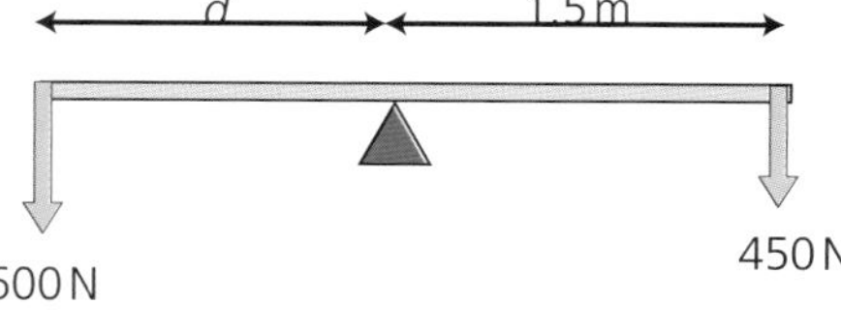

the sum of the anticlockwise moments = the sum of the clockwise moments

$$600\,\text{N} \times 1.5\,\text{m} = 450\,\text{N} \times d$$
$$900\,\text{Nm} = 450 \times d$$
$$d = \frac{900}{450} = 2\,\text{m}$$

a Andy and Caroline are on a seesaw. Andy has a weight of 600 N and is 1 m from the pivot. Caroline's weight is 400 N. How far is Caroline from the pivot if they are balanced?

b Canan sits 2 m from the pivot of a seesaw and balances Yasmin. Yasmin weighs 400 N and sits 3 m from the pivot. What is Canan's weight?

Counterbalance

We have seen how moments working in opposite directions can be either balanced or unbalanced. The principle of moments is important to people who use cranes in building sites or when loading ships. The photo shows a crane picking up a heavy weight from the ground. The crane has a large weight called a **counterbalance** at the other end of the arm. This helps to balance the load the crane is going to pick up and stops the crane falling over.

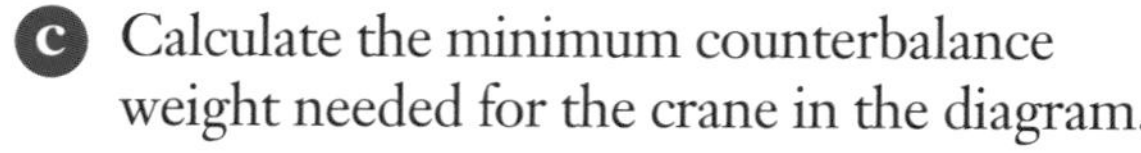

c Calculate the minimum counterbalance weight needed for the crane in the diagram.

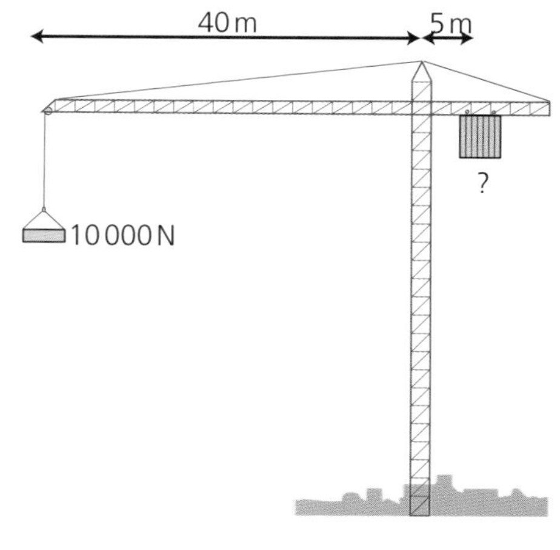

Gymnasts need to balance their weight when they are doing beam or ring exercises. They use different parts of their body to balance them for different moves.

d Explain how a gymnast keeps stable.

e For each photo, draw a stick person in the position shown and label the pivot, the lever and the counterbalance.

Human pivots

In your body, the points where the bones meet are called joints. The joints are the pivots for the bones to turn around. The bones act as the levers when we pick something up. From what you know about moments you can see that the ability to lift something does not only depend on the force exerted by your muscles. It also depends on how long your bone is from your elbow to your wrist, and on the distance from the elbow joint to the place where the muscles are attached to the bone.

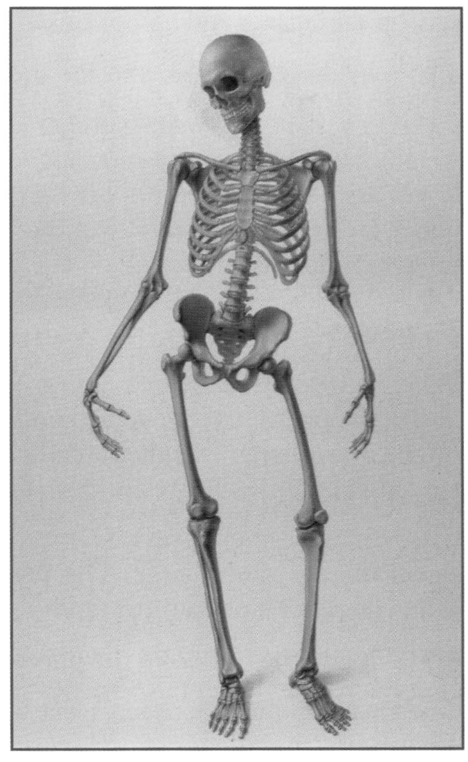

f Look at the skeleton and list as many places as you can where there are pivots.

g Which bones in the body make the best levers?

Lifting safely

It is very important to lift and move objects safely. To reach down to the object you want to lift, you must bend your knees. Then use your knees and hips as pivots to help you straighten up, as shown in the photos. Don't just bend your back down to pick up the object. Bending the back puts a big force directly on the back and can damage it, causing problems such as a slipped disc.

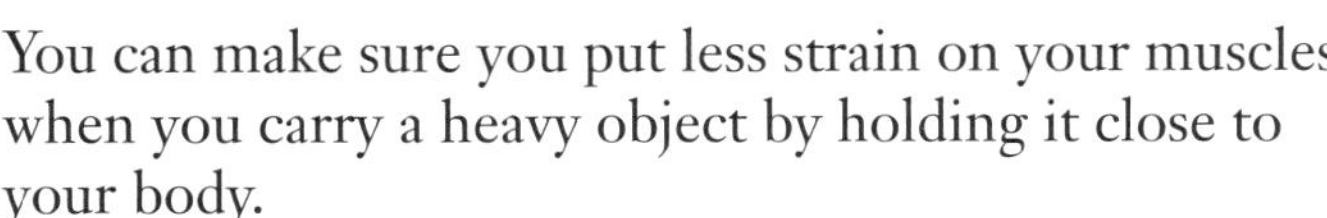

You can make sure you put less strain on your muscles when you carry a heavy object by holding it close to your body.

Questions

1. Explain how weighing things with an old-fashioned pair of pan balances uses the principle of moments.
2. Explain why holding a weight at arm's length would require more strength than holding it close to your body.
3. Russ and Kerryanne are on a seesaw which is balanced. Russ weighs 50 N and is 2 m from the pivot. Calculate the distance Kerryanne is from the pivot if she weighs 40 N.
4. Write a list of rules about how to lift things safely. Include some diagrams.

When you revise

The principle of moments can be used in many everyday situations.

A **counterbalance** is a weight which stops something falling over.

Forces and pressure

Learn about

♦ Pressure

Sinking feeling

Karl and Jackie are both the same weight. They are pushing onto the snow with the same force. Karl's boots sink into the snow while Jackie's feet stay on the surface and do not sink.

a Why does Karl sink into the snow?

Jackie is wearing snowshoes so her weight has been spread out over a larger area. We say that the **pressure** under Jackie's feet is lower than the pressure under Karl's feet.

Pressure at the sharp end

When you push a drawing pin into a board, the pressure from your thumb on the drawing pin is higher at its sharp end. The pressure at the sharp end is very high because the area is so small. The pin is able to move into the board.

The feet of a camel are quite large and flat. The contact area between the camel and the sand is large. This means that the pressure is quite low, so the camel does not sink into the sand.

b Why do the camels in the photo find it easy to walk on sand?

The area of contact between a sharp knife and a piece of cheese is very small. This means that the pressure is very high. The knife is able to cut into the cheese quite easily.

c Explain why a knife does not cut very well when it is blunt. 

What is pressure?

You can see from the examples above that pressure depends on the force applied and the area that it is applied to. For the same force:

- if the area gets bigger, then the pressure gets smaller
- if the area gets smaller, then the pressure gets bigger.

The rectangular block in the diagram has a weight of 15 N. It is lying on its side with its largest face on the floor. The area of this face is $10\,m^2$ ($2\,m \times 5\,m$).

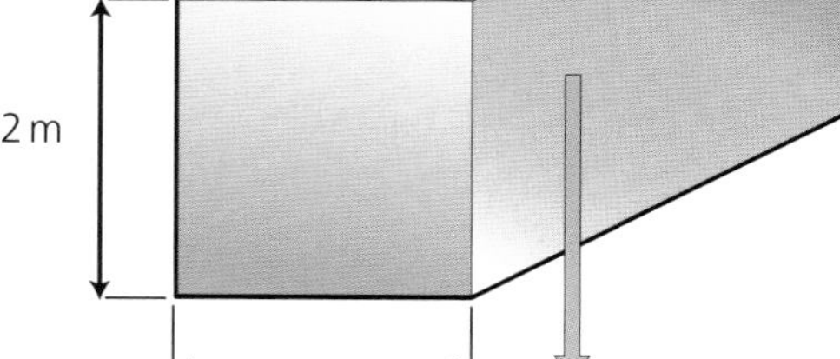

You can calculate the pressure under the face of the block by using the equation:

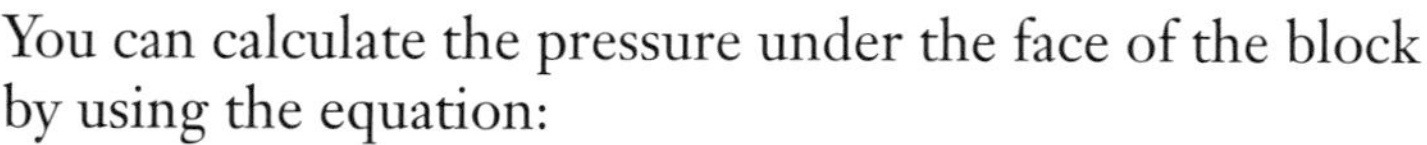

$$\text{pressure} = \frac{\text{force in N}}{\text{area in m}^2}$$

Pressure is usually measured in units of **newtons per square metre** (N/m^2). This unit is also called a **pascal** (Pa). Sometimes units of newtons per square centimetre (N/cm^2) are used instead, for larger pressures.

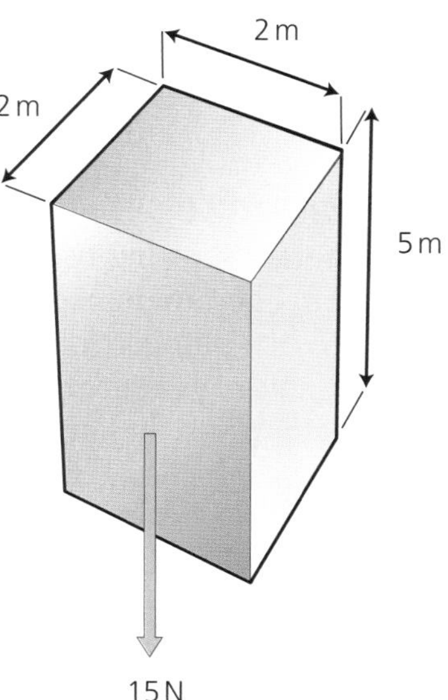

For the rectangular block:

$$\text{pressure} = \frac{15\,\text{N}}{10\,\text{m}^2} = 1.5\,\text{N/m}^2$$

Now the block is placed on its end. The weight is still 15 N, but the surface area in contact with the floor is smaller.

d Calculate the pressure under the block in the diagram opposite. What has happened to the pressure now?

e A woman exerts a force of 600 N over the area of her two feet, 0.005 m^2. An elephant exerts a force of 60 000 N over the area of its four feet, 0.8 m^2. Which of them exerts the higher pressure?

Changing things around

Sometimes you may want to calculate the force or the area rather than the pressure. You can use the pressure triangle to help you with pressure calculations.

You put your finger over the thing you want to calculate, say force, and the rest of the triangle shows pressure multiplied by area. So to find the force you multiply the pressure by the area. In the same way, to find the area, you divide the force by the pressure.

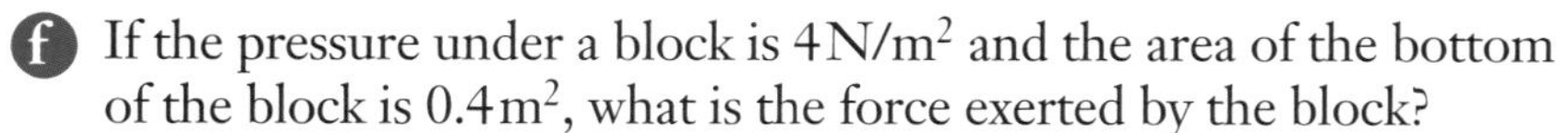

f If the pressure under a block is 4 N/m^2 and the area of the bottom of the block is 0.4 m^2, what is the force exerted by the block?

Questions

1. Copy the table opposite and use the pressure triangle to complete it.

	Force	Area	Pressure
a	30 N	10 m^2	
b	40 N	0.5 m^2	
c	10 N	2 m^2	
d		4 m^2	2 N/m^2
e	20 N		0.5 N/m^2

2. Navjit was watching some people trying to rescue a child who had fallen through the ice into a lake. She noticed that one of the rescuers lay flat on the ice and moved forward slowly. Explain why he did this instead of walking across the ice.
3. Use your knowledge of pressure to explain:
   - **a** why you will hurt yourself if you push down on the pointed end of a drawing pin, but not if you push down on the flat end
   - **b** why the wheels of a tractor need to be large and wide but the blades on the plough it is pulling are very thin
   - **c** how a woman can damage a wooden floor when wearing stiletto heels but not when she wears trainers.
4. The area of one of Siena's shoes is 200 cm^2. His weight is 800 N.
   - **a** What is the pressure beneath Siena in N/cm^2 if he stands on one leg?
   - **b** What is the pressure beneath Siena in N/cm^2 if he stands normally?
   - **c** Siena stands on his toes. Does the pressure go up or down? Explain your answer.

When you revise

Pressure is calculated using the equation:

$$\text{pressure (in N/m}^2) = \frac{\text{force (in N)}}{\text{area (in m}^2)}$$

For a given force, if the area gets bigger the pressure gets smaller, and if the area gets smaller the pressure gets bigger.

3.6 Pressure in liquids

Learn about

- Hydraulics

The big squeeze

Look at the diagram showing two syringes filled with water. They are joined together by a plastic tube. When plunger **A** is pushed in, the liquid is put under pressure. Plunger **B** is pushed out. The pressure has been transmitted through the liquid from plunger **A** to plunger **B**. The pressure is the same throughout the liquid, because it acts equally in all directions. The two syringes are the same size, so the force on plunger **B** is the same as the force on plunger **A**.

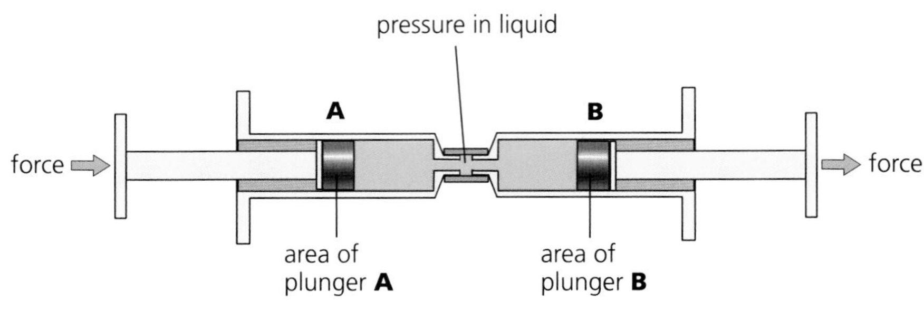

a Explain what happens in a liquid when you try to squash it. Use the particle model to help you.

Different sizes

Think what would happen if the two plungers were different sizes. The pressure is still the same throughout the liquid, but the force on each plunger is different. Look at this example. Plunger **A** is pushed in with a force of 10 N. Because the pressure on plunger **B** is the same, we can work out the force that pushes out plunger **B**.

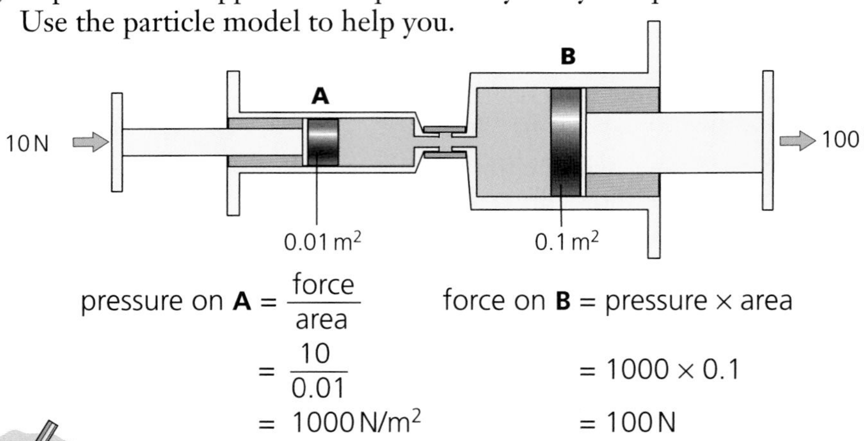

$$\text{pressure on } \mathbf{A} = \frac{\text{force}}{\text{area}} = \frac{10}{0.01} = 1000\,\text{N/m}^2$$

$$\text{force on } \mathbf{B} = \text{pressure} \times \text{area} = 1000 \times 0.1 = 100\,\text{N}$$

b Compare the force on each plunger, and their areas.

If you exert a force of 10 N on plunger **A**, then plunger **B** has a force of 100 N on it. The force has got bigger. A hydraulic system can magnify the force you put into it.

$$\frac{\text{small force}}{\text{small area}} = \frac{\text{large force}}{\text{large area}}$$

Hydraulics

The two syringes make up a type of machine called a **hydraulic machine**. 'Hydraulic' comes from the Greek word for water, as many hydraulic systems use water, though some use oil. A hydraulic machine can magnify the force you apply. The liquid-filled syringes are called **cylinders** and the moving plungers are **pistons**. If a small force is applied to a small input piston, a much larger force can be produced on a larger piston connected to it.

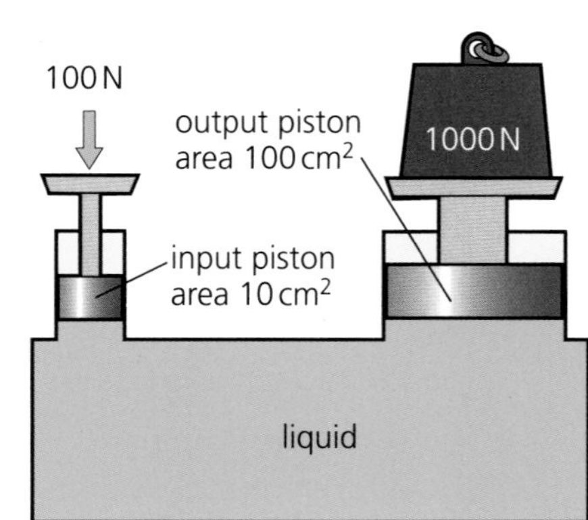

If the area of the output piston is twice the area of the input piston, then the output force will be twice as big as the input force. If the area of the output piston is 10 times bigger, then the output force will be 10 times bigger. This is shown in the table below.

You calculate the pressure on the input piston. Then you use the pressure triangle to calculate the force on the output piston, or its area.

Input piston		Pressure in system in N/m²	Output piston	
Force in N	Area in m²		Force in N	Area in m²
100	0.1	1000	1000	1

Look at the table on the opposite page. This machine makes it easier to lift the weight. You only need a force of 100 N to lift up a heavy weight of 1000 N. Many machines use hydraulics to move and lift heavy things. You can see some of the cylinders on this photo of a digger.

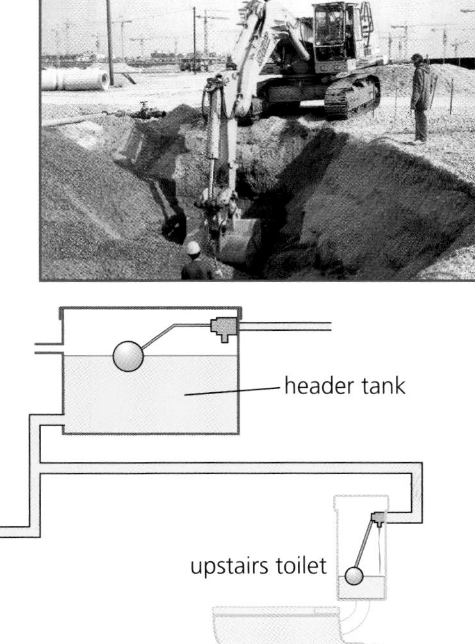

Water pressure

In these hydraulic machines we have thought about pushing a liquid, which applies a pressure on it from outside the liquid. But a liquid also has its own internal pressure. You may have experienced this if you have swum deep down in a swimming pool. Sometimes this pressure makes your ears hurt. The deeper you go, the heavier the weight of water there is over you, pushing on you in all directions. This force over the area of your body exerts a pressure called **water pressure**. When you get to 10 000 m under the ocean, the pressure is equivalent to about eight elephants standing on one plate!

C Submarines dive much deeper than 120 m under the ocean. What design features do you think they need to have to cope with the water pressure?

Raising water up high increases the water pressure and makes it flow faster because of the difference in height. This idea is used in houses to give us better water pressure in taps, showers and toilets. In most houses, the cold water goes to the taps from a 'header' tank. The header tank is in the roof to achieve a higher pressure.

Questions

1. Copy and complete this table. Each row shows a different hydraulic machine.

Input piston		Pressure in system in N/m²	Output piston	
Force in N	Area in m²		Force in N	Area in m²
10	2	a	b	4
15	3	c	d	6
10	0.1	e	50	f
5	2	g	h	5
i	0.2	j	300	2

2. In a digger arm, the area of the output piston is 20 times bigger than the area of the input piston. A force of 25 N is applied to the input piston. What is the force on the output piston?

3. A car brake system has one input piston connected to the brake pedal and four output pistons connected to the four wheels. An input force of 10 N is applied to the brake pedal. The area of the input piston is 0.01 m². The area of each output piston is 0.05 m².
   - **a** How much force is exerted on one output piston?
   - **b** What is the total force exerted on all four output pistons?

4. Cheryl the milkmaid weighs 500 N and Ermintrude, her cow, weighs 5000 N. Design a hydraulic system that would allow Cheryl to raise the cow in the air to make milking easier.

When you revise

Liquids cannot be squashed. The pressure in a liquid is equal in all directions at a particular depth in the liquid. A **hydraulic machine** uses this property of liquids.

A hydraulic machine magnifies the force. If a small force is applied to a small input **piston**, a much larger force can be produced on a larger piston connected to it.

3.7 Pressure in gases

Learn about

- Pneumatics

Squeezing gases 

If you have ever played with a bicycle pump, you know what happens if you put your finger over the hole and then push the plunger in. You exert a force on the plunger and the plunger moves in a little.

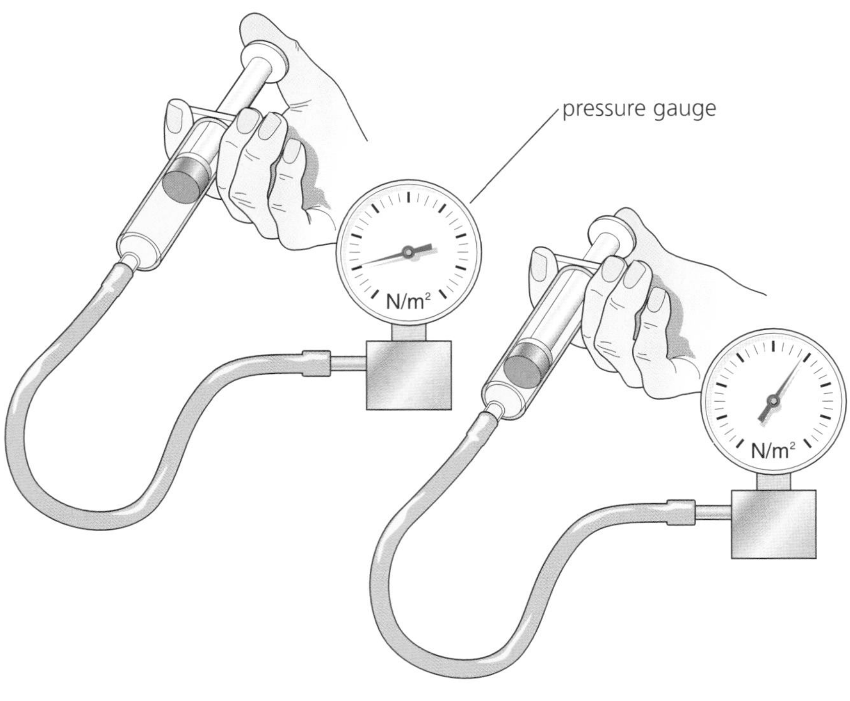

a Use your knowledge of the particle theory to explain what happens to the particles in a gas when the gas is squashed, and why this happens.

When you squeeze or compress a gas in a syringe, the volume it takes up decreases. The number of gas particles doesn't change. When the volume goes down, the pressure goes up. When the volume goes up, the pressure goes down.

The pressure also goes up if you pump more air into a fixed volume, because there are more gas particles squeezed together.

b Think about what happens when you pump up a bicycle tyre. Compare the pressure in the tyre before and after you pump it up. Explain why there is a difference.

c Explain why a balloon or a tyre may explode if you blow it up too much.

We use gas pressure in many ways. Think about a rubber suction pad which sticks to smooth surfaces. When you press the suction pad into place, the rubber flexes and some of the air inside it is squeezed out from underneath. When you let go the rubber springs back, so the volume inside the pad increases. The pressure inside the pad is now lower than the air pressure outside. The air on the outside exerts greater pressure than the air inside. So the pad stays in place.

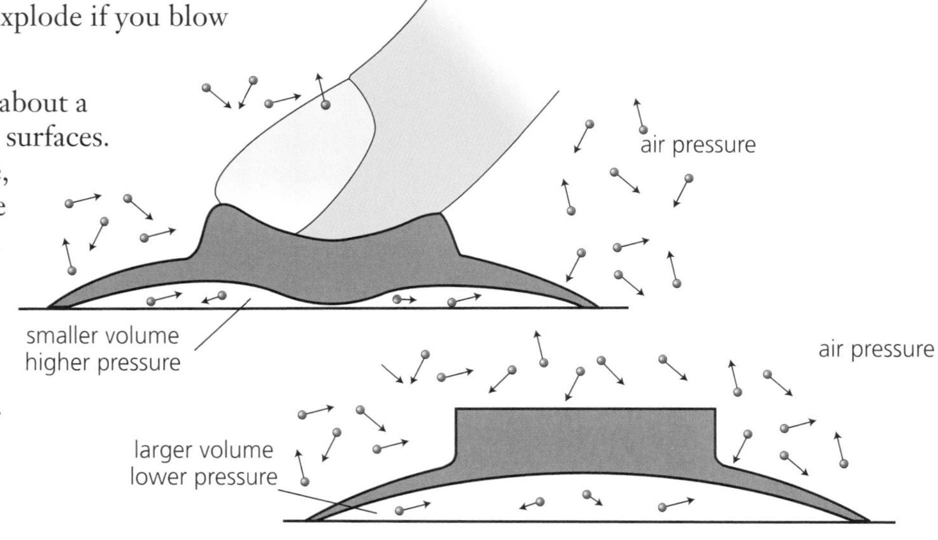

Releasing pressure

If you compress a gas into a small volume and then release it, it expands quickly to a larger volume again. Imagine letting the air out of a bicycle tyre. The air gushes out until the pressure inside the tyre is the same as the air pressure outside the tyre. This expansion of gases is used in aerosols of whipped cream. Inside the can is a mixture of cream and pressurised carbon dioxide. When you push down on the nozzle, the volume gets bigger and the carbon dioxide expands very quickly. A little of the gas, mixed with the cream, rushes out very quickly.

Pneumatics

The sudden expansion of a compressed gas is also used in machines that use cylinders and pistons, like hydraulic machines. Machines that use compressed gas in a cylinder and piston are called **pneumatic machines.** 'Pneumatic' comes from the Greek word for air or breath.

A pneumatic drill has a very fast-moving piston that can move many times a second. It is used for breaking up pavements and drilling holes for explosives. A motor-driven pump called a compressor forces the air at high pressure into a cylinder. The air expands and pushes the piston down. The piston hits the drill bit and forces it down into the pavement.

Air pressure

Like water, air has internal pressure which is called air pressure. The air pressure changes with depth like water pressure does. On the ground at sea level, the air pressure is greatest because there is a large weight of air above, pushing down. The higher up in the air you go, the lower the pressure becomes, because the weight of air gets less. On high mountains the air pressure is half that at sea level.

Aeroplanes fly at about 10 000 m above the ground where the air pressure is even lower. You cannot breathe at this height because there is too little air. The inside of an aeroplane is pressurised to approximately the same pressure as it is on the ground, so that the passengers can breathe.

d In what ways are air pressure and water pressure similar?

e The air pressure exerted by the atmosphere is about 100 000 N/m^2 at ground level. If you assume that the area of your head is 0.1 m^2, calculate the force on your head.

Questions

1. Explain the following statements:
   a Air pressure gets lower the higher up a mountain you go.
   b Aeroplanes have pressurised cabins.
   c A rubber suction pad can be used to unblock sinks.
2. In a carefully controlled experiment, a can with air inside it is sealed and heated.
   a Describe how the molecules move inside the can before heating.
   b Explain what happens to the molecules inside the can after heating.
   c What do you think might happen if the can is heated strongly for a long time?
3. The local university wants more students to take its pneumatics course. Produce a leaflet for them explaining the importance of air pressure in our everyday lives.

When you revise

Gases can be squashed because there is space between the particles. When squashed, the volume goes down and the pressure goes up. When a compressed gas is released, the volume goes up and the pressure goes down.

The fast expansion of released gases is used in aerosols and **pneumatic machines**.

Getting balanced

Think about

- Equilibrium

Number balances

Mustapha was using a beam balance. He wondered why it balanced sometimes but not at other times. He experimented with 1 N weights. When the beam is balanced, it is in **equilibrium**.

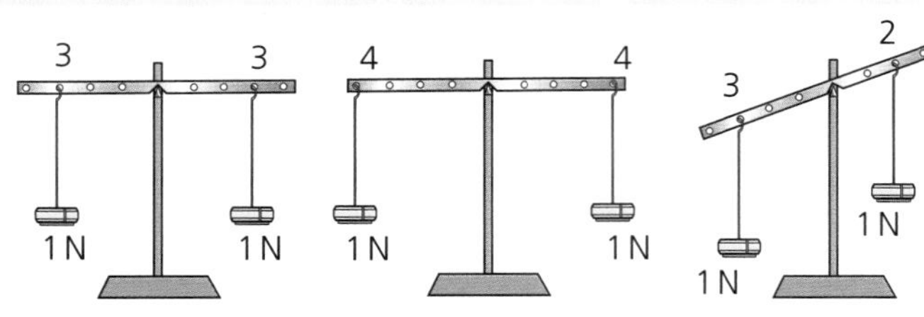

Next Mustapha decided to use 4 N and 8 N weights and see what happened. He made a table to show what weights he used to balance the beam.

	Left-hand side		Right-hand side	
	Distance	**Weight in N**	**Distance**	**Weight in N**
A	1	8	2	4
B	2	8	4	4
C	2	4	1	8
D	4	4	2	8

The beam balance is working just like a seesaw. We can calculate moments for the left-hand side and right-hand side just as we did for the anticlockwise and clockwise moments of a seesaw. The weight is the force. The numbered holes in the beam give the distance.

a Look at the diagrams above. What variables affect whether the beam is in equilibrium?

b Calculate the moment for each side of the balance in the table and check whether the beam will balance for each of rows **A** to **D**.

c Describe the relationship between the distance and weight on one side and the distance and weight on the other side in these four examples.

A bigger balance

Next Mustapha did an investigation using 1 N weights and a bigger balance with eight holes on either side. He decided to investigate what happened when he hung the weights at two or three different holes.

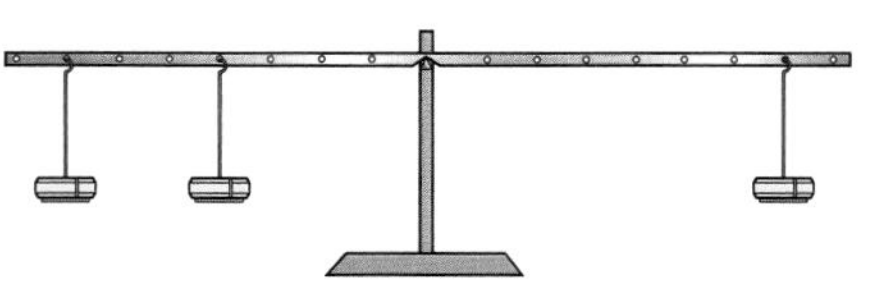

Left-hand side		Right-hand side		
1 N in hole 5		2 N in hole 2		**i**
1 N in hole 8		1 N in hole 4		**ii**
3 N in hole 7		**iii**		**iv**
2 N in hole 5	3 N in hole 2	4 N in hole 3		**v**
1 N in hole 7	4 N in hole 5	5 N in hole 5		**vi**
6 N in hole 8	2 N in hole 4	8 N in hole 7		**vii**
3 N in hole 3		2 N in hole 1	2 N in hole 2	**viii**

d Mustapha's second table is shown opposite. It shows the weights and distances when the beam balanced. Copy and complete the table, giving the weight and which hole it should hang in for each of **i** to **viii**.

Variables

As you have discovered, the combination of distance and weight on the left-hand side of the beam has to be equal to the combination of distance and weight on the right-hand side of the beam. This means a moment has two variables which you can change, distance and weight, for each side of the balance.

There are many situations in life where you can change two variables.

Soft sand

Ginny and Jenny are identical twins. They both weigh the same. Ginny found it easy to walk along the soft sandy beach in her flip-flops, while Jenny sank into the sand in her high-heeled shoes.

e What variables affect whether Ginny and Jenny may sink into the sand?

For Ginny and Jenny, the pressure they exert depends both on the area and the force they exert. If they change either the area or the force they exert, then they change the pressure they exert too. To work out whether they exert the same pressure, like keeping the balance in equilibrium, you have to think about both the area and the force.

f Ginny wants to keep the pressure the same while she carries her little brother across the sand. What variable would she need to change, and how?

g Jenny's brother is lighter than Jenny, but he wants to exert the same pressure as her. What variable would he need to change, and how?

Hydraulic equilibrium

Look at the simple hydraulic system in the diagram. There are two syringes containing a liquid. The liquid is under pressure.

h When you push on one of the syringes, what stays the same in the system all the time?

i What are the other variables in the system?

j Look at the diagrams opposite.
- **i** In **A**, predict whether the output force will be bigger or smaller than the input force.
- **ii** In **B**, is the area of the output plunger bigger or smaller than the area of the input plunger?

k Calculate the missing values to check your answers.

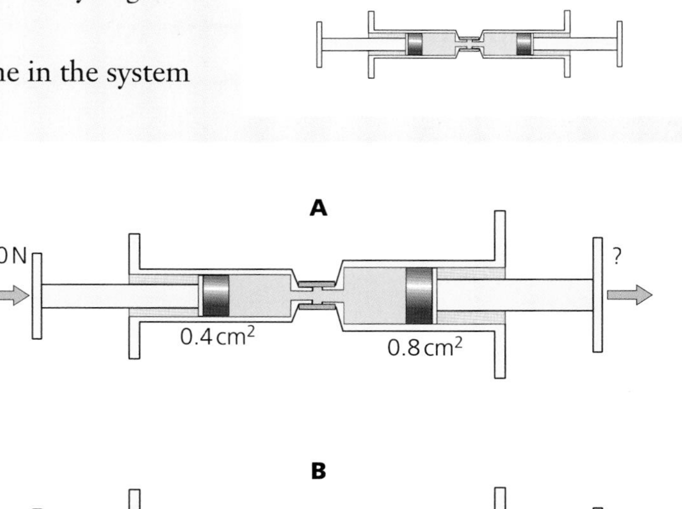

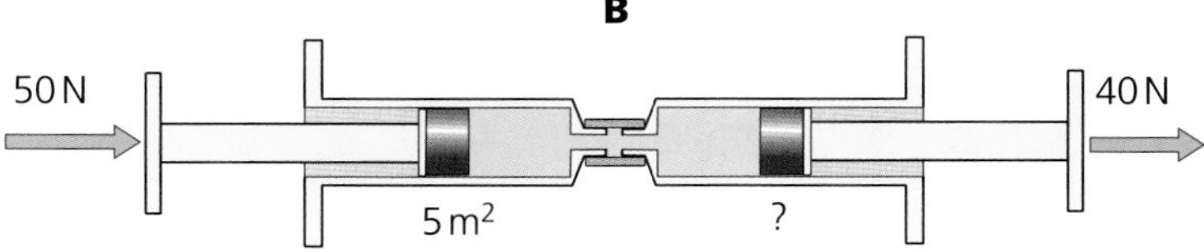

Pressure is a variable made up of two other variables, force and area. If either the force or the area changes, then the other one has to change too if you want to keep the pressure the same. If you only change one out of force and area, then the pressure will change. You have already met other variables made up of a combination of two variables, for example, speed and density.

Questions

1. Name the two variables that make up:
   a speed **b** density.
2. Explain the following:
   a Ice floats. **b** A boat made of iron floats in water.
3. Explain the meaning of the word 'equilibrium', giving examples.

4.1 Finding the pattern

A multitude of elements

Before 1860, elements were big news amongst chemists. In the previous 100 years, 41 new elements had been discovered. Scientists became famous by discovering an element. Some elements were solids, some liquids and some gases. Some elements were metals and some non-metals. Every element seemed different from every other element. Scientists struggled to find any order or patterns in the elements.

a What makes a substance an element?

b What makes the element carbon different from the element sulfur?

In 1860, there was the first ever international meeting for chemists. During the meeting, one chemist reminded the others that each type of atom has a different mass. Some of the chemists realised that they could put the elements in order by the mass of their atoms. Hydrogen, with the lightest atoms, would go first. Lithium would go second because lithium atoms are the second lightest. These chemists rushed home after the meeting, each keen to find the pattern that explained the elements. The race had started!

Finding a pattern

One of these chemists was Dmitri Ivanovich Mendeleev. He made a card for each element. On each card was the element's name, its symbol and the mass of its atoms. He ended up with a pack of over 60 cards.

He arranged the cards by the mass of the atoms, with hydrogen first and lithium second. Mendeleev then looked for patterns using the cards. He took the cards everywhere, laying them out on any convenient table and looking for a pattern.

Mendeleev's next idea was to leave out hydrogen. Hydrogen was strange, as its properties were different from those of any other element. He put aside the card for hydrogen, so that the pack now started with lithium (Li).

He then started to deal the cards out in rows, like a game of patience. In a game of patience you start a new row after seven cards. The question was, when should Mendeleev start a new row?

The question was answered when Mendeleev reached the card for sodium (Na). Sodium is very like lithium in many ways. Mendeleev started a new row with sodium, placing it below lithium. He then dealt the rest of the row. Mendeleev could see that each element in the second row was similar to the element above it.

Then he came to potassium (K), which is very similar to lithium and sodium. Potassium was the first element in the third row and calcium (Ca) was the second. The pattern was too clear to be ignored.

c Why did Mendeleev decide:

i to use the masses of the atoms?

ii to set aside hydrogen?

iii to start new rows with sodium and then potassium?

Inspiration

The pattern was less clear after calcium, but Mendeleev did not give up. He had his next big idea. He decided that not all the elements had been discovered, so there might be gaps in the pattern. He continued putting elements under similar elements, even if it meant leaving a gap. Mendeleev came up with the first version of the periodic table, shown opposite. As you can see, it becomes rather complicated when you reach the last two rows, with two elements in each column rather than one, and an extra column (VIII) for the six elements that would not fit.

I	II	III	IV	V	VI	VI	VIII
H							
Li	Be	B	C	N	O	F	
Na	Mg	Al	Si	P	S	Cl	
K Cu	Ca Zn	gap gap	gap Ti	As V	Se Cr	Br Mn	Fe Co Ni
Rb Ag	Sr Cd	In Y	Sn Zr	Sb Nb	Te Mo	I gap	Ru Rh Pd

d Why did Mendeleev leave gaps in his table?

Using the model to make predictions

Mendeleev's table was a scientific model, a useful way of looking at the world. He first showed it to other scientists in 1869. The elements were arranged in increasing atomic mass. The vertical groups contained elements that were similar. There was a pattern that repeated every time you moved from left to right across the table. In many ways it was similar to the periodic table we use today.

Mendeleev used his periodic table (his scientific model) to make predictions. In 1871, he made a famous prediction about the element missing from the yellow gap in the table. He predicted the mass of the atoms of the missing element, and the compounds the element would make. In 1885, Clemens Winkler discovered an element which he named germanium. Germanium had exactly the properties Mendeleev had predicted.

e Why was it important that Mendeleev's predictions turned out to be accurate?

Questions

1. Imagine you are Mendeleev. You are going to a conference to give a talk to other scientists. The title of the talk is 'My periodic table: an important new way of looking at elements'. Make a list of bullet points that would prompt you to say the most important things you need to tell them, in the correct order.
2. Look at the modern periodic table on page 46. Write a comparison between Mendeleev's periodic table and the modern version.

4.2 The modern periodic table

Learn about

- The periodic table

The present situation

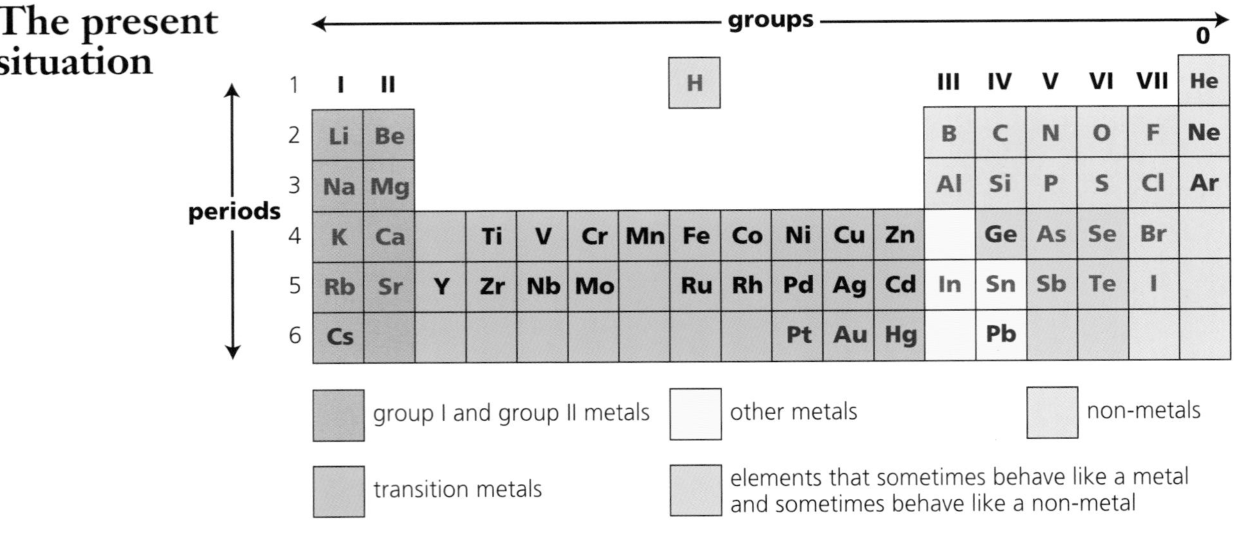

We now know of 118 elements. There is a place in the modern periodic table for each of these elements. The diagram above shows only the top part of the table. The red symbols are the elements that made up Mendeleev's main repeating pattern (see page 45). The **black** symbols are the elements which Mendeleev had problems fitting into his table. The blue symbols are other elements mentioned in this book.

A group is a vertical column in the periodic table.

A period is a horizontal row in the periodic table.

Groups

Elements in a vertical column, or group, are similar to each other. On the far left of the table is **group I**. The table shows five members of group I: lithium (Li), sodium (Na), potassium (K), rubidium (Rb) and caesium (Cs). They are similar in many ways.

- They are all metals.
- They are soft like cheese, so they can be cut with a knife.
- They have low melting points.
- They all react with the oxygen in the air, so they have to be kept under oil.
- All the compounds they form are solid at room temperature, crystalline and dissolve in water to give colourless solutions.
- The formulae of their compounds are similar, for example, the chlorides (LiCl, NaCl, KCl, RbCl, CsCl) and the oxides (Li_2O, Na_2O, K_2O, Rb_2O, Cs_2O). Even the crystal shapes of the compounds are similar. The photo shows sodium chloride crystals. Crystals of lithium chloride or potassium chloride would look exactly the same.

a The formula for magnesium oxide is MgO. Give the formulae for three other group II oxides.

b Chlorine occurs as molecules with the formula Cl_2. Give the formulae for three other elements in group VII.

Transition metals

Mendeleev was not sure where to put metals like iron and silver in his periodic table. He put some of them in a strange 'sub-row' and some in a group he called 'group VIII'. In the modern periodic table these metals form the large central block called the **transition metals**, which is shaded in red in the

Temperature in °C								
pH	**15**	**25**	**35**	**45**	**55**	**65**	**75**	**85**
0	✗	✔	✔	✔	✗	✗	✔	✔
1	✗	✔	✔	✔	✗	✗	✗	✗
2	✗	✔	✔	✔	✗	✗	✗	✗
3	✗	✗	✔	✗	✗	✗	✗	✗
4	✗	✗	✗	✗	✗	✗	✗	✗
5	✗	✗	✗	✗	✗	✗	✗	✗
6	✗	✗	✗	✗	✗	✗	✗	✗
7	✗	✗	✗	✗	✗	✗	✗	✗

✔✔ = digestion finished at 6 hours ✗ = digestion not finished at 6 hours

e In how many test tubes had digestion finished at 6 hours?

f Are Jezzie's results as you expected? Explain your answer.

g Why does Jezzie's teacher suggest that she repeats the experiment for low pH values without the pepsin?

Jezzie's teacher suggested that she repeat the experiment for pH 0 to 3 without the pepsin present. Here are her results.

Temperature in °C								
pH	**15**	**25**	**35**	**45**	**55**	**65**	**75**	**85**
0	✗	✗	✗	✗	✗	✗	✔	✔
1	✗	✗	✗	✗	✗	✗	✗	✗
2	✗	✗	✗	✗	✗	✗	✗	✗
3	✗	✗	✗	✗	✗	✗	✗	✗

✔ = digestion finished at 6 hours ✗ = digestion not finished at 6 hours

h Under what conditions does digestion happen without pepsin?

i Compare the two results tables. Under what conditions does digestion happen with pepsin?

j Suggest what is needed for digestion to happen in the stomach. Give your reasons.

k Write a conclusion for Jezzie's investigation.

Surface area

Jane investigated how surface area affects digestion. She started with 10 mm cubes of egg white, and cut them up to give different surface areas. Jane used 2 cm^3 of 5 mg/cm^3 of pepsin, a temperature of 35 °C and pH 2.

Surface area in mm^2	600	800	1000	1200	1600
Digestion in 6 h?	✔	✔	✔	✔	✔

Jane concluded that surface area does not affect the digestion of egg white.

l How is Jane's conclusion supported by the evidence?

m Do you think Jane's conclusion is correct? Give reasons for your answer.

n Design some further experiments to test Jane's conclusion.

Questions

1. Paul is interested by the fact that food only stays in the stomach for 20 minutes. He wants to investigate whether egg white protein can be completely digested within 20 minutes. Suggest conditions under which complete digestion within 20 minutes would occur. Give a reason for each of your choices.

2. Imagine that you are a scientist working for a company making bolts that are used to build bridges and buildings. Your job is to test all the new bolts to see how rustproof they are. Rusting is a slow process, so you need to set up conditions which will make the bolts rust as quickly as possible. Design a 'rusting box' for maximum rusting.

5.1 Great medical breakthroughs

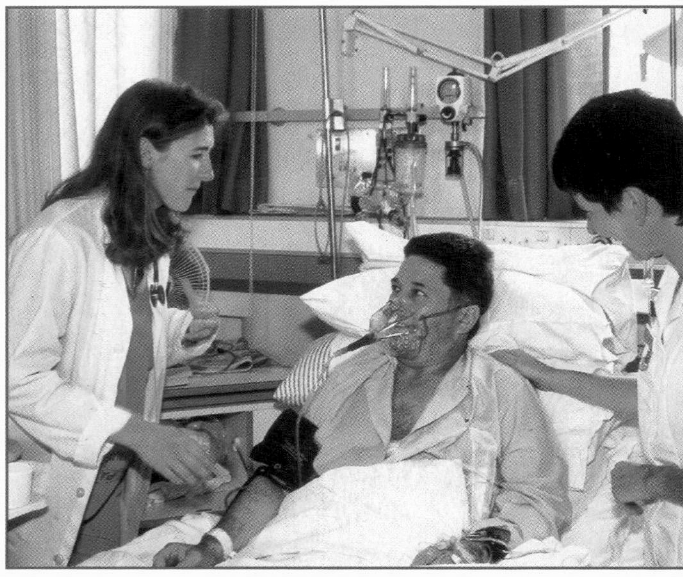

Treating and preventing disease

Over 2000 years ago, the people who lived in the Middle East used over 200 different plants to treat illnesses. The Greeks also used many different plants. The famous Greek doctor Hippocrates used the bark from willow to relieve pain in his patients. We know now that the bark contains a chemical called salicylic acid. We still use this chemical today, and we call it aspirin. Many of the medicines we use today come from plants. One of the reasons why scientists are concerned about the destruction of the rainforests is that we could be losing plants that may produce life-saving medicines.

Over the past 400 years many medical discoveries have been made. Because of these we are now able to cure or prevent many diseases which used to kill people.

In 1867, Joseph Lister, an English doctor, discovered carbolic acid. This was the first widely used antiseptic. Lister thought that it could be microbes that turned wounds bad after operations. He used carbolic acid to kill microbes on the wounds and instruments. Previously tar had been applied to amputated joints, and Lister discovered that it was the carbolic acid in the tar that killed bacteria from the air settling on the wound.

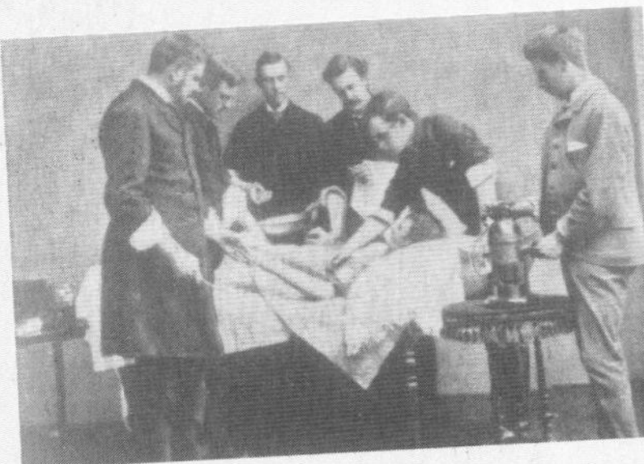

Using a carbolic acid spray during an operation.

Sir Frederick Banting was a Canadian doctor who found that insulin could be used to treat diabetes. He shared the 1923 Nobel prize for medicine with John McLeod for his discoveries.

Alexander Fleming made one of the greatest medical breakthroughs by chance in 1928. Fleming was studying bacteria and noticed that mould growing on an agar plate stopped a particular type of bacterium from growing. He grew more of the mould and obtained a substance from the broth called penicillin. He found it could destroy a number of different bacteria. In 1941, Howard Florey and Ernst Chain found a way of making penicillin in large amounts to use as a medicine.

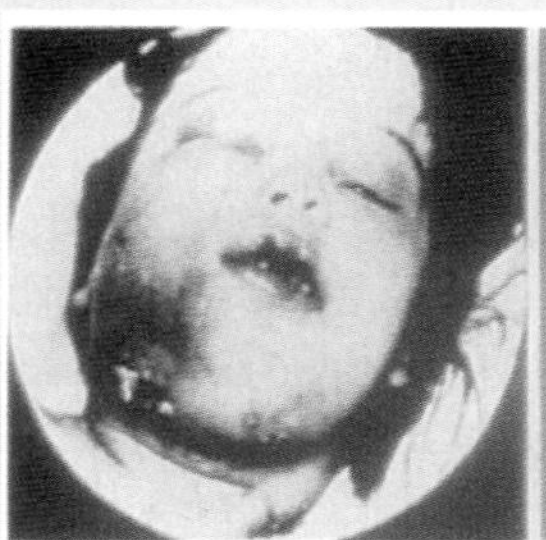

The first child to be treated with penicillin. Four weeks after treatment the infection was gone.

In 1796, the English doctor Edward Jenner performed the first vaccination against smallpox. Jenner had noticed that milkmaids did not get smallpox, but got a milder form of the disease called cowpox. Jenner took the pus from cowpox spots on a sterile needle and scratched it into the skin of a boy called James Phipps. The boy developed cowpox, but he did not develop smallpox. He was protected against smallpox.

Edward Jenner.

How the human body functions

The study of medicine, or being a doctor, is more than just treating patients with drugs. It is also about understanding how the human body works. **Anatomy** is the study of the structure of the body and **physiology** is the study of the functions of the organs and how they work. Our knowledge of the human body has improved a great deal over the last 500 years.

The English doctor William Harvey published a full account of how the blood circulates around the body in 1628. He even deduced that capillaries existed, although he could not see them. It is now known that the first person to give an account of blood circulation was Ibn an-Nafis, an Arab doctor, in the thirteenth century.

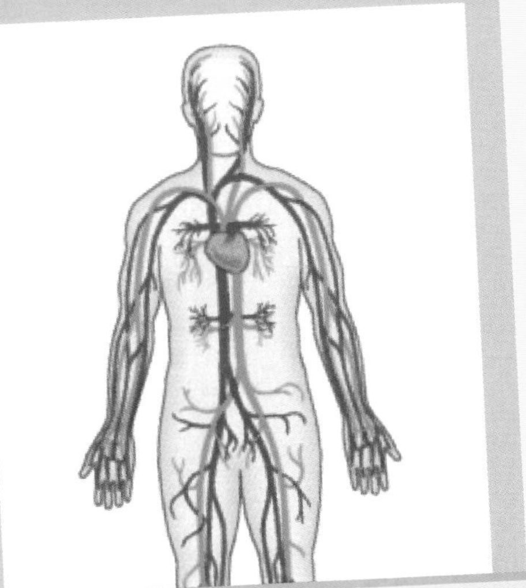

Andreas Vesalius was born in Brussels in 1514 and is known as the 'father of anatomy'. He gave the first full description of the human body in his book *Concerning the Fabric of the Human Body* in 1543.

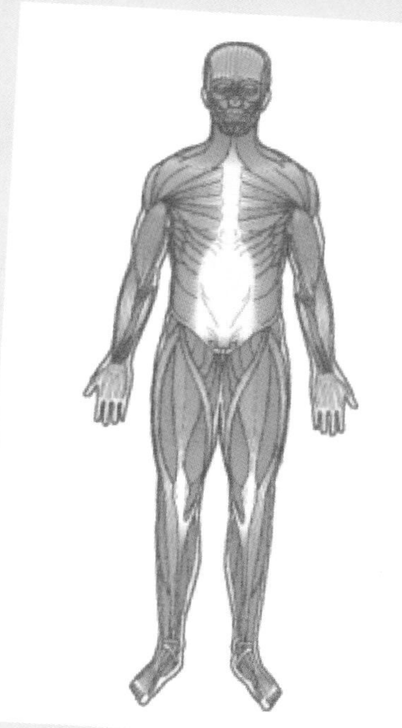

Albrecht von Haller in the eighteenth century was the first to realise that all nerves join the spinal cord and the brain. Thus he realised that it was the brain not the heart that controlled the body.

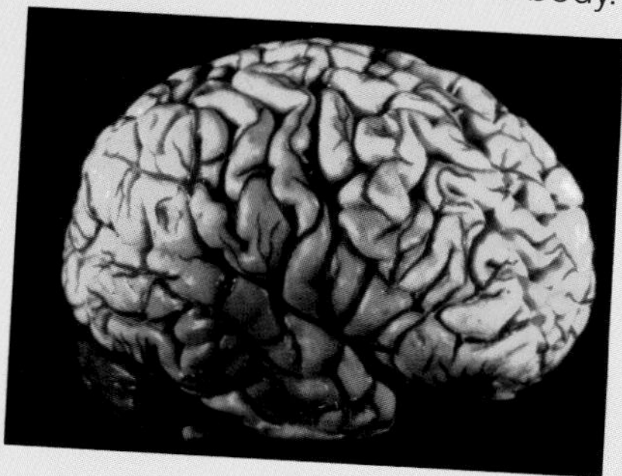

Claude Bernard was a nineteenth-century French physiologist who discovered that glucose was the main source of energy for the body. He also found that the glucose was stored as glycogen in the liver.

The discoveries above represent some of the main highlights of medicine in previous centuries. During the last century in particular, there were too many new discoveries to mention all of them.

a Which important medical discovery from the last century would you add to the list?

Questions

1. Why are the rainforests so important in our fight against disease?
2. Discuss the following statement: 'Luck is an important part of scientific discovery'.
3. **a** What is the purpose of a vaccination?
   b List any vaccinations you have had or that you know about.
4. 'Prevention is better than cure' is a common saying. Classify the discoveries of the four doctors on the opposite page under two headings, 'Prevention' and 'Cure'.
5. Why do you think there were so many more medical discoveries in the twentieth century than there had been before?
6. Make a time line of all the medical breakthroughs mentioned on these pages.

5.2 Keeping fit

Learn about

- Fitness
- Exercise

What is fitness?

When you are asleep you breathe very slowly, but after exercise you breathe much faster. You don't have to decide how to breathe, it happens automatically. Your brain changes how quickly you breathe, your **breathing rate**, without you having to think about it. Your breathing rate depends on the amount of carbon dioxide in your blood.

Respiration

When you breathe in, you take in oxygen to be used in respiration. Respiration is the process in which glucose and oxygen react to release energy from your food. The products are carbon dioxide and water vapour. As you breathe out the body gets rid of these two waste gases.

oxygen + glucose → water + carbon dioxide

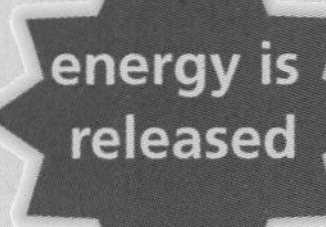

Exercising

The graph shows how the breathing rate may change during the day for two different people.

When you exercise, your muscle cells need to carry out more respiration to release energy. This means they need more oxygen and they also produce more carbon dioxide. When the level of carbon dioxide in your blood rises, your breathing rate goes up to provide the extra oxygen and to get rid of the excess carbon dioxide from your blood. When you are sleeping or at rest, your body needs energy only for the life processes that keep the body functioning. There is less carbon dioxide in your blood so your breathing rate slows down.

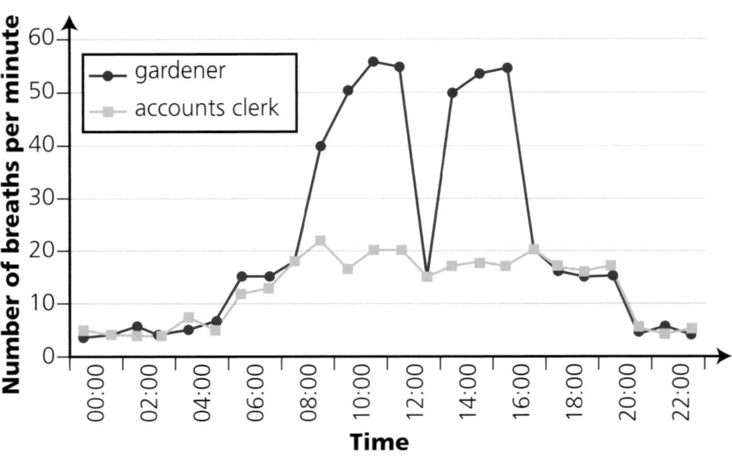

a Why do you think the breathing rate is low between midnight and 6 a.m. for both lines on the graph?

b Why do you think that the breathing rate goes up and down during the day?

c Describe how the two lines on the graph are different, and suggest an explanation.

Measuring your fitness 

Unfit people get out of breath easily. But how you breathe is just one measure of fitness. One of the easiest ways to measure your fitness is to use your pulse rate to show how quickly your heart is beating. Your heartbeat changes depending on the need for oxygen to be transported round the body in the blood, and for carbon dioxide to be expelled. In a fit person, the heart pumps more efficiently because it has grown larger with regular exercise. This means:

- Your resting pulse rate is quite low.
- During exercise, your pulse rate does not increase too much.
- After exercise, your pulse rate quickly returns to normal.

Your fitness also depends on:

- **stamina**: your ability to keep going when you exercise
- **strength**: the ability of your muscles to exert a force to pull your bones
- **suppleness**: your ability to move your body and limbs easily.

Keeping fit and healthy

Exercise is a very important part of a healthy lifestyle. It has been suggested that we should exercise regularly about three times a week to stay healthy. Exercise helps to keep your heart healthy and prevent heart disease. It also keeps the lungs and the rest of your body fit.

Regular exercise keeps your body working efficiently by improving your muscle tone, improving the circulation of the blood and helping keep your weight at a healthy level. It can make your lungs bigger so you breathe more efficiently. Regular exercise also keeps your bones and joints working well.

Different types of exercise can improve your fitness in different ways. Some types of exercise, such as swimming, are good at improving your strength. Others, such as gymnastics, are good at improving suppleness. Jogging can improve your stamina. The table rates some exercises in terms of how they can improve different parts of your fitness.

d Which types of exercise are excellent for building up your stamina?

e What difference does it make to your fitness to walk quickly instead of slowly?

f If you only had time to do one type of exercise a week, which one would you choose? Explain your answer.

As well as taking regular exercise, we should also make sure that we eat a balanced diet. Food provides us with energy and allows our bodies to grow and repair themselves. We need to make sure we don't over-eat or under-eat. Both are bad for our health. To be healthy we should avoid drugs such as nicotine and alcohol. It is also important to get enough rest and sleep.

Exercise	Strength	Suppleness	Stamina
Walking slowly	1	1	2
Tennis	2	3	2
Gymnastics	3	4	2
Walking quickly	1	1	3
Jogging	2	2	4
Football	3	3	3
Swimming	4	4	4
Yoga	3	4	3
Cycling fast	3	2	4

1 = poor 2 = fair 3 = good 4 = excellent

Questions

1. Why do we keep on breathing even when we are not conscious?
2. Explain the following statements:
   a A marathon runner's resting pulse rate is very low.
   b Tasha's pulse rate got back to normal after exercise more quickly than Nicole's.
3. Why does the breathing rate go up when we exercise and go down when we stop?
4. Use the information in the table above to produce a weekly training plan for a teenager to improve overall fitness. Include a range of activities.
5. Design a brochure for a sports centre describing to people why they need to stay fit and use the sports centre more often.

When you revise

The **breathing rate** increases during exercise to supply the muscle cells with the oxygen they need for respiration.

Regular exercise is good for your muscles, your lungs, your circulation, your bones and your joints.

A healthy lifestyle includes a good balanced diet, keeping the right weight, taking enough rest and avoiding drugs.

5.3 Breathe in and out

Learn about

- The structure of the lungs
- Gas exchange

The respiratory system

If you put your hands on your chest, you can feel it move up and down as you breathe in and out. The gases oxygen and carbon dioxide are exchanged inside your lungs.

The lungs are organs. Like all organs, the lungs are made of different types of tissue. Each tissue is made up of similar specialised cells. Look at the diagram opposite. The lungs, together with the tubes that take gases in and out of the lungs, form the respiratory system.

The air is taken in through the nose and mouth.

It passes through the **larynx** and down the **trachea** (or windpipe).

The trachea splits into two tubes called the **bronchi**, one bronchus going to each lung.

The bronchi then split into smaller and smaller tubes called **bronchioles**. Each bronchiole finishes up in tiny air sacs known as **alveoli** (singular alveolus).

nose
mouth
larynx (voicebox)
trachea
ribs
left lung (cut open)
heart
left bronchus
right lung
diaphragm
bronchiole

In and out

At the bottom of your chest cavity is a domed sheet of muscle called the **diaphragm**. When you breathe in, your ribs move upwards and outwards. At the same time your diaphragm becomes flatter. When this happens, the volume inside the chest cavity gets bigger. This makes air rush into the lungs. When you breathe out, the opposite happens. The ribs move downwards and inwards and the diaphragm domes upwards. The volume of the chest cavity gets smaller and air is forced out of the lungs.

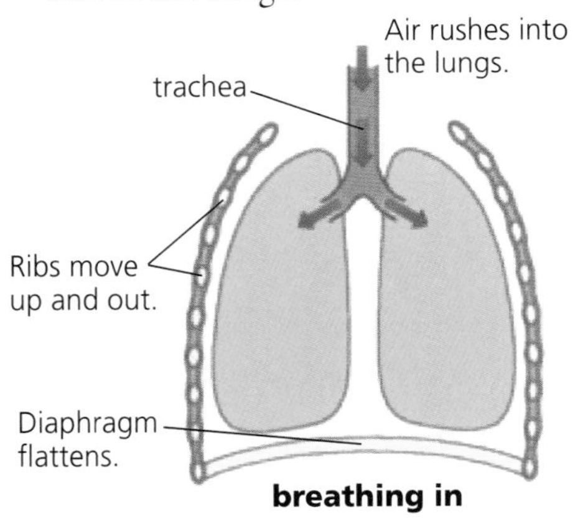

breathing in

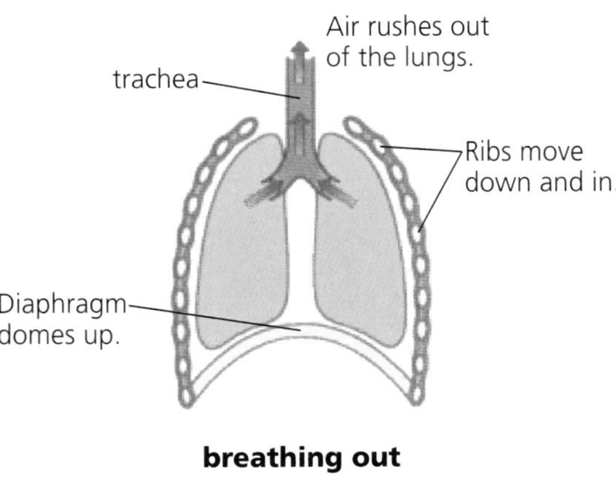

breathing out

a Copy and complete the table below to show what happens when you breathe in and out.

	Ribs	Diaphragm	Effect on volume of chest cavity	Movement of air
Breathing in	Move up and out		Increases	
Breathing out		Domes upwards		Out of lungs

Even when we become adults our cells are still dividing. New cells are constantly needed to replace or repair lots of our body's cells, such as skin cells and blood cells.

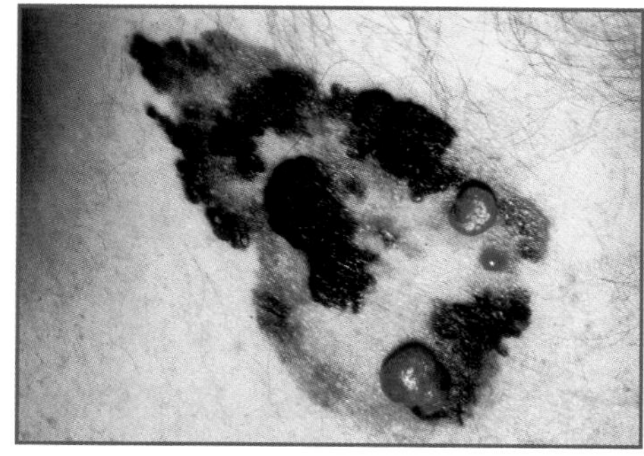

The photo shows skin cancer, which can be caused by over-exposure to ultraviolet rays in sunlight. The dark patch on the skin is called a melanoma.

Cancer

Cell division is usually very carefully controlled. Sometimes, however, cells can begin to divide out of control. This is called **cancer**. The rapidly growing group of cells is called a **tumour**. Many types of cancer can be treated successfully if they are detected in time. Some types of cancer are very difficult to treat and the tumours can spread throughout the body.

b Cell division enables the body to grow and repair itself. Explain why cell division can also cause illness.

Useful microbes

Some microbes are very useful to us. The table shows some of ways that we can use them. It would be impossible for us to survive without microbes.

Microorganism	Uses
Fungi	Yeast is used to produce beer and wine. Yeast is used to make bread rise when it is baked. Fungi are used in making medicines such as antibiotics. Mould is used in making blue cheese. Fungi decompose dead plants and animals and their waste. Fungi called Quorn can be eaten.
Bacteria	Bacteria are used in making yoghurt and cheese. Bacteria are also used in making medicines. Bacteria decompose dead plants and animals and their waste. Bacteria are used in sewage farms to break down sewage. Some bacteria live inside humans' and other animals' intestines and help to digest their food.

Questions

1. Paul and Angela carried out an experiment to monitor the growth of yeast. Here are some of their results.

Time in hours	0	1	2	3	4	5	6	7	8	9
No. of yeast cells	1	2	4	8						

   a Predict how the number of yeast cells will grow over the next 6 hours.
   b Plot these results as a line graph.
   c Describe the shape of your graph.
   d Do you think the population of yeast will continue to grow like this? What might happen to affect the yeast population as it gets bigger?

2. Explain why cell division is important to help us grow.
3. Give three differences between viruses and bacteria.
4. Describe the differences between fermentation in yeast and respiration in humans.
5. Imagine that scientists have discovered a way to kill every single type of microbe on the planet. Write a story about how this would have a serious effect on our lives.

When you revise

There are three main groups of **microbe**: bacteria, viruses and **fungi**.

Bacteria and fungi reproduce by **cell division**.

Cell division makes it possible for humans to grow and repair their bodies.

When cell division goes wrong, it can cause **cancer**.

Microorganisms can be very useful to us.

Defence against disease

Learn about

- How the body fights infection

Disease

Although many microbes are harmless, there are a lot of microbes that can cause diseases if they get inside our bodies. When microbes grow inside our bodies, they cause an **infection**. Organisms that cause disease are called **pathogens**.

The yellow parts of the lungs have been damaged by TB.

Bacteria attack body cells and they also release poisonous chemicals (toxins) which kill cells and make you feel ill. Diseases caused by bacteria include tuberculosis (TB), food poisoning, bacterial meningitis and tetanus.

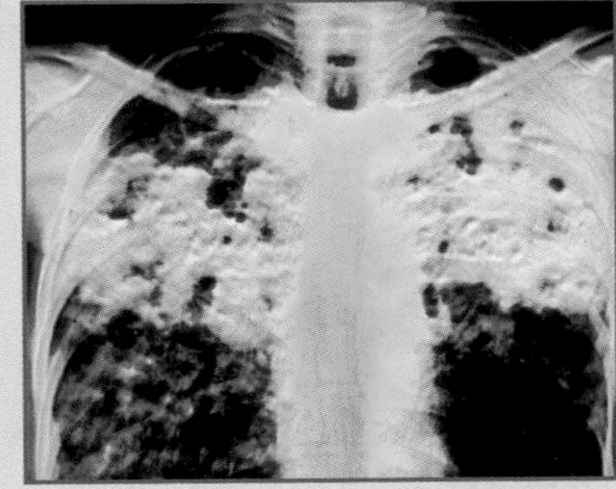

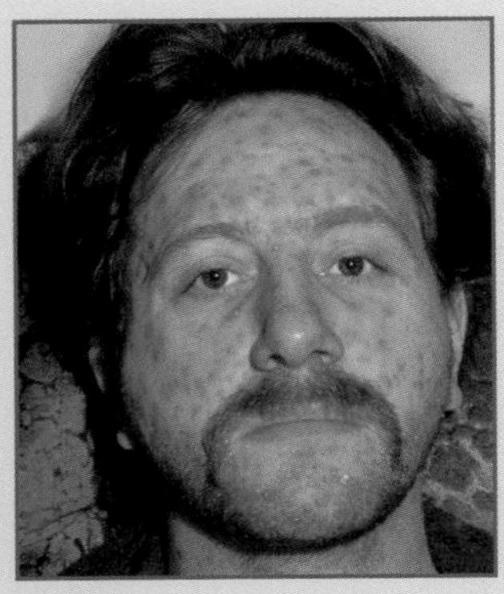

Chickenpox is caused by a virus.

Viruses take over body cells and force the cells to make millions of copies of the virus. These then burst out and invade other nearby cells. They can also release chemicals which make you feel ill. Diseases caused by viruses include colds and 'flu, rabies, chickenpox, German measles, viral meningitis and AIDS.

Athlete's foot is a fungal disease.

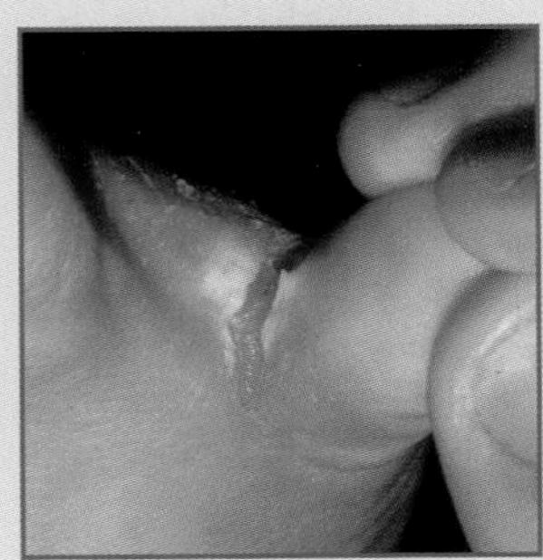

Fungi often grow on skin and release chemicals that digest skin cells. They can make the skin red and sore. Diseases caused by fungi include athlete's foot, ringworm and farmer's lung.

How microbes enter the body

The human body is very good at keeping microbes out and preventing infection. The skin is a good barrier and stops microbes from getting into the blood. Your tears contain a chemical that destroys bacteria. But there are several ways that microbes can get past these defences and enter the body.

- Cuts in the skin allow microbes in.
- The food you eat can contain harmful microbes.
- The water you drink can carry water-borne microbes.
- Air has lots of microbes in it, which you can breathe in.
- **Sexually transmitted diseases** such as AIDS can be caught from sexual intercourse without protection.
- Animals can carry diseases and pass them on by biting you.

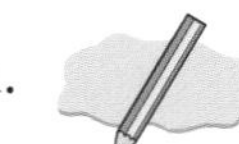

a Make a table to show examples of disease the three types of microbe can cause.

b Weil's disease is caused by bacteria that are sometimes found in canals and rivers. People who canoe there are quite likely to catch the disease. Explain how they might get infected.

Fighting infection

Once microbes get inside the body, there is still another line of defence which can attack them. This is called the **immune system**. **White blood cells** help in the fight against microbes. They work in three different ways.

1. Some white blood cells can engulf microbes.
2. White blood cells produce special chemicals called **antibodies** which attach themselves to the outside of the microbes. Antibodies may kill the microbes directly, or they may make them clump together, which makes it easier for white blood cells to engulf them. The diagram on the next page shows this.
3. White blood cells can destroy the toxins produced by microbes.

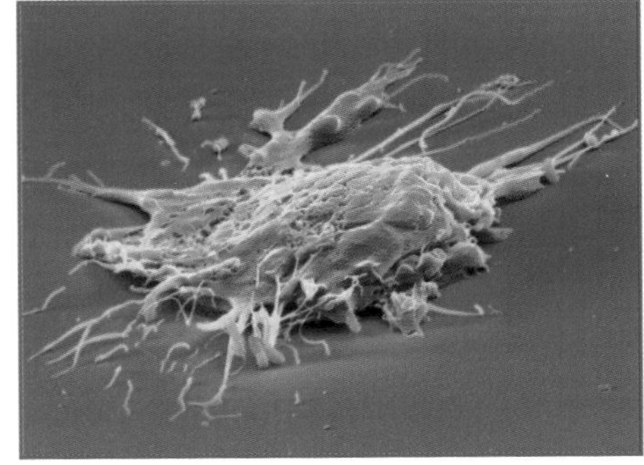

A white blood cell engulfing bacteria (pink rods).

AIDS (acquired immune deficiency syndrome) is a disease that stops the immune system from working. This means that the body is unable to fight infection. People do not die directly from having AIDS, but they are likely to catch lots of other diseases such as pneumonia.

microbe
antibody
antibodies attach to microbes and make them clump together
white blood cell

Immunisation

An antibody is only able to recognise and fight one type of microbe. Once your immune system has met a microbe, the antibodies can be made quite easily and the body can fight the infection a lot quicker. This makes you **immune** to the disease.

You can be **vaccinated** to make you immune to a disease before you catch it. Dead or inactive microbes can be injected into your body. They do not make you ill, but your body will produce antibodies against them. This is called **active immunity** because you have made the antibodies yourself.

Antibodies can be passed from a mother to her baby across the placenta and also in breast milk. For their first few months after birth, babies are protected from some diseases like measles, because they have antibodies from their mother in their blood. You can also be injected with ready-made antibodies. Putting ready-made antibodies into your body gives you **passive immunity**.

Vaccinations control diseases

Many diseases that are a danger to public health have been controlled by vaccinating as many people as possible. Smallpox was a very dangerous disease that killed many people. It has been totally wiped out by vaccination. Polio is now very rare in many countries, thanks to a vaccination programme introduced in the late 1950s.

Rubella (German measles) is a mild disease that gives you a slight rash. In most people it is not particularly serious. But if a woman catches rubella while she is pregnant, the infection may spread to the embryo and leave the baby blind, deaf or possibly brain damaged. It is important that girls are vaccinated against rubella so that they and their babies are protected against the disease.

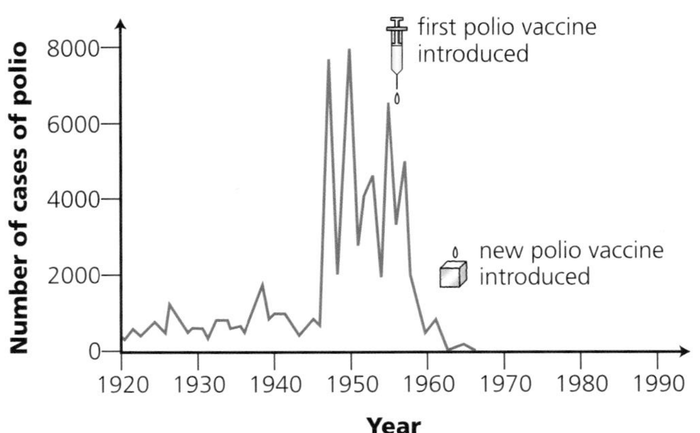

C Every year the virus that gives you a cold changes slightly. This means that the immune system does not recognise it, so it makes you ill again. Explain why it is hard to vaccinate against a cold.

Questions

1. Give four routes by which diseases can enter the body, and describe for each one how the microbes can get in and make you ill.
2. Describe how white blood cells protect the body from infection.
3. Explain the difference between active immunity and passive immunity.
4. Survey your class to find out who has had chickenpox, measles, mumps, colds and 'flu. Find out how many times each person has had each disease. Present this data graphically. For each disease:
   - **a** How many people have had the disease once?
   - **b** How many have had the disease more than once?
   - **c** What does this tell you about this disease?

When you revise

Microorganisms that cause **infection** are called **pathogens**.

The first line of defence in the body is the skin.

The **immune system** can fight off infection using **white blood cells** and **antibodies**.

The immune system can be helped by **vaccinations**.

5.7 Medicines and drugs

Learn about

- How drugs can affect the body

What is a drug?

A **drug** is any substance that is taken into your body and alters it physically or mentally. A drug may affect the way that you think or feel. Nicotine and alcohol are examples of drugs. It is legal to take some drugs, such as nicotine and alcohol. Society tolerates the use of these drugs by adults. Coffee and tea contain a legal drug called caffeine. Many drugs are addictive.

A **medicine** is a drug that if used correctly can make your body work properly or get better. Medicines are usually prescribed by a doctor. Medicines can cause serious problems if you use too much, or if you take them when you are not ill.

Antibiotics

Antibiotics are very commonly used drugs that can kill some types of bacteria. Penicillin is an antibiotic. Antibiotics will not work on viruses. This is why your doctor may give you an antibiotic for a sore throat, but not for 'flu.

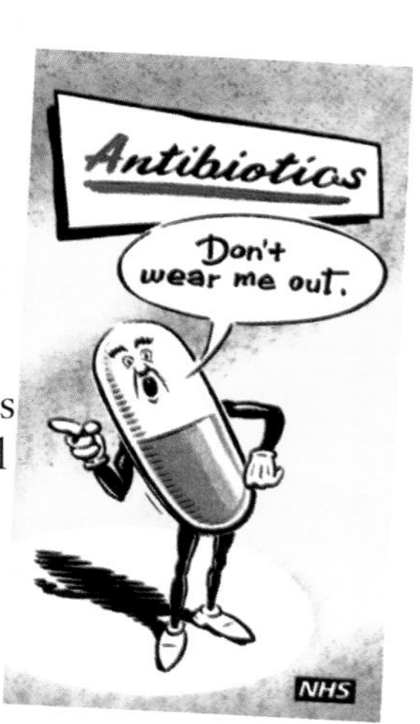

When your doctor gives you a course of antibiotics, it is important that you take all of it, even if you start to feel better. If you don't, then some of the stronger bacteria will survive and begin to reproduce again. Eventually these bacteria may become **resistant** to the antibiotic. Some diseases such as tuberculosis are difficult to treat because the bacteria have become resistant to most of the antibiotics generally in use.

a Explain why a doctor may not always give you antibiotics if you are ill.

Illegal drugs

Many drugs are **illegal**, which means it is against the law to use them. They can all have harmful effects on the body, and most are addictive. These drugs are usually grouped according to the effect they have on the body.

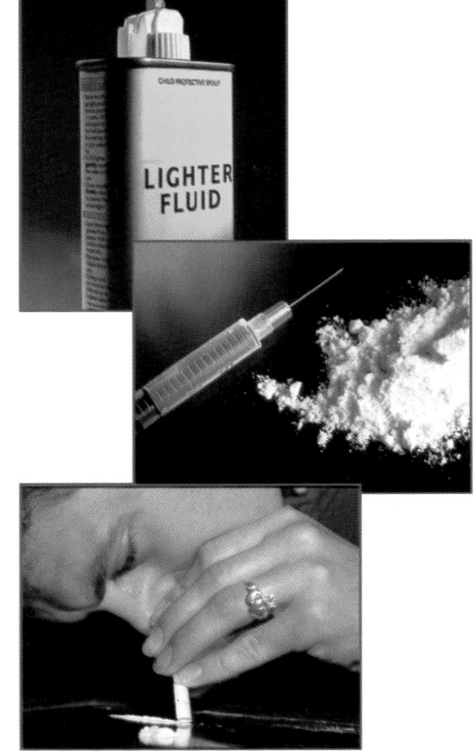

Some solvents in glue, paints and lighter fluid give off vapours that can be breathed in through the nose and mouth. This is called **solvent abuse**. It can make you act in very irrational ways and cause harm to yourself and others. Solvent abuse can damage your brain, kidneys and liver. It can kill you even if you are a first-time user.

Depressants such as heroin slow down your body's reactions and make you feel drowsy and relaxed. They can cause mental problems and constipation. Over-use can lead to unconsciousness and coma, and even death by stopping you breathing. Alcohol is an example of a legal depressant drug.

Stimulants such as cocaine and amphetamines speed up your body's reactions and make you feel as if you have lots of energy. They can leave the body vulnerable to infections and may cause heart failure. Sniffing cocaine can also damage the lining of your nose and cause it to rot away. Legal stimulants include caffeine, found in coffee, and nicotine, found in cigarette smoke.

Rising and sinking

Justin and Yasmin were taking part in a Science Challenge. The challenge was to make a balloon that would float where it was put, neither rising nor sinking.

Each team was given 12 balloons that had been set up by the organisers. Each balloon was labelled with the type of gas inside, the volume of gas inside and the total mass of the balloon. Some of the balloons sank and some of them rose up towards the ceiling.

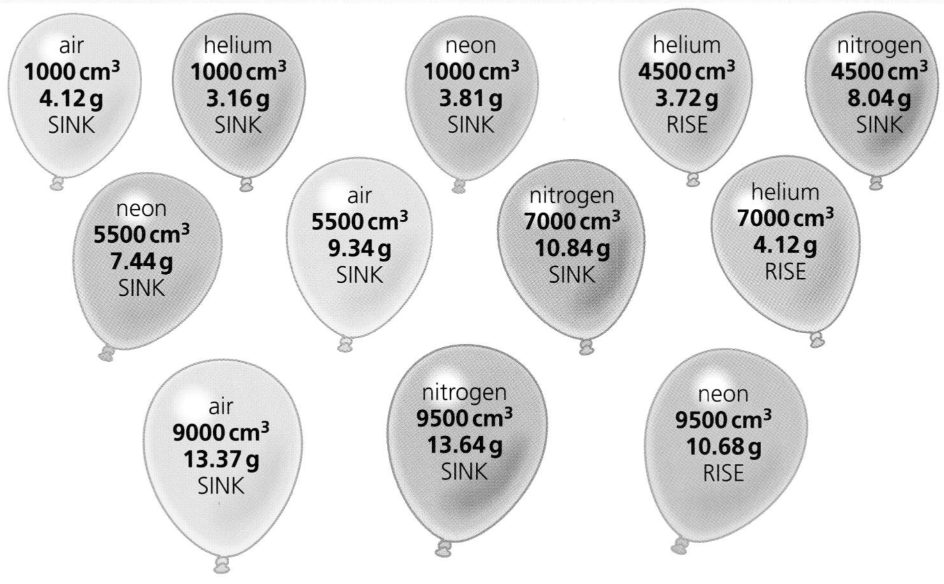

g What are the input and outcome variables for this investigation?

h How does volume affect whether the balloon rises or sinks? Make pairs of balloons from the diagram to explain your answer.

i How does mass affect whether the balloon rises or sinks? Make pairs of balloons from the diagram to explain your answer.

j Choose a balloon from the diagram and suggest ways of making it float rather than rise or sink.

Density

For a balloon to rise it must be less dense than the air around it. If it is less dense it rises up, like hot air in a convection current. During the Science Challenge, the density of air in the room was 0.001 15 g/cm³. Balloons with a density lower than 0.001 15 g/cm³ rose, and balloons with a density higher than 0.001 15 g/cm³ sank.

Density is a variable that depends on two other variables, mass and volume.

$$\text{density} = \frac{\text{mass}}{\text{volume}}$$

Justin and Yasmin decide to make a floating balloon by adding extra mass to the balloon containing 4500 cm³ of helium.

k What is the density of Justin and Yasmin's chosen balloon without the extra mass?

l What density must the balloon have to float?

m What mass must be added to the balloon to make it float?

Questions

1. All the air-filled balloons in the experiment sank. This would be true no matter how big the balloon. Explain why a balloon filled with air would always sink.
2. Hydrogen has a density of 0.000 08 g/cm³. The balloon itself weighs 3.00 g.
   - **a** What volume must 3.00 g occupy before it will float in air with a density of 0.001 15 g/cm³?
   - **b** A balloon filled with 2799 cm³ of hydrogen 'hovers'. Explain why this is different from your answer for **a**.
   - **c** Explain why hot air balloons float. Use the words 'mass', 'volume', 'density' and 'particles' in your answer.

How to revise

Key Stage 3 tests

At the end of Year 9 you will do a Key Stage 3 test which covers everything you have studied over the last three years. It is an opportunity for you to show how much you have learned over the course. To help you get a good mark and feel confident about doing the test, it is a good idea to revise thoroughly before the test. Your teacher will probably help you with this in science lessons, but there is a lot you can do yourself using the revision section of this book.

What to revise

You need to revise everything that you have learned over the last three years. This book will help you.

- It contains three revision units covering biology, chemistry and physics topics from Years 7 and 8 which you need to revise.
- It also contains six units of new Year 9 material which you need to revise. Look back at the 'When you revise' boxes at the ends of the spreads in the first six units – these give you the key points to remember. The blue revision boxes on the pages also revise some material from Years 7 and 8.

Where to revise

- It is best to revise in a room with no distractions like a TV, music or people busy doing other things.
- Most people find it best to have a quiet place for revising.
- Use a table or desk which gives you plenty of space to lay out your books and notes.
- Make sure you have a good source of light to read by.
- Get yourself organised – have plenty of blank paper and a selection of pens and pencils in different colours as well as the notes or books you need.

When to revise

- Try to set aside some time early each evening. Don't leave it too late so that your brain is tired.
- Revise for about 15 minutes and then take a 5-minute break. You could perhaps allow yourself to listen to a song (only one!). Then do another 15 minutes' revision and have another short break. Revise for another 15 minutes, and then have a longer break.
- Breaking up your revision into small chunks like this is much better than revising for a solid hour without any breaks. You will remember more this way.
- Keep a clock close by to help you keep track of the time.

Revision timetables

- Don't try to revise your entire science course in one night!
- Plan your revision long before your test.
- Work out how you will divide the material up, and how much you will revise each night.
- Work out how many evenings you will have available for revision.
- Make a timetable something like this to make sure you cover every topic at least once.

Day	What I will revise	Tick when done
Day 1	Topic 1	
Day 2	Topic 2	
Day 3	Topic 3	

How to revise

There are many different techniques that you can use. Here are just a few.

1 Read – Cover – Write – Check

Read an entire double page spread in the book. Then close the book and write notes on as many key points as you can remember. Then open the book again, check what you wrote down and go over the things you didn't remember. Repeat this until you can remember everything on the pages.

2 Make a memory map for each section. Then try to learn the memory map – think about the way each part of it is linked together. Then cover the map up and try to redraw it. The last question on each revision spread suggests you do this.

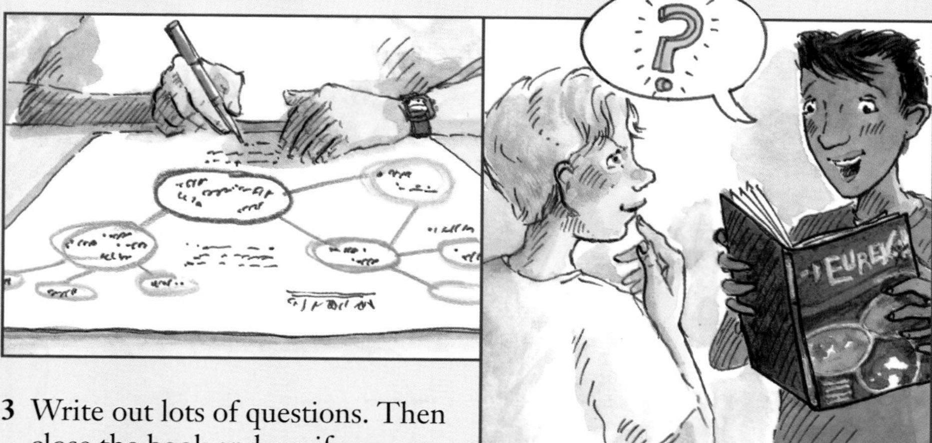

3 Write out lots of questions. Then close the book and see if you can answer them. You can also get someone else to ask you the questions. There are some questions on the revision pages to get you going. At the end of each revision unit are example test questions with tips from the examiners about the best way to answer.

4 Make sure you know the meanings of all the key words you come across. The first question on each revision spread suggests you do this.

5 Make up silly rhymes or mnemonics for important facts or patterns. The sillier they are, the easier it will be for your brain to remember them.

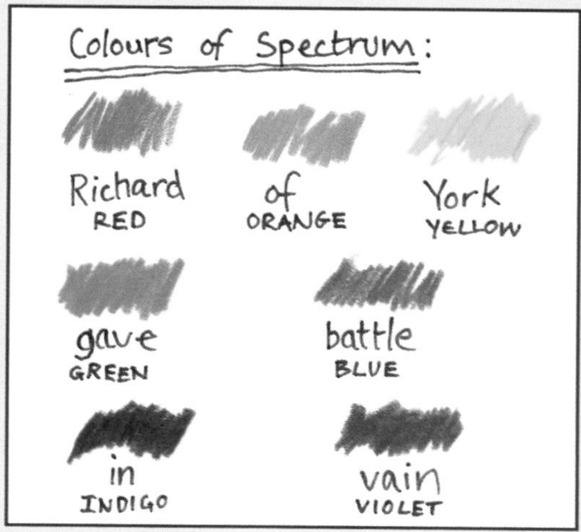

Don't just sit there with a book in front of you. It's not the best way to learn. The best way to revise is by actively doing tasks to make your brain work. This will make it much easier to remember things. Then you can go into your test confident that you will do the best you can.

7.1 Cells and organs

Cells

All living things are made up of small building blocks called **cells**. There are two main types of cell: **animal cells** and **plant cells**. These have a lot in common, but there are also some differences.

Remember: you must be able to label diagrams of cells.

Animal cells

Animal cells, like the one shown opposite, have three main structures that you have to remember: the **cell membrane**, the **nucleus** and the **cytoplasm**.

- The **cell membrane** lets substances in and out of the cell.
- The **cytoplasm** is the place where all the chemical reactions take place.
- The **nucleus** controls everything that happens in the cell.
- There may be stored food inside the cell.

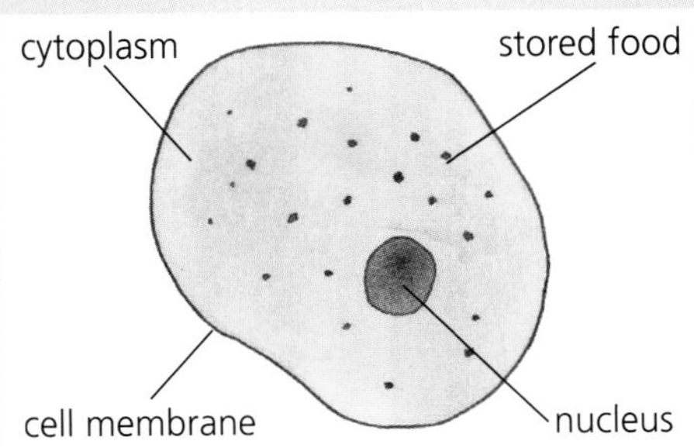

Plant cells

A plant cell, like the one shown opposite, also has a cell membrane, a nucleus and cytoplasm. You will also have to know that, unlike animal cells, it has a **cell wall**, **chloroplasts** and a **large vacuole**.

- The **cell wall** gives support to the cell and makes it strong.
- The **chloroplasts** contain chlorophyll. Photosynthesis takes place in the chloroplasts.
- The cell **vacuole** contains cell sap.
- There may be stored food inside the cell.

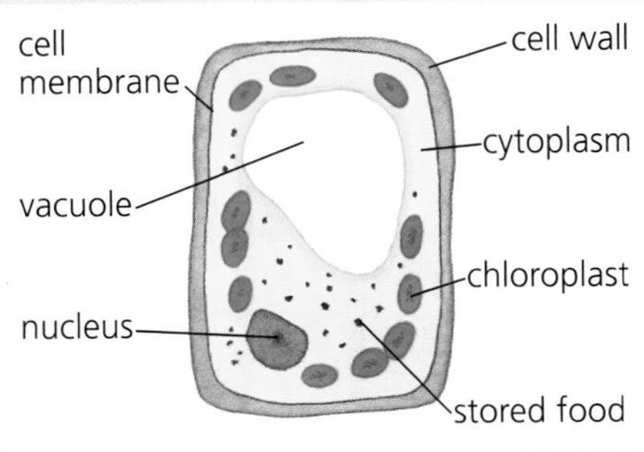

a How would you identify a cell as an animal cell or a plant cell?

Cells adapted to their functions

Cells are adapted to their functions in different ways. You need to know about the examples shown in the diagram opposite.

b Make a table of these different types of cell and their adaptations to their functions.

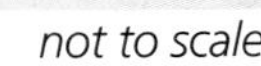

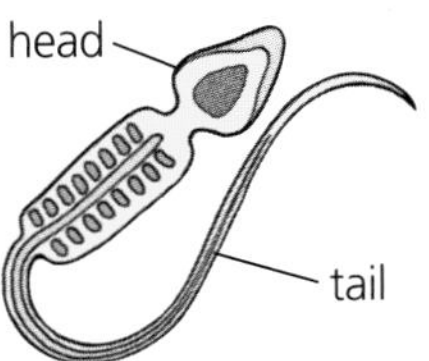

Sperm cells have long **tails** to swim to the egg and a **pointed head** which helps them burrow into the egg.

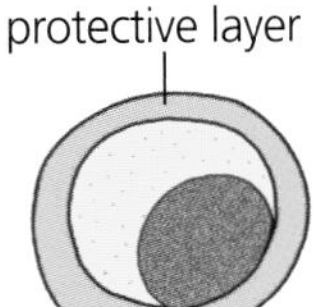

Egg cells have a **protective layer** so that just one sperm can get through.

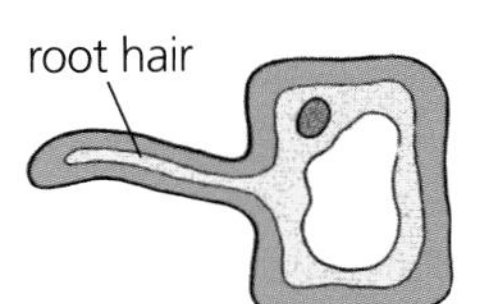

Root hair cells have a long finger-like **root hair** which gives a very large surface area to absorb water.

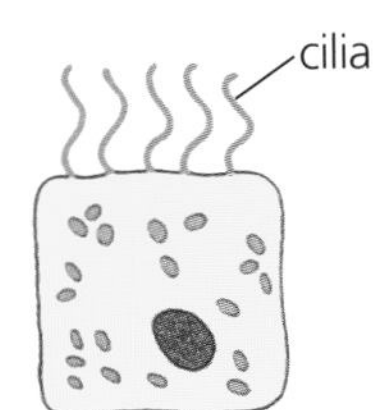

Epithelial cells in your nose and throat produce mucus to trap dust and germs.

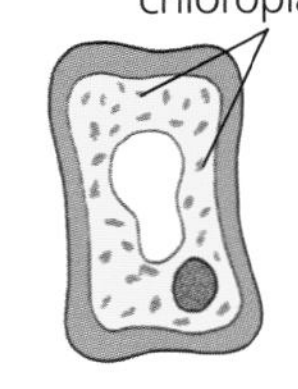

Palisade cells have lots of chloroplasts and are at the tops of leaves to absorb as much light as possible.

Red blood cells have no nucleus and are flexible so they can pass through small blood vessels. They have a large surface area so they can carry lots of oxygen.

Tissues

When a group of similar cells carries out a particular function we call the group of cells a **tissue**, for example:

- muscle tissue and nerve tissue in humans
- onion skin tissue and palisade tissue in plants.

Organs

When a group of two or more tissues work together they form an **organ**, for example:

- the heart, lungs, stomach, eyes and brain in humans
- leaves, stems, roots and petals in plants.

Organ systems

When a group of organs work together they form an **organ system**.

- Examples of organ systems in animals, such as humans, include the circulatory system, the reproductive system, the skeletal system, the digestive system and the respiratory system.
- A flower is an example of an organ system in plants.

cell (heart muscle cell) → tissue (heart muscle) → organ (heart) → organ system (circulatory system) → organism (human)

c Make a table showing two different animal examples of cells, tissues, organs and organ systems, and one plant example of each.

The skeletal system

The **skeletal system** or skeleton is an organ system in animals such as humans. The skeleton is made up of over 200 **bones** and is important because it:

- allows the animal to move
- protects important organs like the brain
- provides the animal with support, for example, so humans can stand upright.

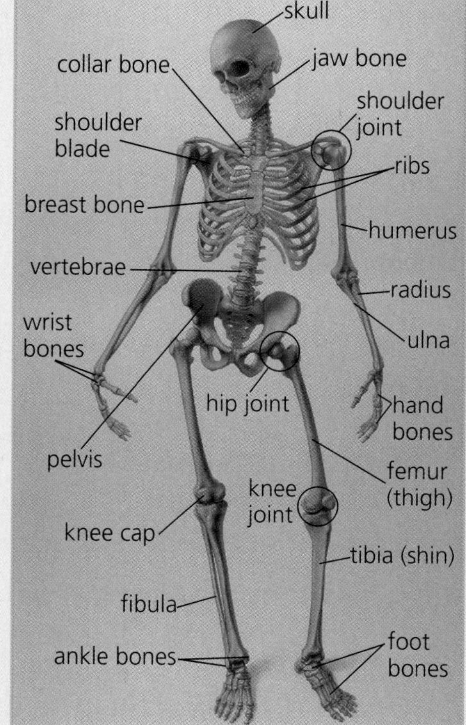

Bones come together at **joints**, which allow the bones to move.

- The bones are held together at a joint by **ligaments**.
- There are three types of joint: **hinge**, **ball and socket** and **pivot**.
- Friction is reduced at the joints as they contain **cartilage** and **synovial fluid**.
- Bones need **muscles** to move them.

d Write a paragraph to explain about how the bones allow us to move. Use the following words: bones, muscles, ligaments, cartilage and synovial fluid.

- Muscles are joined onto bones by special fibres called **tendons**.
- Muscles are made of muscle tissue, which can **contract** and **relax**.
- Bones move when a muscle contracts.
- Muscles can only pull, they cannot push, so they work in **antagonistic pairs.**
- The biceps and triceps in the arm are an example of an antagonistic pair.

e Explain, using diagrams and examples, how an antagonistic pair of muscles works.

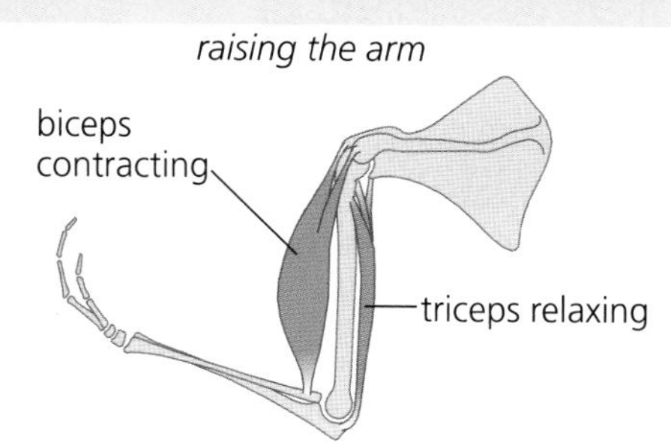

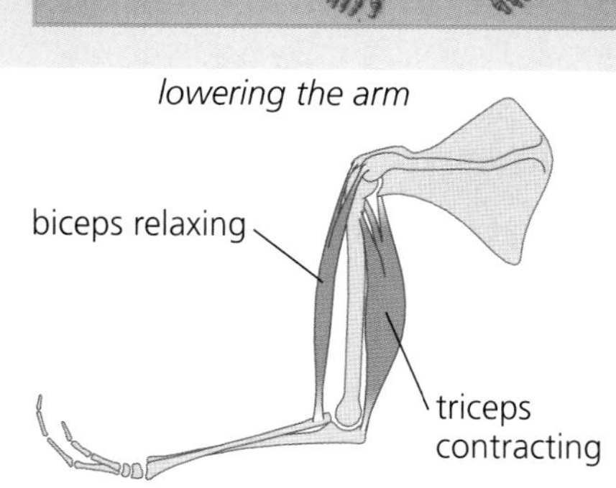

Questions

1. Make sure you know the meanings of all the key words on this spread.
2. Explain what makes the respiratory system an organ system.
3. Which organ systems carry out the following processes?
   a reproduction **b** the breakdown of food
   c the transport of blood around the body
4. **a** Red blood cells are flexible and have a large surface area. Explain how this helps their function.
   b Ligaments can stretch more than tendons. Explain how each of these tissues is suited to its function.
5. Draw a memory map to help you remember the information about cells, tissues, organs and organ systems.

Nutrition

Food

Food contains many different substances. The useful substances that food contains are called **nutrients**. Plants and animals get their food in different ways. Plants make their own food by a process called **photosynthesis**. Animals are **consumers** and eat plants, other animals or both plants and animals. Animals and plants get energy from their food by the process called **respiration**.

Balanced diets

Your body needs nutrients to give it energy and to keep it working properly. A diet that gives the body the right amounts of all the nutrients is called a **balanced diet**. This consists of:

- **carbohydrates**, for example in bread, for energy
- **fats**, such as those in milk and butter, for energy and insulation
- **proteins**, for example in meat, fish and nuts, for growth and repair
- **vitamins** and **minerals** to keep different parts of the body healthy
- **water**, in which all the chemical reactions in our bodies take place
- **fibre** to keep the food moving through the gut.

Vitamins and minerals

When the body doesn't get the required amount of a nutrient, such as a vitamin or a mineral, it is **deficient** in that nutrient. This can cause ill health, for example:

- vitamin C, found in fruits such as blackcurrants and green vegetables such as cabbage, stops people getting scurvy
- the mineral calcium, found in milk, is needed for strong bones and teeth
- the mineral iron, found in liver and eggs, is used in making blood. If iron is missing from the diet it can cause anaemia.

a Make a table to show all the nutrients needed for a balanced diet. Include examples of each type of nutrient and give their importance to the diet.

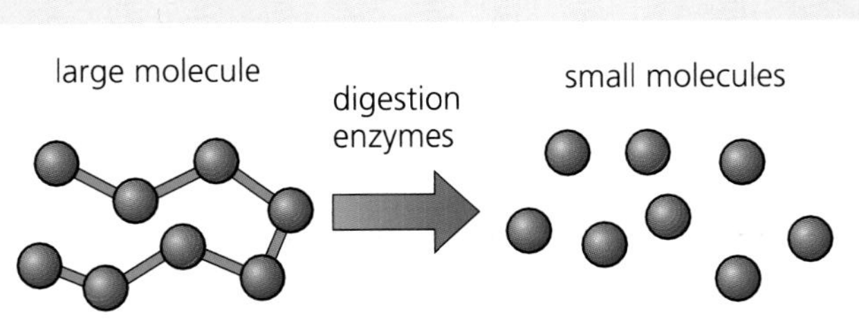

Digestion

- The large molecules you eat are broken down into very small molecules. This is called **digestion** and it takes place in the **digestive system**.
- Only small molecules can dissolve and pass through the lining of the small intestine into the blood. Large molecules that are insoluble cannot pass through the lining, and need to be broken down further.

b Write a paragraph explaining why large food molecules have to be broken down in the body.

Where does digestion happen?

- Digestion starts in the **mouth**, and carries on all the way through the **stomach** and **small intestine**.
- Food spends several hours in the stomach, where acidic digestive juices help break the food down.
- The food is pushed through the gut by a process called **peristalsis**.

Remember: we cannot digest fibre because we do not have the enzymes to do it.

- In the small intestine, pancreatic and intestinal juices digest several different types of nutrients.
- In the small intestine, alkaline **bile** neutralises the acid from the stomach and helps to break down fats.
- Any waste food that is left is removed from the body through the **anus**.

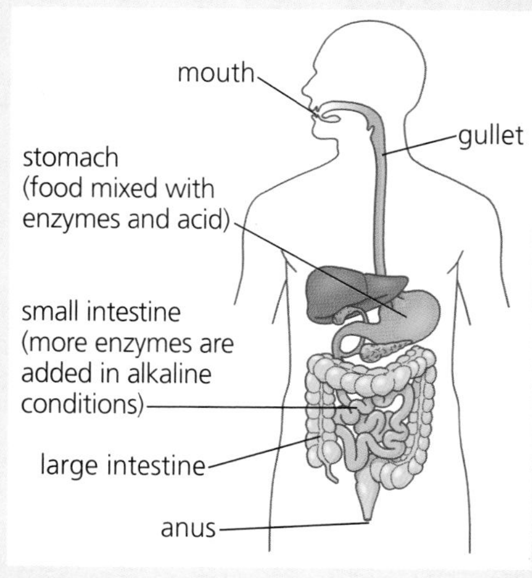

How is food broken down?

- In the mouth, the teeth help break up the food into smaller pieces. This mechanical breakdown of the food is a **physical process**.
- In digestion, substances called **enzymes** help to break the larger molecules into smaller molecules. Breaking down food in this way is a **chemical process**. It starts in the mouth with the enzymes in the saliva, and continues through the stomach and small intestine. For example:
  Large **starch** molecules (carbohydrates) are broken down into small **glucose** molecules.
  Proteins are broken down into **amino acids**.
  Fats are broken down into **fatty acids** and **glycerol**.

c Make a table to show the reactants and products in the digestion of proteins, fats and starch.

Absorption

- The small intestine has a very large surface area as it is made up of millions of tiny finger-like structures called **villi** (one villus).
- The large surface ensures that the digested food passes from the intestine into the blood quickly. This process is called **absorption**.
- Small molecules of food pass through the villi and are carried away by the blood to where they are needed by the body.
- The undigested food, that is mainly fibre, passes into the large intestine because its molecules are too large to be absorbed.
- Water is absorbed in the **large intestine** and waste food can be stored here before it is **egested** from the body through the anus.

d Draw a flow diagram of the digestive process. Add labels to explain briefly what happens to the food at each stage.

Questions

1. Make sure you know the meanings of all the key words on this spread.
2. How is the small intestine adapted to its function?
3. Why is fibre important to your diet, and what foods have a high fibre content?
4. The table shows some nutritional information for 100 g of some common foods.
   a Which food would give you most energy?
   b Which food contains the most of the nutrient needed for growth and repair?
   c Which food would be best for a growing child as part of a balanced diet? Explain your answer.

Food	Protein in g	Fat in g	Carbohydrate in g	Energy in kJ
Nuts, e.g. peanuts	24.3	49.0	8.6	570
Vegetables, e.g. carrots	0.7	0	5.4	98
Fish, e.g. white fish	17.1	0.9	0	324

5. Draw a memory map to help you remember the information about food and digestion.

Photosynthesis and respiration

Photosynthesis

- **Photosynthesis** happens in the green parts of a plant, usually the leaves.
- The green parts contain **chloroplasts** which are green because they contain the chemical **chlorophyll**.

Photosynthesis can be summarised by the word equation:

carbon dioxide + water → glucose + oxygen

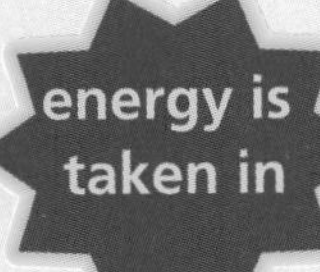

Remember: you must learn this word equation.

- Plants take in carbon dioxide through holes in the leaves called **stomata**.
- Water is taken in from the soil through the **root hairs**.
- Light energy from the Sun is absorbed by chlorophyll.
- Glucose and oxygen are produced. Oxygen leaves through the stomata. The glucose is used to provide energy for the plant.
- Photosynthesis produces the **biomass** of the plant. Biomass is the total mass of a living thing not including the water.

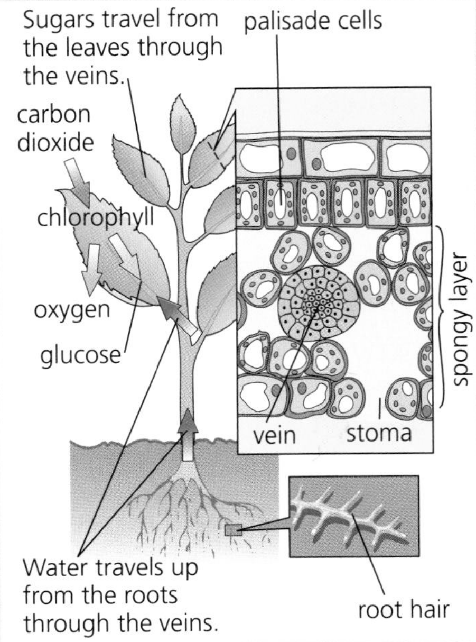

Transport in plants

- Glucose is transported from the leaves to the rest of the plant in the veins.
- Water for photosynthesis is transported from the roots to the leaves in the veins.

Plant nutrients

Minerals are also taken in by the root hairs. The most important plant minerals are:

- **nitrogen**, as nitrate salts, needed to make proteins for growth
- **phosphorus**, as phosphate salts, needed to make the roots grow properly
- **potassium**, needed to make chlorophyll. Without potassium the leaves would turn yellow so photosynthesis could not happen.

a Describe where the plant gets the reactants for photosynthesis, and what happens to the products that are formed.

b Make a table listing the main plant nutrients and their importance.

Respiration in plants

Plants break down the glucose they produce to release the chemical energy stored in it. Glucose reacts with oxygen to produce carbon dioxide and water. Energy is given out in the reaction. This is called **respiration** and can be summarised by the word equation:

glucose + oxygen → carbon dioxide + water

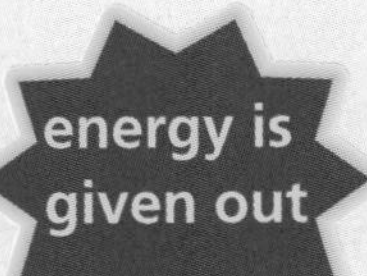

Remember: you must learn this word equation.

- Glucose comes from photosynthesis. Oxygen comes from photosynthesis during the day and from the air at night.
- Carbon dioxide and water are released through the stomata.

Respiration in humans

Food gives you energy. Carbohydrates, fats and proteins provide the body with the sources of energy you need to stay healthy. Energy is released from food by respiration. The word equation is the same as for plants. Respiration takes place inside all living cells of plants, animals and bacteria.

- The fuel used in respiration is glucose. It is obtained from the digestion of food.
- The oxygen for respiration comes from breathing in. **Aerobic respiration** is the type of respiration that needs oxygen for it to take place.
- Carbon dioxide and water are produced and are released when you breathe out.
- The energy is used for many things, such as working your muscles.

c Write a paragraph describing what happens in respiration in plants and animals.

Transport in the blood

- The oxygen and glucose for respiration are transported to the cells by the blood.
- Oxygen is attached to the **haemoglobin** in red blood cells and glucose is dissolved in the blood.
- Oxygen and glucose can pass out from the blood through the thin-walled capillaries to nearby cells where they are needed.
- Carbon dioxide and water are made during respiration. They are taken away from the respiring cells in the blood. Carbon dioxide is dissolved in the blood.
- The blood carries carbon dioxide and water to the lungs where they are released.

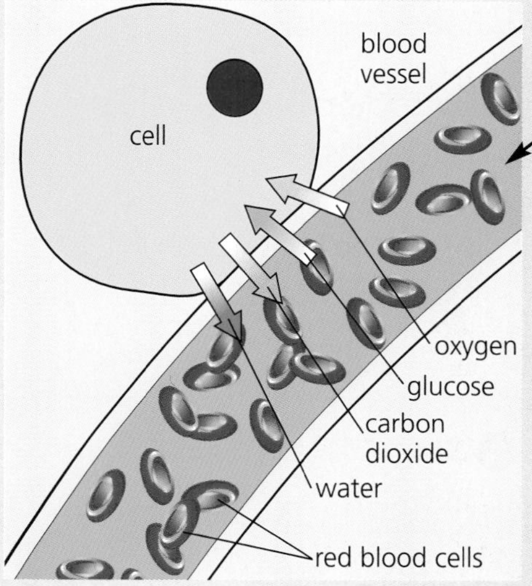

d Use a flow chart to explain what happens to the oxygen and carbon dioxide in respiration.

Questions

1. Make sure you know the meanings of all the key words on this spread.
2. What do you think is most likely to happen to photosynthesis if the plant is:
   a kept in an atmosphere that has a low concentration of carbon dioxide?
   b kept in bright light?
3. What differences might you expect to find in air that you breathed in and air that you breathed out?
4. The following graph shows how light intensity affects photosynthesis in plants.

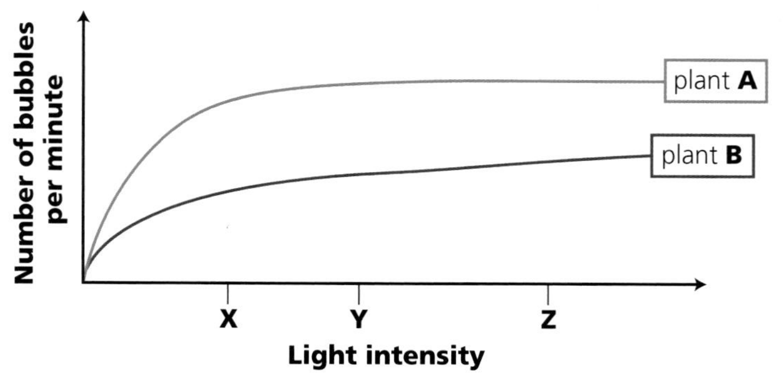

   a What gas makes the bubbles?
   b Which plant produces the most bubbles at low light intensity?
   c Is there a relationship between the amount of light and the number of bubbles produced? If so, describe it.
   d Which letter **X** to **Z** shows plant **A** at its maximum rate for photosynthesis?
   e Another plant, **C**, is found in woodlands. What do you think the graph for this plant would look like compared with the other plants? Explain your answer.
5. Draw a memory map to help you remember the information about photosynthesis and respiration.

7.4 Reproduction

Human reproduction

Male reproductive system:

- Sperm are made in the **testes**. There are two of these (one **testis**).
- The testes are in a bag of skin called the **scrotum**.
- The sperm leave the testes through a tube called the **sperm tube**.
- Glands add a special liquid to the sperm to make **semen**.
- Eventually the sperm travel down the **penis**. This is where they leave the man's body.

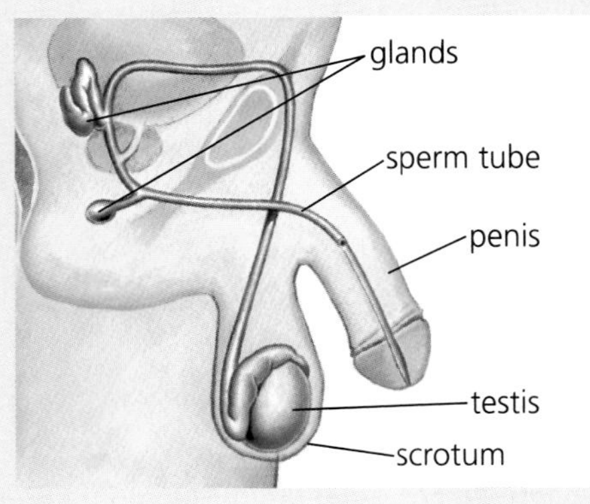

Female reproductive system:

- The eggs or ova are made in the **ovaries**.
- Once a month an egg leaves one of the ovaries and travels down the **oviduct** to the **uterus**.
- The uterus (womb) is where the baby will develop if the egg becomes fertilised.
- The opening of the uterus is called the **cervix**.
- Sperm enter the woman's body through the **vagina**.

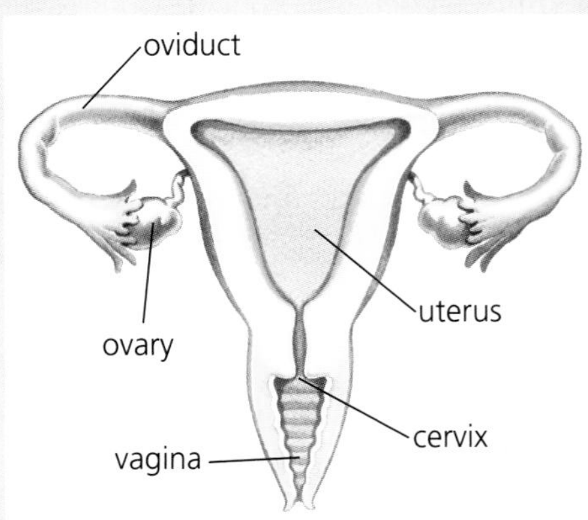

a Draw diagrams of the male and female reproductive systems. Add labels to show the functions of all the main parts.

Adolescence

Adolescence is a time in everyone's life when physical and emotional changes take place to prepare us to be young adults. **Puberty** is the first part of adolescence, when most of these changes take place.

b Make a list of four changes that happen during puberty to:
i boys **ii** girls.

Changes in boys	Changes in girls
Body hair, including pubic hair, starts to grow	Body hair, including pubic hair, starts to grow
Voice deepens	Breasts grow
Testes start to make sperm and hormones	Ovaries start to release eggs and make hormones
Shoulders broaden	Hips widen
Sexual organs get bigger	Periods start
Behaviour changes	Behaviour changes

Menstruation

At puberty, girls begin a monthly cycle called the **menstrual cycle**. Each cycle lasts about 28 days.

c Draw the main stages of the menstrual cycle. For each stage, describe what happens.

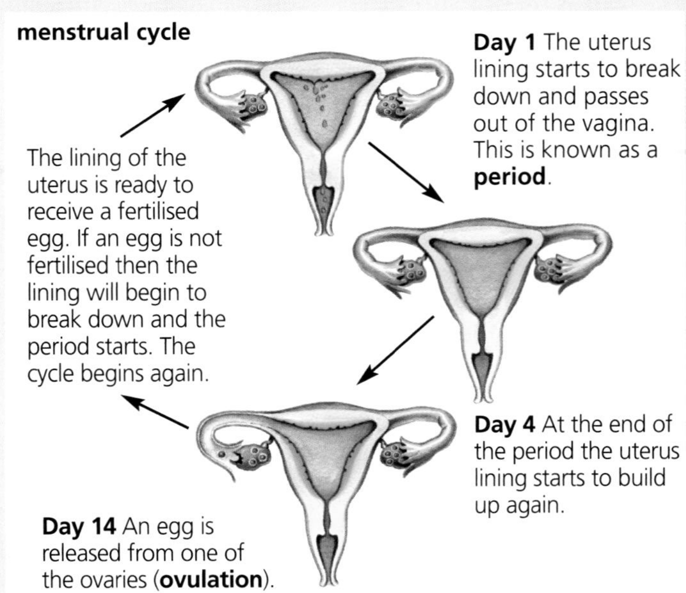

Human fertilisation

- After **sexual intercourse**, the sperm start to swim from the vagina into the uterus. The sperm swim up into both oviducts. Many sperm will die on the way.
- If there is an egg in the oviduct:
  The sperm will surround it and the first sperm to reach the egg burrows into it. The nucleus of the sperm joins with the nucleus of the egg. This is called **fertilisation**. The fertilised egg will become a baby. The woman is **pregnant**. The menstrual cycle stops.
- If there is no egg in the oviduct:
  All the sperm will die in a short time. No baby will be produced. The menstrual cycle continues.

Pregnancy

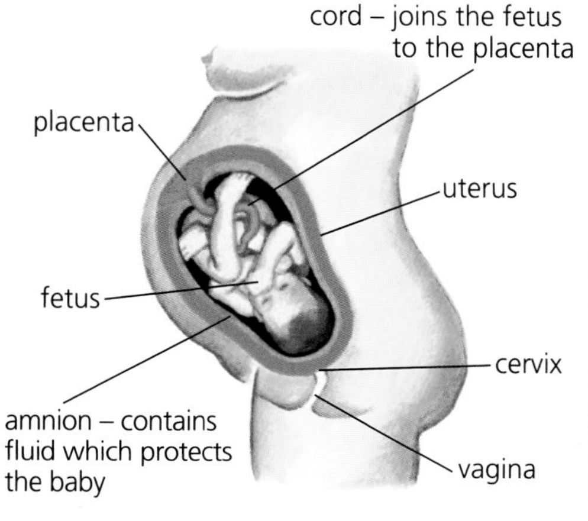

- **Cell division**: about 24 hours after it has been fertilised, the egg divides into two cells, then into four cells. After four days it has divided into 32 cells. It is now called an **embryo**.
- **Implantation**: about a week after fertilisation, the embryo attaches to the lining of the uterus. This is called **implantation**.

The placenta

- The **placenta** provides the fetus with all the substances it needs from the mother.
- The **cord** joins the placenta to the fetus.
- The baby receives oxygen and food from the mother and gets rid of carbon dioxide and other waste through the placenta.

d Explain how the placenta is like a life-support system to the fetus in the uterus.

Plant fertilisation

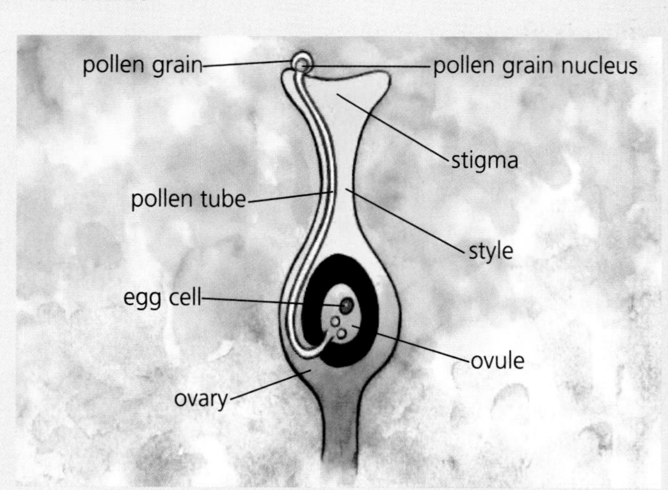

After pollination, a **pollen tube** grows to carry the **pollen grain** to the **egg cell**. Fertilisation takes place when the nucleus of the male sex cell, the pollen grain, joins with the nucleus of the female sex cell, the egg cell. This produces a fertilised egg cell.

e Produce a flow diagram showing what happens in plant fertilisation.

Questions

1. Make sure you know the meanings of all the key words on this spread.
2. What function do hormones have in adolescence?
3. Explain the function of the placenta.
4. What is the function of the amnion?
5. List the similarities and differences between fertilisation in flowering plants and fertilisation in humans.
6. Draw a memory map to help you remember the information about reproduction in plants and animals.

Classification and variation

Classification

- All the living things can be sorted into different groups depending on their features. The four main groups are **animals, plants, microorganisms** and **fungi.**
- The grouping of things is called **classification**.
- Animals are grouped into two main groups: **vertebrates**, animals with a backbone and **invertebrates**, animals without a backbone.

Vertebrates

Vertebrates are divided in to five smaller groups:

- **Mammals**, such as humans and lions, develop inside the mother. The young are fed on milk from the mammary glands of the mother.
- **Birds**, such as eagles and penguins, lay eggs with hard shells and look after their young when they are born. They have feathers and wings and most can fly.
- **Reptiles**, such as crocodiles and lizards, lay eggs with a leathery skin on land. They breathe air and live mainly on land.
- **Amphibians**, such as frogs and newts, lay jelly-like eggs in water. They breathe air and live part of their life in water and part on land.
- **Fish**, such as sharks and cod, lay their eggs in water. They breathe through gills and live only in water.

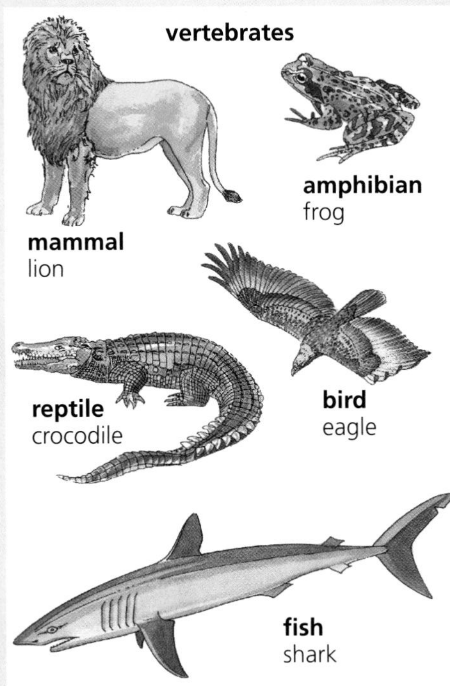

a Make a table to summarise the differences between the five groups of vertebrates.

Invertebrates

- There are seven main types of invertebrate: jellyfish, starfish, flatworms, roundworms, segmented worms, molluscs and **arthropods.**
- Arthropods are invertebrates with segmented bodies and lots of jointed legs.
- Arthropods themselves can be divided into four smaller groups, depending on their body type and the number of legs. The groups are crustaceans, centipedes and millipedes, spiders and insects.

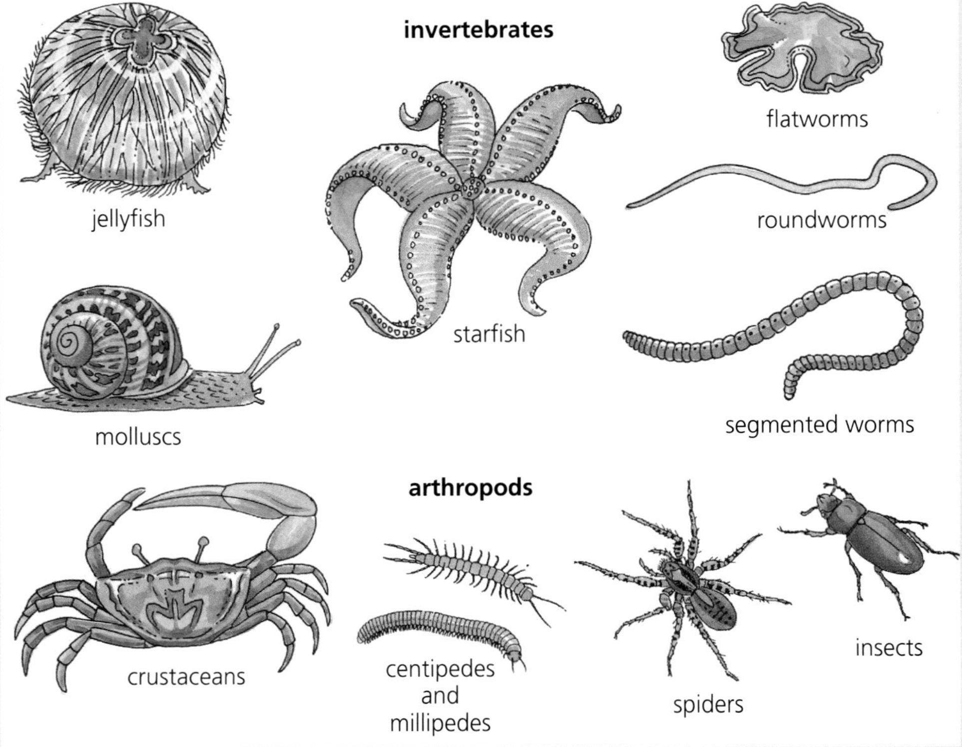

Plants

There are many different types of plant on Earth. They are classified into four main groups that are found in different habitats:

- **Flowering plants**, such as grasses and trees, are the biggest group. They reproduce using seeds formed after fertilisation. They live in a great variety of habitats depending on what kind of leaf, stem and root they have.
- **Mosses** are small-leaved plants that reproduce using spores. They live in damp habitats.
- **Ferns** have leaves called fronds and reproduce using spores. They live in damp, shaded habitats.
- **Conifers** are trees that reproduce by making seeds inside cones. They have long needle-shaped leaves. This helps them survive in cold or dry habitats.

b Describe how you would classify a plant into one of these four main groups.

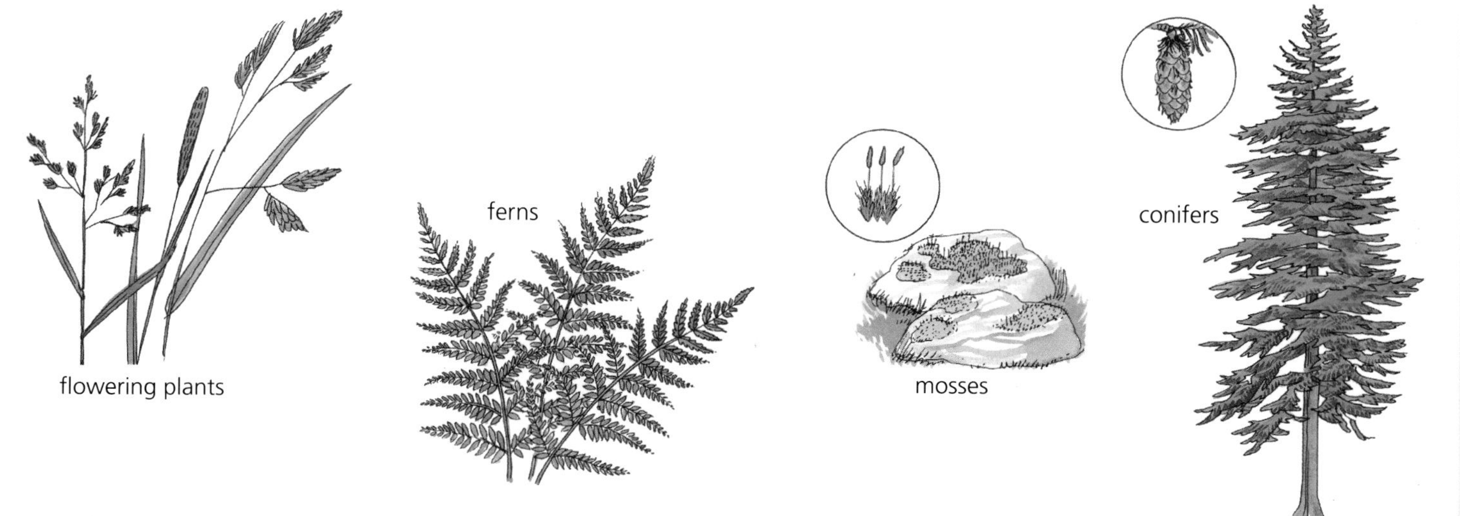

Variation

- The differences between living things are called **variation**.
- When there are enough differences between groups of organisms we call them different **species**. The many different kinds of dog are all the same species because they can mate and produce offspring. A dog and a cat are different species, as they cannot breed together.

Questions

1. Make sure you know the meanings of all the key words on this spread.
2. Explain how you know that:
   a a whale is a mammal
   b a crocodile is a reptile
   c a shark is a fish.
3. Why can't cats and dogs breed together?
4. List ways that the human population shows variation.
5. Make a memory map to help you remember the information about classification and variation.

The environment

Adaptation

- A **habitat** is the place where an organism lives.
- An **ecosystem** is an area like a pond or a forest including all the living things in it and its soil, air and climate.
- Different organisms are suited or **adapted** to their environment to help them survive in it.
- Polar bears have thick, white fur coats to insulate them from the cold. It is difficult to see the white polar bear against the snow because it is **camouflaged** against the snow so it cannot be seen by its prey.
- Camels are able to store water to help them survive in the hot desert. They have large feet to stop them sinking into the sand. They face the hot Sun at midday to expose the minimum body surface to the Sun's rays.

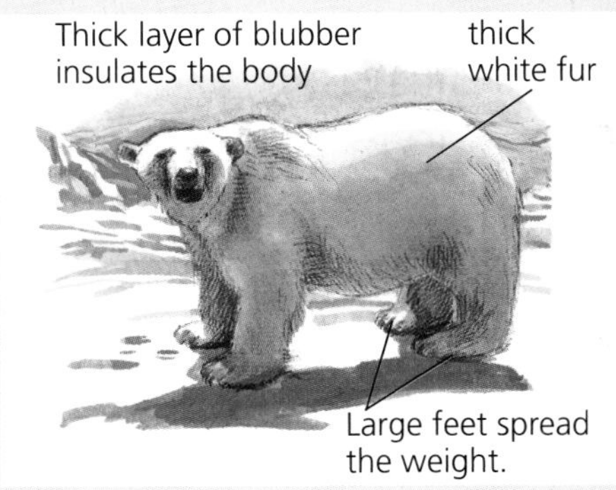

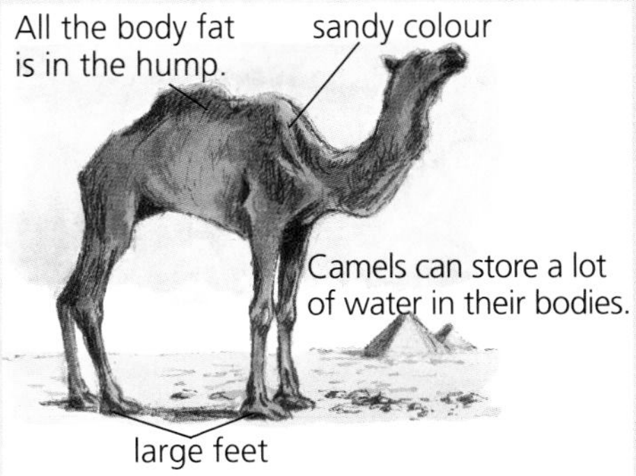

a Copy and complete the table below. Replace the numbers with a reason for the adaptation.

Organism	Habitat	Adaptation	Reasons for adaptations
Polar bear	Arctic	White fur	Keeps it camouflaged and warm
Seal	Arctic	Black coat Layer of fat	1 2
Wading bird e.g. curlew	Mud flats	Wide feet Pointed beak Long legs	3 4 5
Reptile e.g. lizard	Desert	Lives underground during the day	6
Primrose	Woodland	Flowers with brightly coloured petals and nectar	7

Destroying habitats

If habitats are destroyed, then food chains can be disrupted and in the end some species can become extinct. Human activity can destroy habitats in different ways.

- Building roads and bigger towns destroys areas of countryside and new developments cause noise and pollution.
- Factories, power stations and cars create a lot of gases such as sulfur dioxide which cause air pollution. These gases produce **acid rain** which can poison trees and lakes.

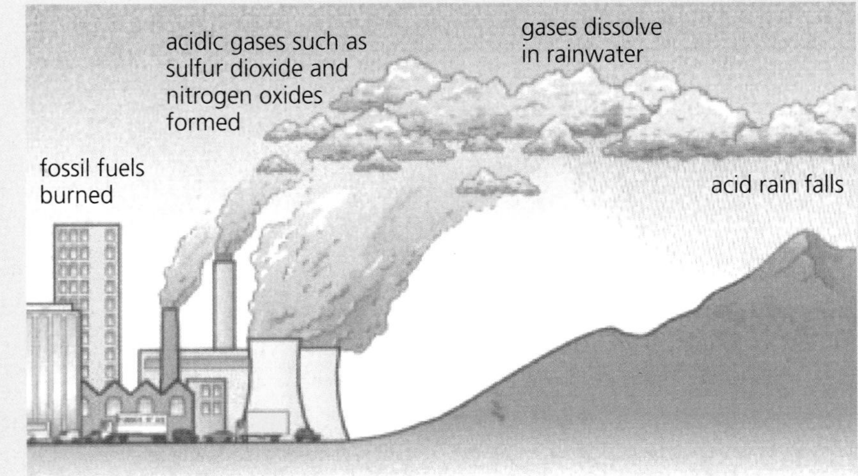

- Gases such as carbon dioxide which increase the **greenhouse effect** are also produced, making the Earth's atmosphere warmer and changing climates, which can threaten habitats.
- Some industries dump waste into rivers and seas. **Toxic** substances, such as pesticides like DDT and some metals like mercury, can be passed through food chains. They build up in animals and poison them.

b In Minamata Bay, Japan, in the 1950s, many people were killed when they ate fish that had been poisoned with mercury from a nearby factory. Draw a food chain to explain how the Minamata incident affected the food chain.

Protecting and sustaining the environment

It is important to protect all organisms and their habitats. There are many ways humans can try to do this:

- Sampling different habitats allows scientists to find out what lives there and which species may become endangered, so they can be protected.
- For each development, people should consider the needs of the environment and balance them against the human needs for food, products and services.
- People need to learn to use fewer resources, such as energy and materials, or to use renewable sources of energy.
- We should recycle as many resources as possible, such as glass and plastic, and make compost so that **decomposers** (bacteria and fungi) can recycle the dead matter from plants and animals.
- Regulations can be used to limit air and water pollution, such as international agreements on greenhouse gases.
- People need to be educated about the importance of protecting the environment.

Questions

1. Make sure you know the meanings of all the key words on this spread.
2. Explain why it is important for organisms to adapt to their environment. Give an example.
3. Give four ways in which a fox is adapted to its way of life.
4. Explain the following statements:

   Pesticides can kill birds of prey such as falcons and eagles.

   Decomposers are important for the cycling of nutrients.
5. Make a list of five things you would try to persuade your friends to do to protect the environment. Explain why you chose each one.
6. Draw a memory map to help you remember the information about adaptation and the environment.

7.7 Biology example questions

The example questions show you how to write good answers to make sure you always get all the marks available.

The main reasons why pupils do not do as well as they think they should is that they give answers that are too general, or that are incomplete and do not give a full answer to the question.

Do not fall into this trap. Read these extra comments round the questions for useful tips that will help you get all the marks and make sure you are successful in your KS3 Test.

2 The diagram shows a plant cell.

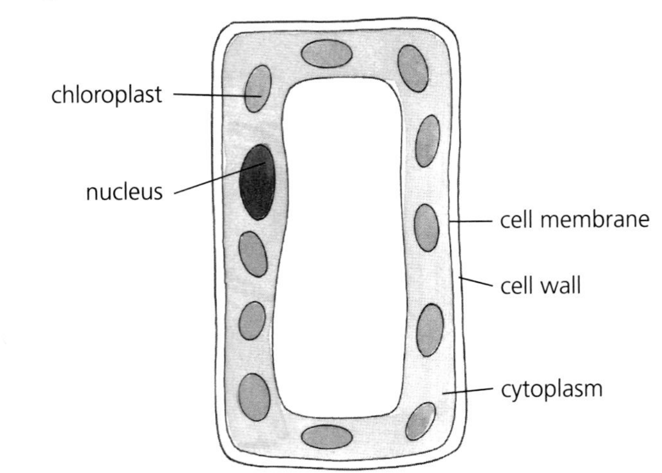

a Where in the plant would you find this type of cell? (1)

In the leaf ✓

b Most animal and plant cells have a nucleus. Give two other parts, labelled on the diagram, which are present in both animal and plant cells. (2)

Part 1 Cell membrane ✓

Part 2 Cytoplasm ✓

c i What is the function of the cell wall? (1)

To give shape to the cell ✓

ii What is the function of the chloroplasts? (1)

Photosynthesis occurs in the chloroplasts. Carbon dioxide and water are converted into glucose and oxygen ✓

Total (5)

a The cell is called a palisade cell. It makes up the tissue under the upper surface of the leaf. This is one of several types of cell you need to know about and to recognise in diagrams.

b Remember, plant cells have chloroplasts, a cell wall and a large vacuole, which animal cells don't.

c i The cell wall is made of cellulose. It provides support for the plant cell. Cell walls do not hold the cell contents together – this is the function of the cell membrane. Cell walls allow plant cells to stack together to make the plant.

c ii 'Photosynthesis' is the word that will get you the mark. Do not write 'to make food for the plant', as this is too vague.

Light is absorbed by the chlorophyll in the chloroplasts. This provides the energy for the photosynthesis reaction.

4 Ben copied the following information from the labels of two packets of food.

Food	Energy in kJ/100 g	Protein in g/100 g	Fat in g/100 g	Sugar in g/100 g	Fibre in g/100 g	Vitamin C in mg/100 g
X	424	6.9	0.6	3.6	6.2	0
Y	736	20.2	10.6	0	0	0

a Food Y contains a smaller variety of nutrients than food X. Give **two** reasons why food Y might be chosen instead of food X as part of a balanced diet. (2)

Reason 1

The rest of the person's diet might be low in protein ✓

Reason 2

The person could be underweight or ill and need a high energy intake to build them up ✓

b Ben made a curry. The label on the curry power showed:

	Calcium in mg/100 g	Iron in mg/100 g	Vitamin C in mg/100 g
curry powder	640	58.3	0

i Give one reason why calcium is needed by the body. (1)

For healthy bones ✓

ii Give one reason why iron is needed by the body. (1)

To make red blood cells ✓

c With his curry, Ben also had:

boiled rice; chopped-up, boiled egg;
a glass of water; a slice of lemon.

Which one of these foods provided Ben with vitamin C? (1)

Lemon ✓

Total (5)

a The question 'Why choose food Y?' requires reasons or explanation to be given.

You need to make comparisons between food X and food Y in order to give reasons why you would choose Y. Just stating 'Food Y is much higher in energy, protein and fat' is a poor answer.

b i 'Strong *or* healthy bones *or* teeth' is a good, complete answer.

Writing the word 'bones' or 'teeth' would probably get you the mark, but the question asks for a reason.

b ii Iron is needed to make the haemoglobin in red blood cells. If you do not have enough iron you become anaemic.

Do not write just 'blood' or 'blood cells' – this does not give enough detail to get you the mark.

c Vitamin C comes from fruit, particularly citrus fruit such as lemons and oranges.

Physical changes

States of matter

Everything around us is made of **matter**. There are three **states of matter**: **solid**, **liquid** and **gas**. Each state has different properties.

- Solids are hard, dense, have a fixed volume and fixed shape, cannot be squashed and are difficult to stir.

- Liquids are runny, have a fixed volume, change shape to fill the bottom of their container, cannot be squashed, are easy to stir and can flow and be poured.

- Gases are not very dense, change volume and shape to fill all of their container, are easy to squash and can flow from place to place.

a Make a table with three columns headed 'Solid', 'Liquid' and 'Gas'. List all the properties of each state of matter.

Made from particles

Everything is made from tiny **particles**. The reason why solids, liquids and gases behave in different ways is because their particles are arranged differently.

- In a solid the particles are very close together. They are held together in an orderly **lattice arrangement** by **forces of attraction**. Solids are usually dense because there are a lot of particles in a small volume. Because the particles are very close together, a solid cannot be squashed easily.

solid

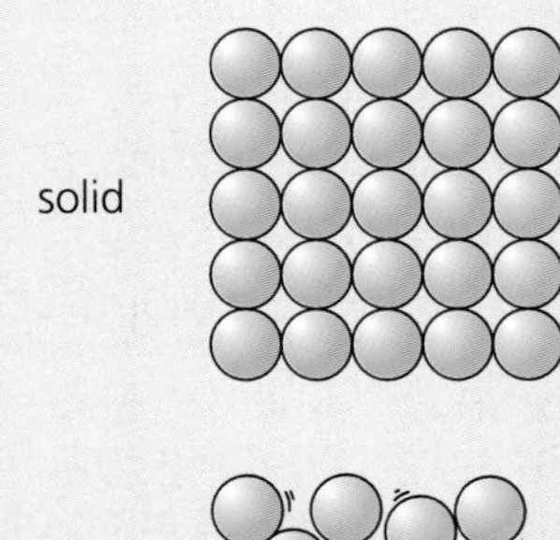

- In a liquid the particles are very close together. There are some forces of attraction, but they are only strong enough to hold the particles in a random arrangement. The particles are able to slide over each other and change position. Liquids are usually quite dense as there are a lot of particles in a small volume. Because the particles are very close together, a liquid cannot be squashed easily.

liquid

- In a gas, the particles are very far apart. There are no forces of attraction between the particles so they move quickly and randomly in all different directions. Gases have a low density as there are not many particles in a small volume. Because the particles are far apart, a gas can be squashed easily.

gas

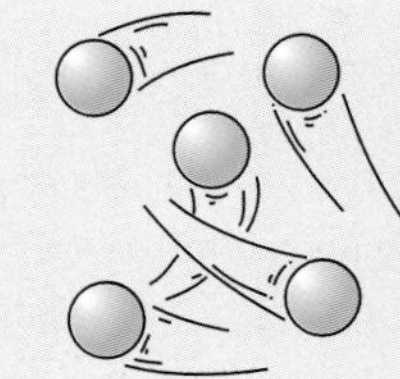

b Make a table with three columns headed 'Solid', 'Liquid' and 'Gas'. Describe the arrangement of the particles in each state of matter.

Changing state

- **Melting** happens when a solid turns into a liquid at a certain temperature called the **melting point**. When a solid melts it takes in energy.
- **Freezing** happens when a liquid turns into a solid at the melting point. When a liquid freezes it gives out energy.
- **Boiling** happens when a liquid turns into a gas at a certain temperature called the **boiling point**. When a liquid boils it takes in energy.
- **Condensing** happens when a gas turns into a liquid at the boiling point. When a gas condenses it gives out energy.
- **Evaporation** happens when a liquid turns into a gas at any temperature. When a liquid evaporates it takes in energy.

c Copy the flow diagram and label the arrows to show the changes of state. Underline the changes of state in green if the particles take in energy. Underline them in orange if the particles give out energy.

Changes of state are explained further in the next spread.

Remember:

Boiling is different from evaporation. Boiling takes place throughout the liquid. Evaporation only happens at the surface of the liquid.

In every change of state mass is conserved. This means that there is the same mass of substance before and after the change of state.

Changes of state are physical changes. They are reversible changes. No new substances are formed.

Melting point and boiling point

Every substance has a specific temperature at which it melts called its **melting point**. This is also the temperature at which it freezes.

Every substance has a specific temperature at which it boils called its **boiling point**. This is also the temperature at which it condenses.

d Look at the bar chart. Make a table with three columns headed 'Solid', 'Liquid' and 'Gas'. Put each chemical in the correct column to show its state at room temperature.

e Make a similar table to show the state of each chemical at 110 °C.

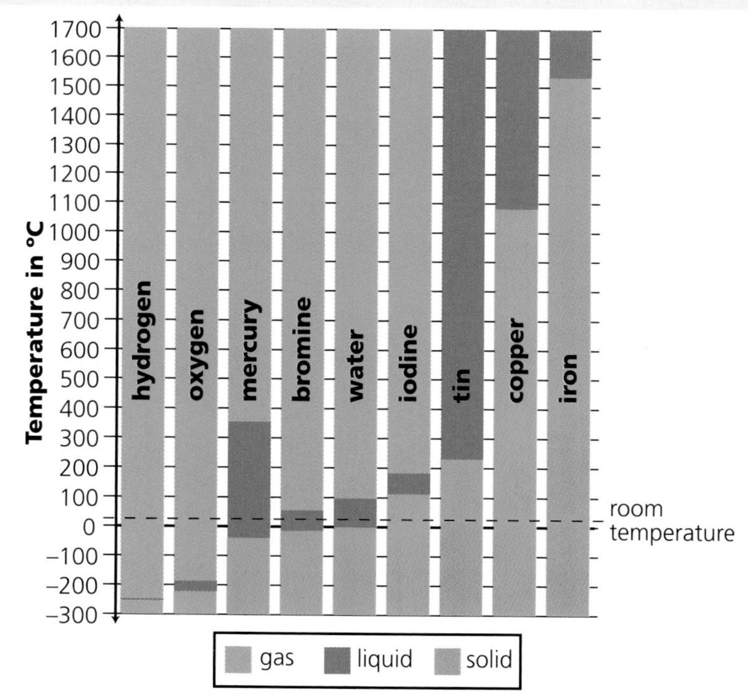

Questions

1. Make sure you know the meanings of all the key words on this spread.
2. Write two sentences to explain why a solid is hard to squash but a gas is not.
3. Write two sentences to explain why a liquid is more dense than a gas.
4. Make a list of changes of state in which matter:
   i takes in energy **ii** gives out energy.
5. Give two ways in which evaporation and boiling are different and two ways in which they are similar.
6. Draw diagrams showing the arrangement of particles in a solid, a liquid and a gas. Describe the differences.
7. Draw a memory map to help you remember the information about states of matter and changes of state.

8.2 The particle model

Melting

- The particles in a solid are close together with forces of attraction between them. The particles vibrate back and forth.
- As the solid is warmed up, the particles vibrate faster. The temperature rises.
- Once the temperature reaches the **melting point**, all the particles are vibrating so much that they overcome some of the forces of attraction between them. The temperature stays the same while the solid melts.
- When all the solid has become a liquid, the temperature starts to rise again.

Remember: if particles are warmed up they move faster. The thermal energy is transferred to kinetic energy.

Boiling

- In a liquid, there are still some forces of attraction between the particles. The particles roll and move around each other.
- When the temperature reaches the **boiling point**, all the particles are moving so much that they break the forces of attraction between them and the particles move away in all directions. The temperature stays the same while the liquid boils.
- When all the liquid has become a gas, the temperature starts to rise again.

Evaporating

- At the surface of the liquid, some particles gain enough energy to break away from all the others and leave the liquid behind.
- The particles break away as a gas. Some of the liquid has **evaporated**.
- Evaporation takes place at any temperature, and only happens at the surface of the liquid.

Condensing

- If a gas is cooled down, the particles lose energy and move more slowly.
- At the **boiling point**, some of the particles get close enough to each other to form forces of attraction between them. The temperature stays the same while the gas condenses.
- When all the gas has become a liquid, the temperature starts to fall again.

Remember: if particles are cooled down they move more slowly. The kinetic energy is transferred to thermal energy leaving the substance.

Freezing

- If a liquid is cooled down, the particles lose energy and move more slowly.
- At the **melting point** they are just vibrating back and forth. Stronger forces of attraction form between the particles and they form a lattice arrangement. The temperature stays the same while the liquid freezes.
- When all the liquid has become a solid, the temperature starts to fall again.

a Describe what happens to the forces of attraction at each of the changes of state.

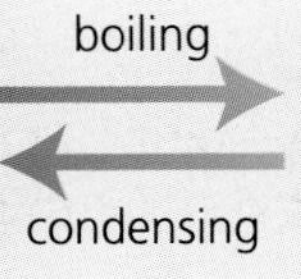

Diffusion

Diffusion happens in gases and liquids when particles spread out and mix with other particles, for example, when the smell of a perfume spreads through the air. The particles move away from their source (the perfume bottle) and mix with the air particles. The smell gets weaker as the particles move further and further apart. The particles move to fill all the available space evenly.

Diffusion is faster in hot gases or liquids because the particles are moving faster.

b Some coloured liquid dye is dropped into a beaker of water. Draw diagrams to show the dye and water particles after:
i 1 minute **ii** 5 minutes
iii 20 minutes.

Gas pressure

The gas particles inside this balloon are moving in all directions and constantly hitting the rubber. Every time a particle hits the rubber, it gives it a tiny push. This keeps the balloon in shape. The sum of all these forces on the area of the balloon is called **gas pressure**.

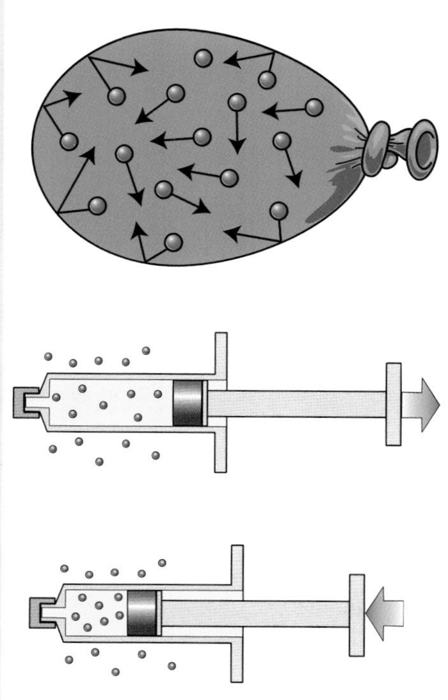

When you heat a gas in a syringe:
- The gas particles move faster.
- They hit the sides more often and so the force on the inside of the syringe is greater.
- If the plunger cannot move, then the gas pressure inside the syringe will rise.
- If the plunger is allowed to move, then it will move out to make the volume inside the syringe greater. The pressure inside falls until it is the same as the gas pressure of the air outside.

When you squash a gas in a syringe:
- Pushing the plunger in makes the volume inside the syringe smaller.
- The particles have less room to move around, and so they hit the sides more often and the force on the inside of the syringe is greater.
- The gas pressure inside the syringe rises.

c Write two sentences to describe why squashing a gas will increase its pressure.

d Write two sentences to explain why cooling a gas will decrease its pressure.

Remember: the particles do not change size when matter expands or contracts.

Expansion and contraction

An increase in temperature makes the particles in matter move more. They take up more space, so the matter **expands**. A decrease in temperature makes the particles move less. They take up less space, so the matter **contracts**.

e Draw diagrams showing the particles before and after you heat:
i a solid **ii** a liquid
iii a gas in a hot-air balloon.

Questions

1. Make sure you know the meanings of all the key words on this spread.
2. Explain why engineers put gaps between slabs of concrete when they are building a road.
3. Explain why power cables seem to have more slack on a hot day than on a cold day.
4. Why does the temperature of crushed ice stay the same while it melts into liquid water?
5. Describe what happens to the particles when a solid melts and forms a liquid and then boils and forms a gas.
6. What is the melting point of water? What is the boiling point of water?
7. Draw a memory map to help you remember how the particle model can explain changes of state, diffusion, gas pressure and expansion and contraction.

Elements, mixtures and compounds

What are substances made of?

- **Atoms** are the smallest particles in an element.
- An **element** is made up of only one type of atom. Examples of elements include copper, iron, oxygen, hydrogen, sulfur, mercury and zinc.
- A **compound** is a substance that is made up of more than one type of atom chemically joined together. Examples of compounds include water, hydrogen sulfide and sodium chloride.
- A **mixture** contains more than one element or compound which are just physically mixed together. They are not chemically joined. Examples of mixtures include air and sea water.

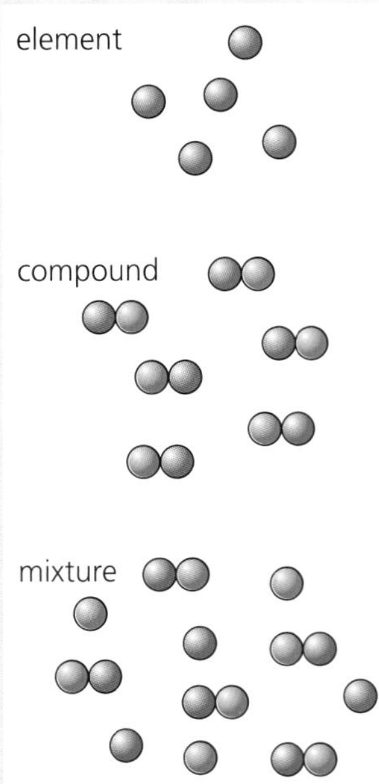

a Describe the difference between an element and a compound.

b Classify each of these substances as an element or a compound.

water **iron** **sugar**
oxygen **carbon dioxide**
hydrogen

Dissolving

- Some chemicals **dissolve**. They are **soluble**. Other chemicals do not dissolve. They are **insoluble**.
- The substance that dissolves is called the **solute**. The liquid that it dissolves in is called the **solvent**. The mixture of solute dissolved in solvent is called a **solution**.
- When no more can dissolve, the solution is **saturated**. The amount of a chemical that can dissolve in a solvent is called its **solubility**.
- The mass of solution is the same as the mass of solvent + solute. Mass is conserved when you make a solution.

When a solid dissolves in water:

- The water molecules surround the particles of the solid.
- The forces of attraction between the particles in the solid crystal are broken. New forces of attraction form between the water molecules and the particles of the solute.
- Energy is given out when the new forces of attraction form between the water molecules and the solute particles. This 'pays back' much of the energy needed to break the forces of attraction between the particles in the solid crystals.

To make the solute dissolve faster you can do the following:

- Use hotter solvent. The solvent particles will have more energy and will be moving around more.
- Stir it. The particles move around more so that the solute is in better contact with the solvent.
- Grind the solute into a powder. More solute particles will be in contact with the solvent.

Remember: dissolving is a physical change. It is reversible.

c How can you tell if a solution is saturated?

d There are three ways that you can make a sugar lump dissolve faster. List them and explain why each one works.

Separating mixtures

Mixtures are made of substances that are not chemically joined together. They can be separated using different techniques based on the physical properties of the elements or compounds in the mixture.

Chromatography is used to separate a mixture of coloured compounds.

- The mixture is put onto a piece of filter paper and then dipped into a solvent.
- As the solvent moves up the paper, it carries the chemicals up with it.
- If a chemical is very soluble, it moves a long way.
- If a chemical is not very soluble, it moves only a short way.

e Why is it possible to separate the different chemicals in a mixture?

Distillation is used to purify liquids by separating the liquid from any solids that are dissolved in it.

f Describe how the water particles gain and lose energy as they change from being in salty water to being in pure water.

1 The salty water is heated until it boils. The water turns into a gas, called **water vapour**, and rises up the flask.

2 The salt starts to form crystals at the bottom of the flask.

3 In the condenser the water vapour is cooled and it condenses back into liquid water.

4 The water drips into the beaker.

5 This water is **pure**. It has no other substances in it. We call it **distilled water**.

Crystallisation

The solubility of a substance depends on the temperature of the solvent. 22 g of copper sulfate will dissolve in $100\,cm^3$ of water at 25 °C. If you heat the water up to 60 °C, then 40 g will dissolve.

If you have a saturated solution of copper sulfate at 60 °C and then cool it down to 25 °C, only 22 g of copper sulfate will stay dissolved. The other 18 g of copper sulfate will form solid crystals. These crystals can be removed by filtering the solution.

If you evaporate all the liquid away then you get all of the solute back that you dissolved at the start. This means that mass is conserved. Crystallisation is the reverse of dissolving.

Remember: hot solvent can dissolve more solute than cold solvent.

Questions

1. Make sure you know the meanings of all the key words on this spread.
2. Explain the differences between making a compound and making a mixture, using the terms 'physical change' and 'chemical change'.
3. Describe how chromatography can be used to separate a mixture of five different inks.
4. You have a sample of muddy salt from which you want to get pure salt. Explain the processes you would use to do this.
5. Draw a memory map to help you remember the information about elements, compounds, dissolving and separating mixtures.

Rocks

The Earth's surface

Rocks form the surface **crust** of the Earth. Rocks are made from a mixture of different chemicals. These chemicals are called **minerals**.

Physical weathering

Physical weathering happens when rock is broken into smaller pieces, but not changed into new substances. It is a physical change. It can be caused by the effect of wind, water and changes in temperature. These types of weathering are very common in mountains and desert regions.

- **Freeze-thaw**: water can get into cracks in the rock. If this water freezes it expands, making the crack bigger.
- **Heating and cooling**: rocks get hot during the day and expand. They get cold at night and contract. This leads to cracking.
- **Wind**: fine grains of sand are carried by the wind and blown against the surface of the rock so they gradually wear it away.

Remember:
You must know the difference between physical and chemical weathering.

In physical weathering, no new substances are formed.

In chemical weathering, new substances are formed.

Chemical weathering

Chemical weathering happens when chemicals in the air and water react with the compounds in the rock to make new substances. It is a chemical change.

- Rainwater is slightly acidic because there is carbon dioxide dissolved in it. Rainwater may also be more acidic because of pollution. Then it is called **acid rain**.
- Many statues and buildings are made of a rock called limestone (calcium carbonate).
- When acidic rain falls on limestone, it reacts with it and produces a new chemical.
- This new chemical is soluble and dissolves.

a Explain why freeze-thaw is a physical process.

b Explain why acid rain causes chemical weathering.

Erosion

Erosion happens when rocks are weathered and then the pieces are carried away. Erosion can be caused by wind, water and glaciers.

Remember:
Weathering + transport = erosion.

Types of rock

The table on the next page summarises the three types of rock.

c Explain how you would distinguish a sedimentary rock from an igneous rock.

d What feature might help you decide if a crystalline rock was igneous or metamorphic?

Remember: the oldest sedimentary layers are at the bottom.

Type of rock	Description	Examples
Igneous	Formed from molten rock, called **magma**, which has cooled and solidified. Sometimes it comes out of volcanoes or cracks in the Earth's crust. This is called **extrusive** igneous rock. Sometimes it solidifies below ground. This is called **intrusive** igneous rock. Igneous rock contains crystals. The bigger the crystals, the slower it cooled. Igneous rocks do not react with acid.	Basalt (small crystals) Granite (big crystals)
Sedimentary	Formed from layers of **sediment** that settle at the bottoms of rivers, lakes and seas over millions of years. The layers are squashed by the weight of the layers above them. The **grains** of sediment are different sizes and become **cemented** together to form rock. Dead animals and plants are covered by sediment and become **fossils**. Limestone and chalk react with acid, but sandstone and mudstone do not.	Limestone Sandstone Mudstone Chalk
Metamorphic	Formed from sedimentary or igneous rocks that have been exposed to high pressure and/or high temperature. This causes changes in the rocks over a very long period of time. Metamorphic rocks may have layers or tiny crystals in them. Fossils are usually destroyed by the heat and pressure. Marble reacts with acid, but slate does not.	Marble (made from limestone) Slate (made from mudstone)

The rock cycle

The **rock cycle** is a continuous cycle of changing rock from igneous rock to sedimentary, to metamorphic and back to igneous rock. This cycle can take many millions of years to complete.

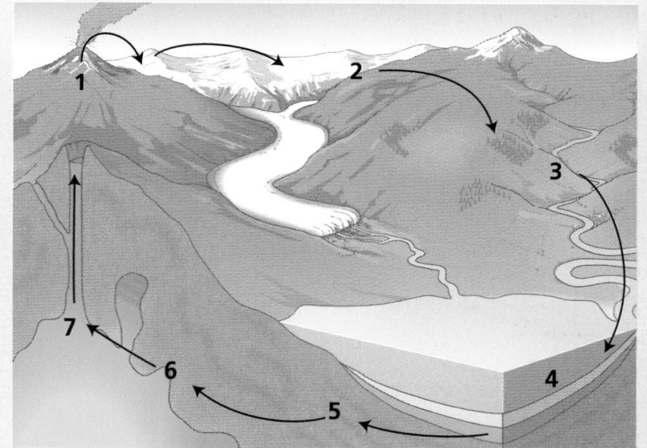

1. Magma **cools** and forms igneous rocks.
2. **Weathering**: rocks are broken down.
3. **Erosion**: weathered rocks are transported away and worn down further.
4. **Deposition**: sediment is laid down in layers at the bottoms of seas and lakes.
5. **Compression**: sedimentary rocks are formed by cementation.
6. **Heat and pressure** can form metamorphic rocks.
7. **Melting**: new magma is formed and a volcano erupts. Then the cycle begins again.

e Igneous and sedimentary rocks are formed underground. Explain how it is possible that mountains are made from igneous or sedimentary rock.

Remember: you must know the rock cycle and what happens at each stage.

Questions

1. Make sure you know the meanings of all the key words on this spread.
2. Explain the difference between physical weathering and chemical weathering.
3. Explain why basalt and granite have different sized crystals.
4. Use your knowledge of the states of matter to describe the changes in the rock cycle.
5. Draw a memory map to help you remember information about types of weathering, different rock types and the rock cycle.

8.5 Chemical changes

Reactants and products

In a chemical change, new substances are formed. The atoms in the **reactants** are rearranged to form new substances, the **products**. Mass is conserved.

There are many different chemical reactions that you need to know. They are summarised here.

Remember: in a chemical change, reactants react and produce products.
reactants → products

Oxidation reactions

When oxygen reacts with a substance and produces an oxide, this is an **oxidation reaction**. Some **non-metals react with oxygen**:

carbon + oxygen → carbon dioxide
$C + O_2 \rightarrow CO_2$

hydrogen + oxygen → water (hydrogen oxide)
$2H_2 + O_2 \rightarrow 2H_2O$

Some **metals react with oxygen**. The general equation is:

metal + oxygen → metal oxide

For example,

magnesium + oxygen → magnesium oxide
$2Mg + O_2 \rightarrow 2MgO$

The **combustion of a fuel** is an oxidation reaction. The general equation is:

hydrocarbon + oxygen → carbon dioxide + water

For example,

methane + oxygen → carbon dioxide + water
$CH_4 + O_2 \rightarrow CO_2 + 2H_2O$

a Write word equations for the following reactions:

i calcium reacting with oxygen

ii zinc reacting with oxygen.

Neutralisation of acids

You can **neutralise** an **acid** to form a **salt**. Different chemicals will neutralise acids, such as alkalis, metals, metal oxides and metal carbonates.

You can **neutralise an acid with an alkali**. The general equation is:

acid + alkali → salt + water

For example,

hydrochloric acid + sodium hydroxide → sodium chloride + water
$HCl + NaOH \rightarrow NaCl + H_2O$

Remember:
Hydrochloric acid makes chloride salts.
Sulfuric acid makes sulfate salts.
Nitric acid makes nitrate salts.

You can **neutralise an acid with some metals**. The general equation is:

acid + metal → salt + hydrogen

For example,

hydrochloric acid + zinc → zinc chloride + hydrogen
$2HCl + Zn \rightarrow ZnCl_2 + H_2$

You can **neutralise an acid with some metal oxides**. The general equation is:

acid + metal oxide → salt + water

For example,

hydrochloric acid + magnesium oxide → magnesium chloride + water

$$2HCl + MgO \rightarrow MgCl_2 + H_2O$$

You can **neutralise an acid with a metal carbonate**. The general equation is:

acid + carbonate → salt + water + carbon dioxide

For example,

hydrochloric acid + calcium carbonate → calcium chloride + water + carbon dioxide

$$2HCl + CaCO_3 \rightarrow CaCl_2 + H_2O + CO_2$$

Remember:
both alkalis and metal oxides are bases.
The general equation is
acid + base → salt + water

b Write word equations for the following reactions:

i nitric acid reacting with sodium hydroxide

ii sulfuric acid reacting with calcium carbonate.

Recipes for making salts

There are three different ways of making salts.

1. Add an alkali to an acid, checking with an indicator, until the mixture is exactly neutral. Evaporate the water to leave the crystals.
2. Add an insoluble metal oxide, an insoluble metal carbonate, or a metal, to an acid. Add extra solid to make sure all the acid has reacted. Filter out the extra solid. Evaporate the water to leave the crystals.
3. Mix solutions of two soluble salts which react together to make an insoluble salt. This is one type of **precipitation** reaction. Then filter and wash the salt. Leave it to dry.

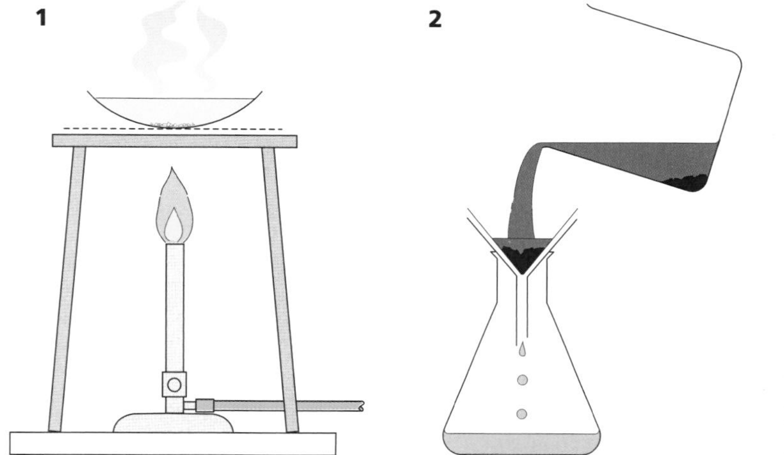

In the reaction shown by the equation, the lead iodide precipitates, as shown in the photo.

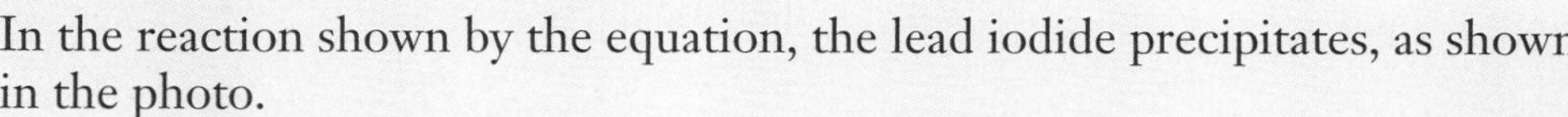

lead nitrate + sodium iodide → lead iodide + sodium nitrate

$$Pb(NO_3)_2 + 2NaI \rightarrow PbI_2 + 2NaNO_3$$

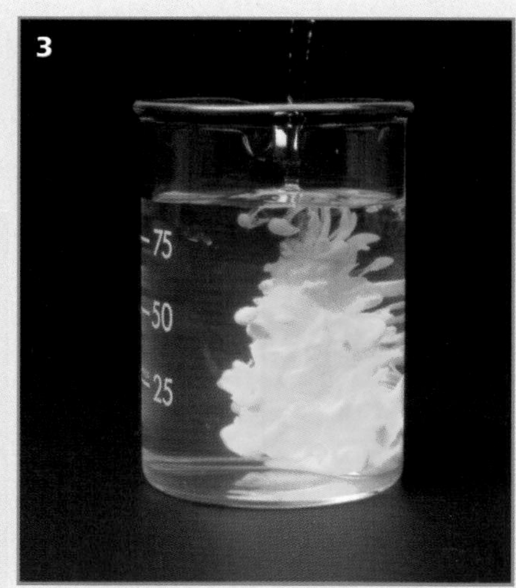

Questions

1. Make sure you know the meanings of all the key words on this spread.
2. Write word equations for three oxidation reactions. Write the same equations using formulae.
3. Write the general word equations for neutralising acid with:
   a a metal
   b an alkali
   c a metal oxide.
4. Draw a flow chart to show three different ways of making a salt. Include diagrams and use colour.
5. Draw a memory map to help you remember the information about oxidation and neutralisation reactions and producing salts.

Chemistry example questions

a These terms are ones you need to remember.

Remember that water melts and freezes at its melting point.

Water boils and condenses at its boiling point.

b Points (1) and (2) refer to the points labelled on the graph.

(1) The ice starts to melt after about 6 minutes.

(2) The temperature does not start to go up until all the ice has melted at 0 °C.

c You will get two marks for each drawing. The ticks show what you will get the marks for.

Remember to draw circles at the size indicated. Try to draw them roughly the same size. You will lose a mark if they are of very different sizes.

The particles in solids are regularly arranged and close packed. The circles can alternate rather than lining up, e.g.

The particles in liquids are random or irregular, but close packed. You cannot squeeze a liquid into a smaller volume. In your drawings make sure there are not too many spaces and that each circle touches at least two other circles.

Gases are mainly empty space with particles racing about and bouncing off each other. Show no more than three circles in your drawing.

3 Water can exist in three physical states: ice, water and steam.

a What is the name given to the process that changes: (2)

i ice into water? melting ✓

ii steam into water? condensing ✓

b A beaker of ice was placed in a warm room. The graph shows how the temperature in the beaker changed from the start of the experiment.

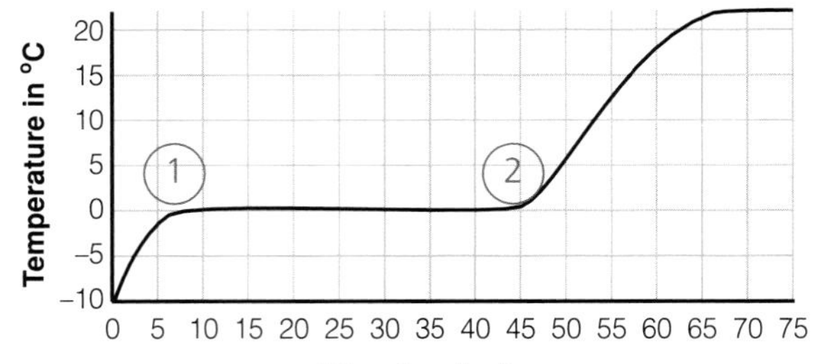

How long after the start had all the ice just gone? (1)

45 minutes

c Draw diagrams, in the boxes below, to show the arrangement of water molecules in ice, water and steam. Use circles, like this ○, to represent the water molecules.

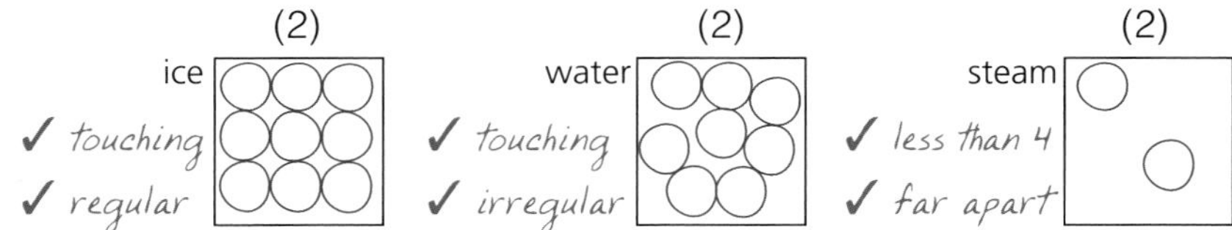

d Water is a compound of two elements. A diagram of a water molecule is shown below. In this diagram the circles represent atoms.

In the circles, write the correct symbols for the elements. (1)

Total (10)

d The formula for water is H_2O. If you think about the number of atoms here, the two smaller circles must be Hs for hydrogen and the larger one must be O for oxygen. You are not expected to remember this shape but you ought to be able to think out the answer.

5 Alex has four solids. They are labelled **W, X, Y** and **Z.** He adds a sample of each one to some dilute acid. The table shows his results.

Solid	Result with dilute acid
W	it reacts slowly and gives off hydrogen
X	it reacts quickly and gives off carbon dioxide
Y	it dissolves and the liquid becomes warm
Z	it remains undissolved as a white powder

a i Which solid could be chalk (calcium carbonate)? (1)

X ✓

ii Give the name of another rock which reacts with acid in the same way as chalk. (1)

Limestone ✓

b i One of the solids is a metal. State which one and give the reason for your choice. (2)

W because it gives off hydrogen with acid ✓

ii The list below gives five metals.

copper gold potassium sodium zinc

Write them in order of reactivity starting with the most reactive. (1)

Most reactive Potassium Sodium Zinc Copper Gold Least reactive ✓

iii Give the name of another metal which would react with acid in a similar way to zinc. (1)

Iron ✓

c As each of the solids reacts, the acid is used up. Describe a test you can use to show whether or not acid is still present. (2)

Add universal indicator. ✓ *It turns from green to red if acid is present. It stays green if the acid has been used up.* ✓

Total (8)

a i All carbonates react with acid to give carbon dioxide.

a ii Chalk and limestone are sedimentary rocks made of calcium carbonate. Marble is another correct answer. Marble is a metamorphic rock made of calcium carbonate.

b i With acid, reactive metals give off hydrogen. They react to form the metal salt. The more reactive they are, the faster they react.

b ii You need to know a reactivity series, e.g.

potassium
sodium
calcium
magnesium
aluminium
zinc
iron
[hydrogen]
copper
silver
gold

Notice hydrogen is in the series to link it with reactions with acids. A metal above hydrogen will react with acids to give hydrogen gas. A metal below hydrogen will not.

c To get the second mark you need to show the result of the test if the acid is still present, as well as the result if the acid is used up.

Writing 'Use indicator' would not get you a mark unless it was obvious from the colour changes you gave which indicator you meant.

b iii If you know your reactivity series, questions like this are very easy. The metal just above or just below zinc will react in a similar way. Metals above aluminium will react much more quickly, and metals below iron will not react.

Energy resources

Non-renewable energy resources

Non-renewable energy resources are not replaced as we use them. These resources will run out in the future. We will need to find other energy resources to use instead.

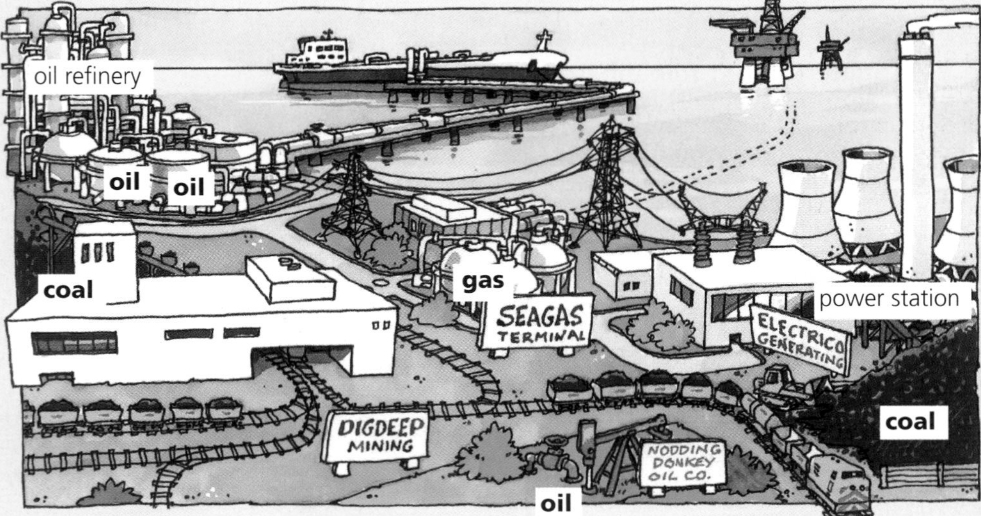

Fossil fuels

Coal, oil and gas are **fossil fuels**. They are non-renewable because they are formed by a process that takes millions of years:

- Animals and plants die.
- They are buried under layers of sediment.
- There is little oxygen, so they rot very slowly.
- They are heated and put under pressure.
- Over millions of years the plants turn into coal and the animals turn into crude oil and natural gas.

Remember: the energy in all fossil fuels originally came from the Sun.

Pollution

Fossil fuels can be burned in power stations to generate electricity, or in vehicles to provide energy to move around. Burning fossil fuels produces gases, mainly carbon dioxide. Burning coal also produces some sulfur dioxide, and burning petrol in vehicles produces other gases. These gases can cause **pollution** problems. These include:

- **acid rain:** some gases, such as sulfur dioxide, dissolve in rain and make an acidic solution.
- **global warming**: some gases in the atmosphere, such as carbon dioxide, keep the heat in, and cause the temperature to rise on the Earth. This changes the climate.
- **smog**: this is a mixture of polluting gases and soot, which collects over cities and can cause breathing difficulties.

a Explain why there will be a problem with using non-renewable energy resources in the future.

b Make a flow chart to show how fossil fuels are formed.

Alternative energy resources

We need to use alternatives to fossil fuels. Many of these **alternative energy resources** are **renewable**, which means they are replaced as we use them.

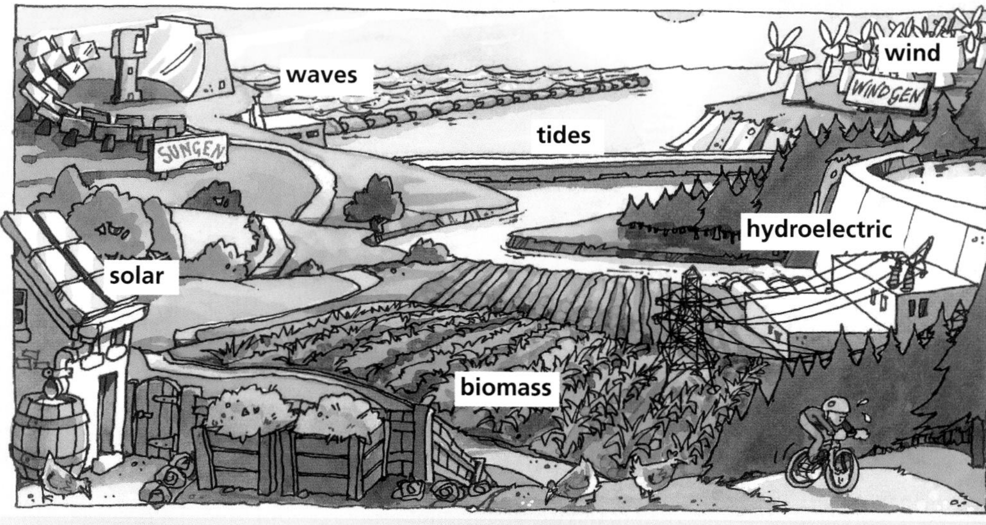

Biomass such as wood or other crops can be burned for heating. Methane is a biomass fuel that is produced by rotting animal and plant material. It can be burned for heating or in vehicles, or used to generate electricity. Ethanol comes from plant biomass, and can be burned in vehicles.

Batteries store chemical energy, which can be used to power vehicles and other devices.

The following alternative energy resources can be used to generate electricity:

- **wind turbines** take kinetic energy from the wind
- **wave machines** take kinetic energy from the waves
- in **hydroelectric power**, a turbine takes kinetic energy from falling water
- **tides** can also use falling water to turn a turbine
- **solar cells** transfer light energy directly into electrical energy
- **fuel cells** transfer the energy released in a chemical reaction directly into electrical energy.

Remember: the energy from all these renewable sources (except tides and fuel cells) originally came from the Sun.

Less polluting

One of the advantages of renewable energy resources is that they do not produce as many polluting gases as burning fossil fuels. Burning biomass produces carbon dioxide, but producing the biomass involves growing plants, which take in carbon dioxide from the atmosphere and use it in photosynthesis.

However, some people feel that alternative energy resources cause other forms of pollution, such as:

- wind turbines produce noise pollution
- tidal barriers and hydroelectric power stations in the mountains disturb the environment as land is flooded and habitats are changed.

Questions

1. Make sure you know the meanings of all the key words on this spread.
2. Make a table with two headings, 'Renewable' and 'Non-renewable'. Put the energy resources on this spread into your table.
3. Give two disadvantages of fossil fuels. Write a sentence about each one.
4. Tides and fuel cells are the only energy resources on these pages not caused by the Sun. For each of the others, write a sentence which explains how the Sun is involved.
5. Draw a memory map to help you remember the information about non-renewable and renewable energy resources and pollution.

Electricity and magnetism

Symbols

Drawing lamps, batteries and switches takes a long time. It is easier to draw circuits using **circuit symbols** to represent the components.

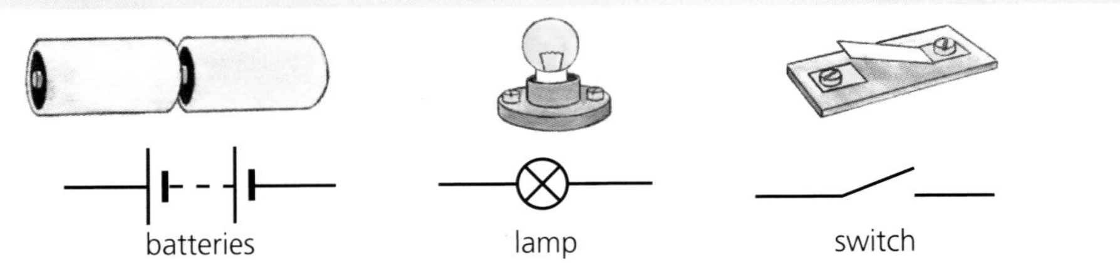

Circuits

Electricity transfers energy to make things work. You need a complete **circuit** for electricity to flow. If there are any gaps then the electricity will not be able to go around the circuit. The diagram shows a simple circuit with a single battery, a lamp and a switch.

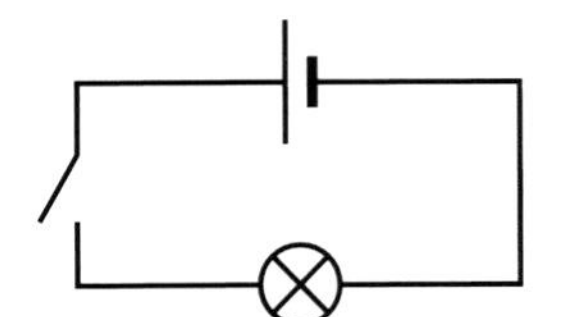

a Draw two different circuits, each with two batteries, two lamps and one switch.

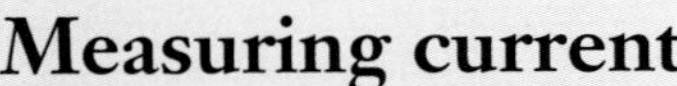

Measuring current

Current is measured in **amps, A**, using an **ammeter**. The ammeter is put in the circuit. The circuit symbol for an ammeter is Ⓐ

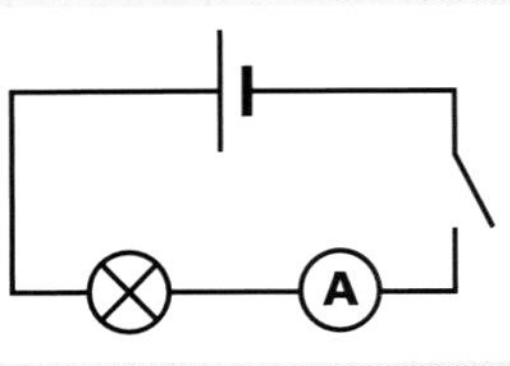

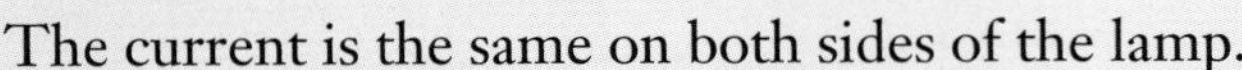

The current is the same on both sides of the lamp.

- Increasing the number of batteries increases the current.
- Decreasing the number of batteries decreases the current.
- Increasing the number of lamps decreases the current.
- Decreasing the number of lamps increases the current.

b Explain why a lamp in a circuit with two batteries gets dimmer after one battery is removed.

c Explain why a lamp in a circuit with two batteries gets dimmer after a second lamp is added.

Measuring voltage

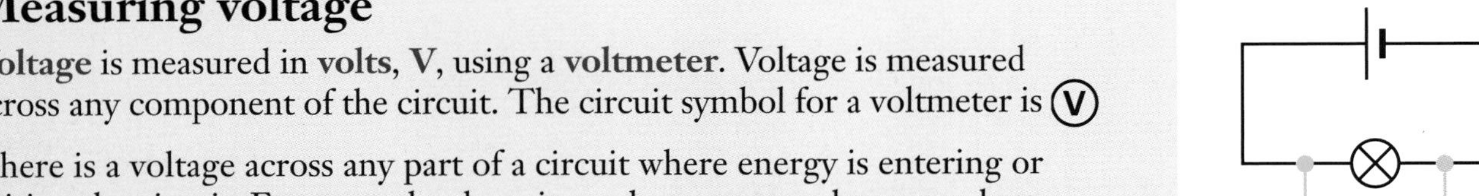

Voltage is measured in **volts, V**, using a **voltmeter**. Voltage is measured across any component of the circuit. The circuit symbol for a voltmeter is Ⓥ

There is a voltage across any part of a circuit where energy is entering or exiting the circuit. For example, there is a voltage across a lamp or a battery, but not across wires. You can increase the voltage in a circuit by adding more batteries.

Series and parallel

There are two ways of connecting two lamps and a battery.

In a **series circuit**:

- The lamps are side by side.
- If one lamp goes out, they will all go out.
- The current is the same all the way around the circuit.
- The voltage is shared between the lamps.

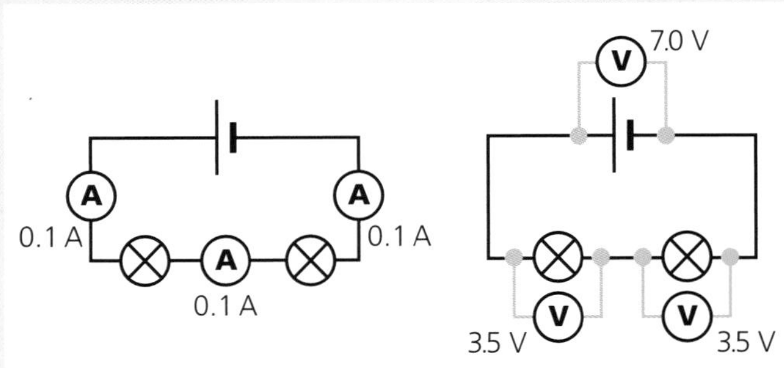

In a **parallel circuit**:

- The lamps are in different loops.
- If one lamp goes out, the rest will stay on.
- The current is shared between the loops.
- The voltage is the same across the battery and each lamp.

d Three lamps are connected to a battery. The voltage across the battery is 9 V. What is the voltage across each lamp if the lamps are connected:

i in series? **ii** in parallel?

Remember: lamps in parallel are brighter than the same lamps in series using the same battery.

Magnets

A magnet produces a **magnetic field**. Magnetic fields can be shown by drawing **magnetic field lines**. These lines run from the **north pole** of the magnet to the **south pole** of the magnet, as shown in the diagram.

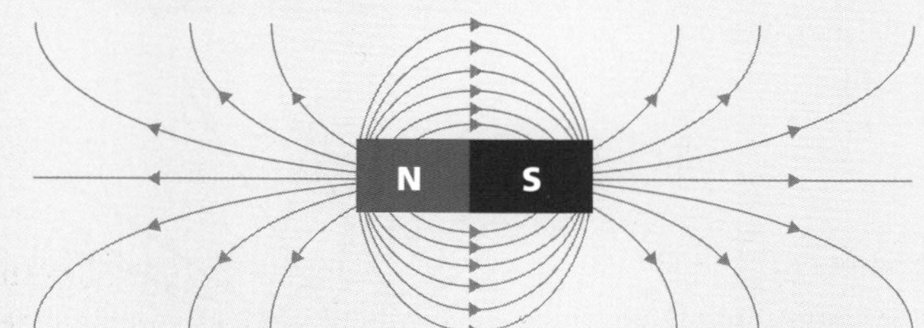

Unlike magnetic poles **attract**.

Like magnetic poles **repel**.

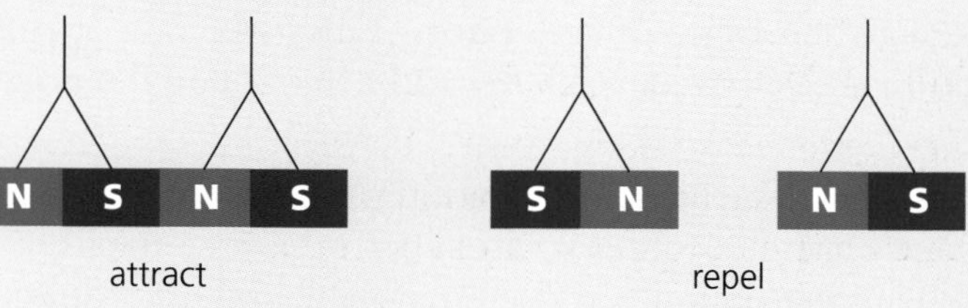

Iron, nickel and cobalt are magnetic metals.

Electromagnets

An **electromagnet** is a coil of wire with an electric current running through it. If the current is switched off, the coil stops being magnetic.

To make the electromagnet stronger you need to do one of these:

- put in an iron core
- increase the current
- increase the number of coils in the wire.

Electromagnets are very useful. They can be used in scrap metal yards for picking up cars. They can also be used in electric circuits as switches and bells.

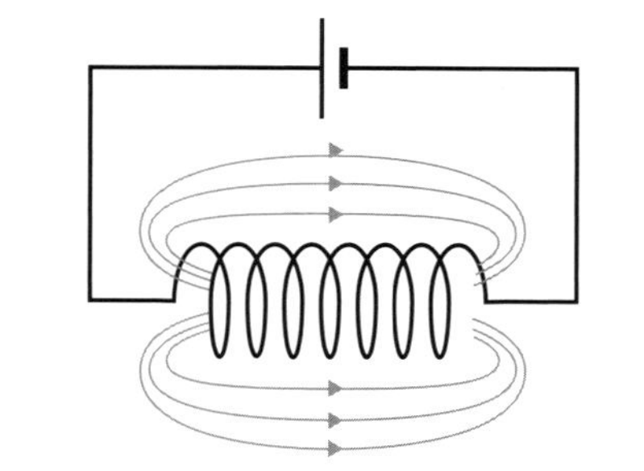

e Give two reasons why an electromagnet is better than a normal magnet for use in a scrap metal yard.

Questions

1. Make sure you know the meanings of all the key words on this spread.
2. Give three ways in which a series circuit and a parallel circuit are different.
3. Give two reasons why it is better to connect Christmas tree lights in parallel than in series.
4. You have been given two lamps and three switches. Design a circuit that will let you switch off both lamps together but will also let you switch off each lamp separately.
5. Explain how a magnet could be used to separate aluminium cans from steel cans.
6. Draw a memory map to help you remember all the information about electric circuits, magnets and electromagnetism.

Light and sound

Light

- Light travels away from its **source** in straight lines in all directions.
- Light travels at a speed of 300 million metres per second in air.
- We see when light enters our eyes.
- Shadows are formed when the light is blocked.

Remember:
You must know the difference between the reflection and the scattering of light.

When you draw ray diagrams you must draw the light rays with a ruler and show the direction of the ray with an arrow.

Reflection

- When light hits a smooth surface, such as a mirror, it is **reflected**.
- The **incoming ray** hits the mirror and is reflected. It is then called the **reflected ray**.
- The top diagram opposite shows that the **angle of incidence** always equals the **angle of reflection**. This is the **law of reflection**. Angles are measured between each ray and a line called the **normal**. For a flat surface, the normal is a line at 90° to the surface.
- When the surface is not smooth, such as paper, the light hits the surface and becomes **scattered**. In this case the light comes in from one direction but is reflected in many different directions.
- Some surfaces **absorb** the light and little or no light is reflected back. Dark surfaces absorb more light, while pale surfaces absorb less light.

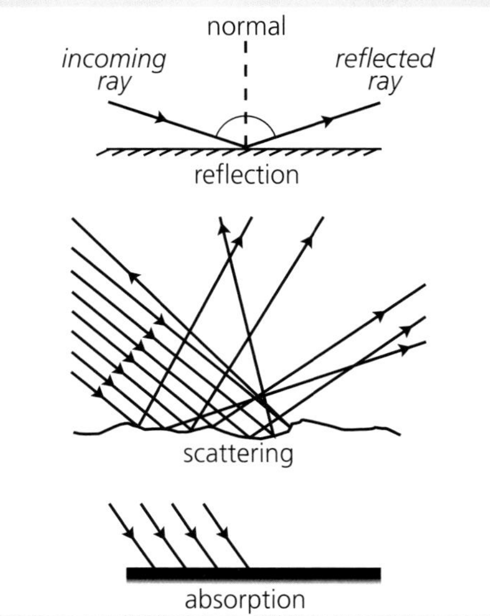

a Make a table to summarise the meanings of reflection, scattering and absorption.

Refraction

Light travels through **transparent** materials but not through **opaque** materials. When light travels from one transparent material to another it may become **refracted**.

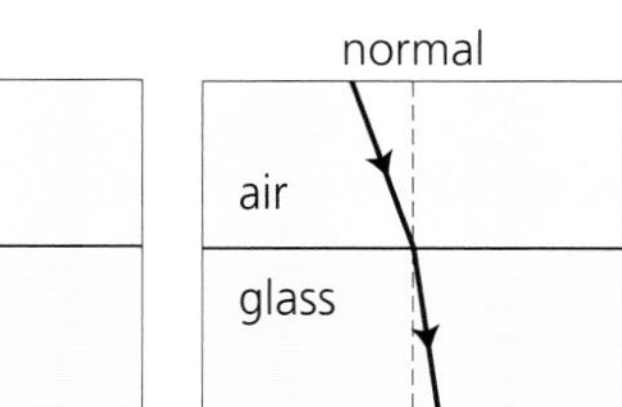

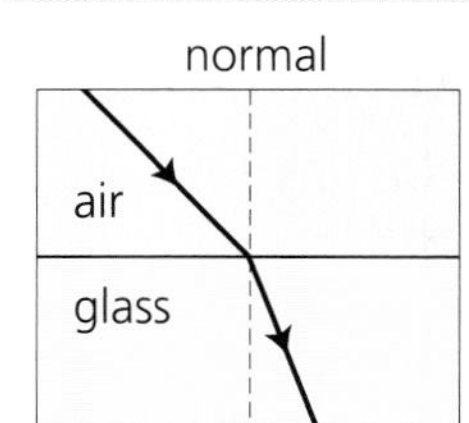

- Light refracts because it travels at different speeds in different materials.
- Light travels faster in air than in water or glass.
- Light bends towards the normal when it travels from air into glass or water.
- Light bends away from the normal when it travels from glass or water into air.
- Light is not refracted if it travels along the normal.

b Draw a diagram showing a ray of light passing from the air through a glass block and out the other side.

Colour

- White light is made of many colours, which can be seen when white light passes through a prism. This produces a **spectrum**.
- This splitting up of light into its colours is known as **dispersion.**
- The colours are always refracted in the same order: red, orange, yellow, green, blue, indigo and violet.
- A coloured filter only allows one colour of light through and absorbs the others.

Remember: the spectrum by using the mnemonic ROY G BIV.

- A coloured object in white light reflects the colour of the object, which we see, and absorbs the other colours.
- Coloured objects appear to be different colours in different coloured light.

c What colour of light will pass through a green filter?

d What colour will a red shirt look in blue light?

Sound

- A sound is made when something **vibrates**.
- We hear sound because vibrations travel through the air to our ears and make the eardrum vibrate.
- Sounds cannot travel through a vacuum because sound needs a material to travel through.

Loudness and amplitude

- The **amplitude** is the height of the vibration from the centre.
- Amplitude can be measured in metres.
- The larger the amplitude of a vibration, the louder the sound.
- The smaller the amplitude of a vibration, the quieter the sound.
- Loud sounds transfer a lot of energy and can damage your hearing.

large amplitude
louder sound
small amplitude
quieter sound

Pitch and frequency

- The **frequency** is how many vibrations there are each second.
- Frequency is measured in **hertz** (Hz).
- Higher and lower sounds have different **pitches**.
- The higher the frequency, the higher the pitch.
- The lower the frequency, the lower the pitch.
- Some people cannot hear very high-pitched or very low-pitched sounds.

6 vibrations in 0.001 seconds
higher-pitched sound
3 vibrations in 0.001 seconds
lower-pitched sound

e Explain how amplitude and frequency affect a sound.

Sound and light

- Both light and sound transfer energy.
- Light and sound can be reflected. Reflected sound is called an **echo**.
- Both light and sound travel at different speeds in different materials.
- Light travels at 300 million m/s, much faster than sound which travels at 330 m/s. Thunder and lightning show that sound and light travel at different speeds.

f Write a paragraph to show the differences and similarities between sound and light.

Questions

1. Make sure you know the meanings of all the key words on this spread.
2. Why does a black object appear black in any colour light you put it in?
3. Explain the following:
   a sound travels quicker through a solid than through a gas
   b it takes 4 seconds after you clap to hear the echo when you are standing 660 m from a wall.
4. Draw a diagram to show a vibration that gives:
   a a low-pitched sound
   b a high-pitched sound
   c a loud sound.
5. Draw two overlapping memory maps, one for light and one for sound. In the overlap will be all the things that sound and light have in common.

Physics revision

9.4 Forces and motion

Forces in action

The effects of forces can be seen everywhere. When you push or pull an object you are exerting a force.

Different types of force include:

- weight
- friction
- tension
- upthrust
- reaction force.

Weight

- **Weight** is the force of **gravity** on an object and like all forces it is measured in **newtons** (N).
- Weight or **gravitational force** pulls an object towards a large object, usually the Earth.
- The further apart two objects are, the smaller the force between them.
- The gravitational force an object exerts also depends on its mass.

a List the factors that affect the size of a gravitational force between two objects.

Remember: weight is a force. It should not be confused with mass, which is a measure of how much matter an object has, and is measured in kg.

Friction

- **Friction** is the force that is exerted when two things rub together.
- Friction slows moving objects down, and causes thermal energy to be given out.
- Friction is useful in brakes in cars and bicycles.
- Friction can cause problems by wearing down machinery.
- Friction can be reduced by using **lubricants**.
- **Air resistance** is an example of friction, which slows down moving objects.
- Cars and planes are **streamlined** to keep their air resistance low.

b Write a paragraph explaining how friction can be useful and not so useful.

Unbalanced and balanced forces

Unbalanced forces:

- When forces act against each other and they are not the same size, they are **unbalanced**.
- If a stationary object has unbalanced forces acting on it, it will start to move in the direction of the biggest force. If you give a push to a trolley and your push is bigger than the forces acting on it, such as friction, the trolley will move in the direction of your push.
- If the unbalanced force on a moving object is in the same direction as the movement, then the object will speed up. If the unbalanced force is in the opposite direction to the movement, the object will slow down.

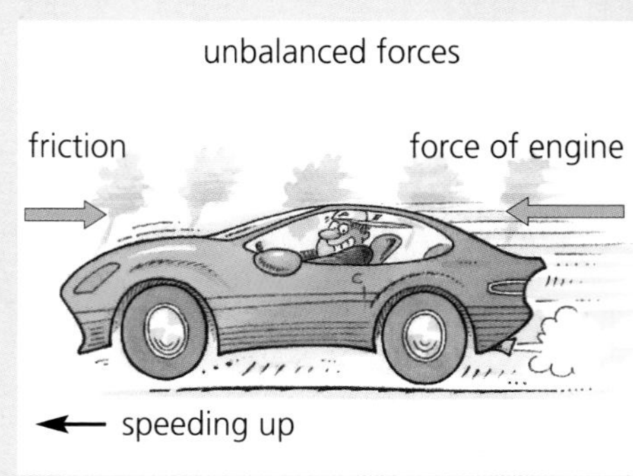

Balanced forces:

- If two forces are the same size and acting in opposite directions, they are **balanced**.

- A vehicle travelling at a steady speed and something standing still both have balanced forces acting on them.
- A floating object has balanced forces acting on it. The **upthrust** (the force of the water pushing up) is equal to the object's **weight** (the force acting down on the water).
- The **reaction force** stops something falling through a solid object. When a person stands on a plank, the reaction force of the plank balances the weight of the person.
- When a weight pulls down on a rope or spring, the weight is balanced by the **tension** force in the rope or spring pulling up.

c A parachutist has a weight of 500 N. As she falls the air resistance is 200 N. Is this an example of balanced or unbalanced forces? Explain your answer.

reaction force of plank

Mr Blue's weight

tension force of spring

weight

Speed

You can tell how fast an object is moving by measuring the distance it travels and the time it takes. **Speed** is measured in metres per second. You can calculate the speed using this equation:

$$\text{speed} = \frac{\text{distance travelled}}{\text{time taken}}$$

Remember this equation.

d Calculate the speed in the following examples.

i Tina rides 20 km on her bike in 4 hours.

ii Charlotte travels 12 km on her horse in 30 minutes.

iii Mike sprints the 100 m in 12 seconds.

A **distance–time graph** shows the distance travelled over a period of time. The steeper the line the faster the object is travelling. A horizontal line shows a stationary object.

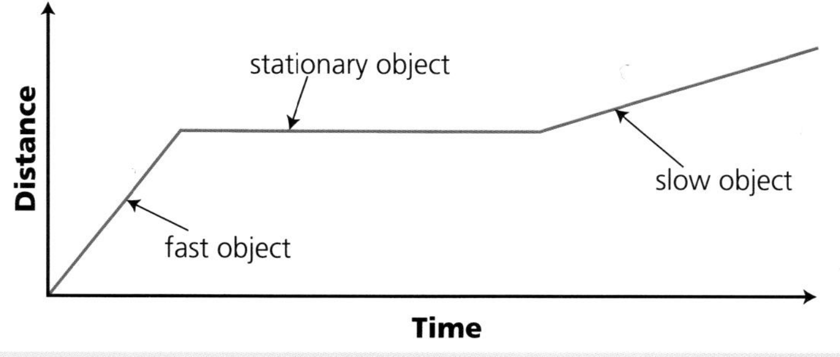

Questions

1. Make sure you know the meanings of all the key words on this spread.
2. For each of the following, draw a diagram to show the forces.
   - **a** a car pulling a trailer forwards
   - **b** a hot-air balloon which is tethered to the ground by a rope
3. **a** The friction of the trailer wheels in question **2a** is 3000 N, while the car pulls it forwards with a force of 5000 N. What is the overall or resultant force on the trailer?
   - **b** The car and trailer travel 20 km in 15 minutes. What is their speed during this journey?
   - **c** What is the mass of the car on Earth if its weight is 8000 N?
   - **d** If the gravitational force at the surface of the Moon is one-sixth that on Earth, what is the weight of the car on the Moon?
4. Draw a memory map to help you remember the information about forces and speed.

physics revision

9.5 Earth and space

The Solar System

- The **Solar System** consists of nine **planets** and their **moons**, and also other objects such as **comets** and **asteroids**, orbiting the **Sun**.
- Planets orbit the Sun and moons orbit planets.
- The nine planets in order from the Sun are Mercury, Venus, Earth, Mars, Jupiter, Saturn, Uranus, Neptune and Pluto.
- The planets differ from each other in many ways, including diameter, surface temperature and distance from the Sun.

a Write a paragraph to explain what is meant by the Solar System.

The Sun and stars

- The Sun is a **star** and it is the source of light for the Earth.
- Like all stars, the Sun is **luminous** which means that it gives out light.
- We can only see the planets and our Moon because they reflect the light from the Sun. They are **non-luminous**.

b Draw a diagram to explain how we see the Moon.

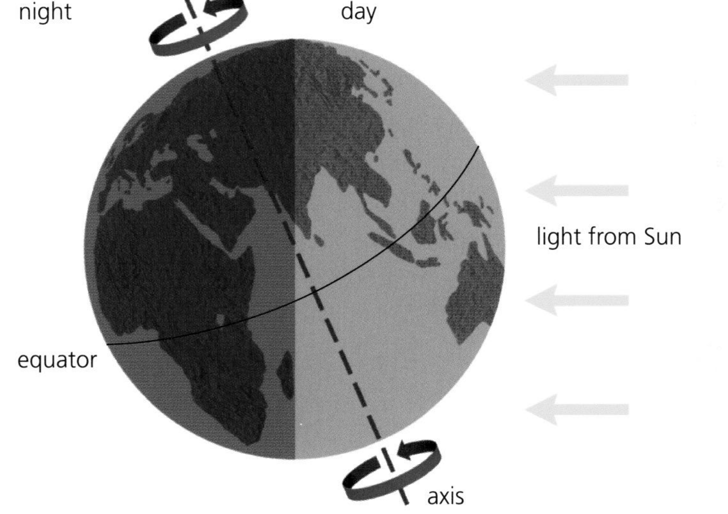

Day and night

- The Earth spins on its **axis**, an imaginary line that runs between the Poles, once every 24 hours.
- As the Earth spins, the UK moves from shadow at night, when it faces away from the Sun, into the light during the day, when it is facing the Sun.
- The Sun appears to rise in the east and set in the west.

c Write a short paragraph to explain what causes day and night.

The seasons

- The Earth orbits the Sun every 365 days. This is called a **year** and during this time in the UK there are four **seasons**: spring, summer, autumn and winter.
- The seasons are caused by the tilt of the Earth on its axis.
- The UK is in the northern hemisphere. In the summer, the UK is tilted towards the Sun, giving warmer weather. In the winter, the UK is tilted away from the Sun, giving colder weather. The diagram on the next page shows this.

- The tilt of the Earth also causes day length to vary at different times of the year. The days are longer in the summer and shorter in the winter.
- The stars we see in the night sky change with the seasons because we are facing a different way out into space.

d What is the weather like in Australia while it is winter in the UK? Explain why.

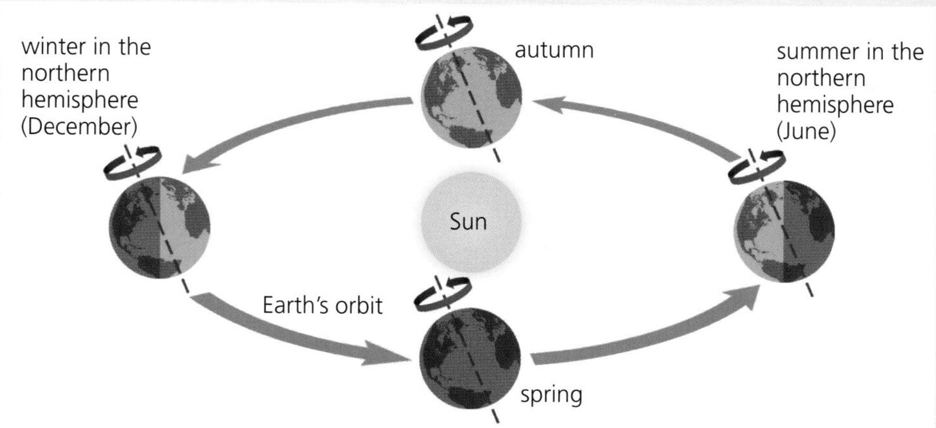

Satellites

- A **satellite** is an object that orbits a larger object.
- The Moon is the **natural** satellite of the Earth. **Artificial** satellites are put into space by scientists.
- Artificial satellites have many uses, for example, communication, exploration, weather forecasting and navigation.
- Artificial satellites can be put into different types of orbit such as **polar** and **geostationary** orbits. Geostationary satellites orbit the Earth once every 24 hours and they stay in the same place over the Earth. Polar satellites orbit over the North and South Poles.
- The planets orbit the Sun and are satellites of the Sun.
- The planets are kept in orbit by **gravitational force** between them and the Sun. The size of this force depends on the size of the planet and its distance from the Sun.

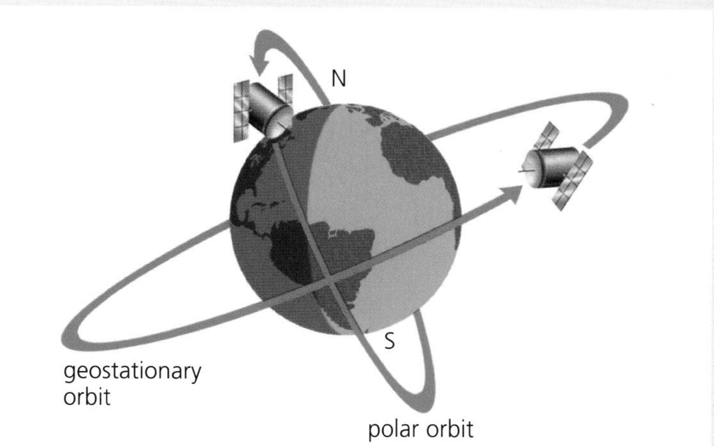

e Explain the difference between an artificial satellite and a natural satellite, giving several different examples.

Questions

1. Make sure you know the meanings of all the key words on this spread.
2. Explain why Pluto is the coldest planet.
3. Explain why Jupiter has a higher surface gravity than the Earth.
4. Explain what would happen if the Earth was:
   a not tilted on its axis
   b not spinning on its axis.
5. What type of weather would you expect at the equator and why?
6. Explain how you can see satellites on clear nights.
7. Explain the difference between a polar orbit and a geostationary orbit.
8. Draw a memory map to help you remember the information about the Solar System, day and night, the seasons and satellites.

Physics example questions

8 Jack is pushing a luggage trolley along level ground at an airport.

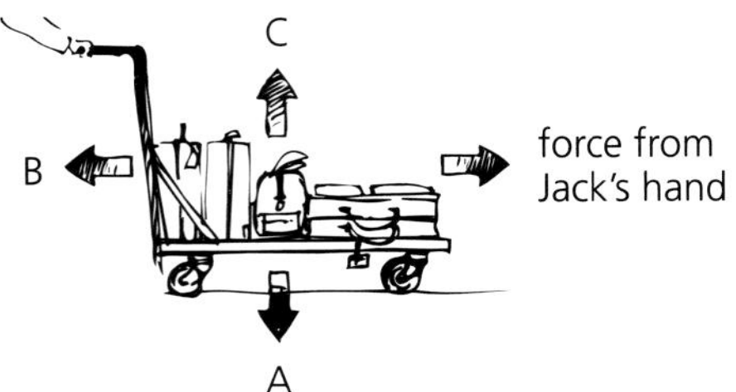

There are four forces acting on the trolley.

a One of the forces is the push from Jack's hands. The others are friction, weight and the reaction of the ground.

Complete the sentences. (3)

Force A is *weight* ✓

Force B is *friction* ✓

Force C is *reaction of the ground* ✓

b What are the units in which force is measured? (1)

newtons ✓

c The trolley is moving forwards, and it is getting faster. One pair of forces is now unbalanced.
Compare the sizes of these two forces. (1)

The forward force of Jack's hand must now be bigger than the backward force of friction. ✓

d Jack has to push the trolley 150 m to the check-in desk.
If he pushes the trolley at 3 m/s, how long will it take him? (1)

$$\text{Speed} = \frac{\text{distance}}{\text{time}} \quad 3 = \frac{150}{?}$$

$$\text{therefore } ? = \frac{150}{3} = 50\,\text{s}$$ ✓

Total (6)

a When choosing an answer from a list, always copy correctly and completely. Do not shorten 'reaction of the ground' to 'reaction'.

b The symbol for the unit of force is N (capital). The word is newton (without a capital letter).

c These answers always require a sentence. You need to include the link that to get faster needs a bigger forward force.

If you were unsure about the name of force B, an answer like 'The force from Jack's hand is larger than force B' is acceptable because it uses the information from the diagram.

Do not write 'It is bigger' because the marker does not know what 'it' refers to.

d In any calculation, write down the equation in the form that you remember it and put the numbers in. Then rearrange the equation. Use small numbers to help you check your rearranged equation. For example, $3 = \frac{6}{?}$ is easier to rearrange than an equation with letters involving algebra.

Many speed calculations can be done using common sense rather than the formula:

$$\text{speed} = \frac{\text{distance}}{\text{time}}$$

It always pays to check your answers using common sense. Think to yourself: if it goes 3 m in 1 second then it goes 30 m in 10 seconds or 90 m in 30 seconds. So it goes 150 m in 50 seconds. Do not forget the units!

11 a The Earth is the third planet from the Sun.

i Which is the second planet from the Sun? (1)

Venus ✓

ii Which is the fourth planet from the Sun? (1)

Mars ✓

b The diagram shows the orbits of the Earth and Mercury. Mercury takes 88 Earth-days to orbit the Sun.

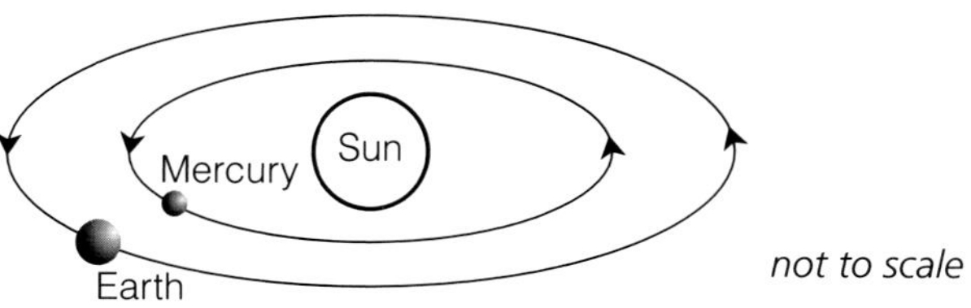

In the diagram, the Earth and Mercury are lined up with the Sun. How long will it take before the Earth and Mercury are lined up with the Sun again? Tick the correct box. (1)

less than 88 Earth-days ☐
exactly 88 Earth-days ☐
more than 88 Earth-days ☑ ✓
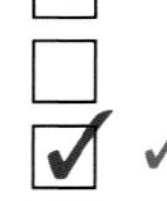
exactly 365 Earth-days ☐

c Mercury and Pluto are both small rocky planets. Mercury is one of the brightest objects in the night sky, but Pluto is so faint that it cannot be seen with the naked eye.

Give **two** reasons why Mercury is much brighter than Pluto. (2)

Reason 1

Mercury is nearer the Sun so gets more light than Pluto ✓

Reason 2

Earth is nearer Mercury than Pluto so light has less distance to travel after being reflected. ✓

Total (5)

a You need to remember the order of the planets in the Solar System from the Sun, at least to Jupiter: Mercury; Venus; Earth; Mars; Jupiter; Saturn; Uranus; Neptune; Pluto.

b Mercury takes 88 days to get back to the same place (where it is shown on the diagram). In this time the Earth will have moved on about one-quarter of an orbit so Mercury will have to cover at least another quarter of its orbit to catch up with Earth.

c The further light, or any form of energy, has to travel, the more the light or energy spreads out.

Mercury is nearer to the Sun than Pluto. It receives much more light. Light also has less distance to travel from Mercury to Earth than from Pluto to Earth, so spreads out less. Good answers include both parts of the explanation.

Investigations using experiments (1)

Learn about

- Planning
- Carrying out

Step 1: finding a question to investigate

Does sugar dissolve quicker in hot tea than in cold tea?

You've made the first step – you have a question you want to answer. Now you have to turn it into an ***investigation****. This is an investigation you can carry out in a school laboratory, by doing experiments.*

Key to understanding these spreads:

black = main text

red = 'Sid the scientist'

blue = 'Pippa the pupil'

Step 2: thinking about the variables

Once you have a question, you should try to ask it as scientifically as possible. This means identifying the variables. When you have a list of **variables**, you need to decide which variable you are going to change, which variable you are going to measure, and which variables you are going to keep the same to make it a fair test.

There are lots of variables: mass of sugar, volume of water, temperature of water, type of sugar, amount of stirring, time to dissolve.

So which is your ***input variable****, the one you are changing, and which is your* ***outcome variable****, the one you are measuring?*

Input variable is … temperature. Outcome variable is … time to dissolve. Everything else has to stay the same.

Good, now ask your question in a more scientific way.

Does the time taken for the sugar to dissolve depend on temperature?

Step 3: the risk assessment

You need to think about the experiments you are planning and the risks involved. If you are using chemicals, you need to find out if they are dangerous and what safety precautions to take.

It's pretty safe. I'll follow the lab rules and wipe up any spills. I'll use a kettle rather than a Bunsen burner to heat the water because I'm less likely to burn myself pouring the water.

Don't forget to write your ***risk assessment*** *down.*

Step 4: equipment and values

You then have to decide how you are going to do the experiments, and what values you are going to use for the input variable, and for the variables you are keeping the same. You will probably have to do some trial experiments to decide if you have all the **equipment** you need, and whether the values you have chosen are sensible.

Start by thinking about the variables. You need to think about the measurements and observations you need to make. This will lead you to the equipment you need.

OK. Input variable is temperature, so I'll need a thermometer. Outcome variable is time, so I'll need a stopwatch. I need to keep the mass of sugar constant, so I'll need a balance, and I'll need a measuring cylinder to measure the water. I'll need a glass rod for stirring. I think I'll do the experiment in a beaker, so I'll need that, and I'll need something to heat the water, so I'll need a kettle. I'm not sure what type of sugar I should use, or the amount of stirring.

So far so good. Time for some trial experiments. Don't forget to write down any ***measurements*** *and* ***observations****. They should be there in your final report.*

Some time later ...

Granulated sugar was best, because I could see the crystals better. I decided to put the beaker on a piece of black paper, to help me see when all the crystals had gone. I've decided not to stir, because it makes it too complicated, and to use 50 cm^3 of water and 2 g of sugar.

Fine. How many values for the temperature are you going to use? Think about what you are hoping to do with your results. Are you hoping to draw a graph?

I think so. To draw a graph I'll need lots of different temperatures. I'll do five different temperature values: 90 °C, 70 °C, 50 °C, 30 °C and 10 °C.

Is one measurement enough for each temperature?

I suppose not. I'll do two. That's 10 experiments, I'll be there ages.

Step 5: making a prediction

Once you have a plan it is a good idea to make a **prediction**. Sometimes you have nothing to go on, and making a prediction is not possible. However, often you will know something about what you expect to happen. It is best if you can explain why you made your prediction using your knowledge and understanding of science.

The sugar will dissolve quickest at the highest temperature.

Why? Think about it. Look back in your notes. Look up dissolving. Come up with a reason.

Some time later ...

It's all to do with particles. The water is made of particles and the sugar crystals are made of particles. The higher the temperature of the water, the more the water particles move and they hit the sides of the sugar crystals more often, knocking off sugar particles. It takes less time to knock off all the sugar particles if the water particles are moving quicker. I've drawn some diagrams.

Step 6: carrying out

You should have a table prepared to write down your results, because there may not be time once you get going. Do not forget to put titles at the top of each column, along with the units you are using. Sometimes, despite all your planning, it will go wrong. You may have to modify what you were going to do, and repeat parts when things go wrong. The most important thing is to write down what you do.

It was a disaster! I couldn't get the temperature of the water to exactly 90 °C and the sugar took ages to dissolve at 10 °C. I tried to repeat it, but the temperatures weren't exactly the same the second time. I had to do one experiment four times – I kept making mistakes.

Just write down all the problems and don't worry too much. Make a neat copy of your table, but put in the messy one as well – a scientist always includes the original copy.

Turn over for Investigations using experiments (2) on analysing, concluding and evaluating.

Investigations using experiments (2)

Learn about

- Analysing and concluding
- Evaluating

Step 7: looking at the data and drawing graphs

Look carefully at your **results**. If your **data** is numbers, then you will probably want to make a chart or graph. You need to make sure it is the correct type of chart or graph, so use a skill sheet or ask someone for advice if you are not sure.

If you repeated experiments, you may be able to **calculate** an **average** (a mean). You can only calculate a mean if the experiments were exact repeats.

There may be other calculations you can do using your results. You may be able to calculate speed, or pressure, or the amount by which something increase or decreased.

However, many investigations do not give results that can be used in calculations. Some investigations will not lead to a chart or graph.

I can't do averages, because my repeats weren't exact repeats. I've got 65 °C and 62 °C, though the others are the same.

Don't worry. Plot all your results on your graph. Do you know what graph to plot?

I think so. The input variable, the temperature, goes along the bottom. The outcome variable, the time, goes up the side. Both variables are numbers that increase continuously, so it's a line graph with a line of best fit. I used the skill sheet.

Good. Are you going to try to plot your times like that, in minutes and seconds? What about turning the times into seconds? They will be easier to plot.

Step 8: looking for patterns and trends

You need to look carefully for **patterns** and **trends** in your results. This is easier if you have made a chart or a graph, because any trend will be more obvious. If you use a line graph, then the line of best fit will show any trends. It is not enough just to draw the chart or graph, you have to describe the pattern or trend in words. This is even more important if there is not a chart or graph.

I've written, 'The higher the temperature the faster the sugar dissolved. This is shown in my graph.'

Step 9: explaining and interpreting

You then need to **explain** what you have found out, using your scientific knowledge and understanding. This is particularly important if you found out something you did not know, or if the investigation turned out differently from what you expected.

But it turned out exactly as I said it would. I've already written about particles and drawn diagrams in my prediction.

You still have to mention it. Your conclusion will not be complete without it.

OK. 'Increasing the temperature increased the speed of the water particles, so they knocked the sugar particles off the crystals more quickly, so the crystals dissolved quicker.'

Step 10: do your conclusions fit with your prediction?

Look back at your prediction, if you made one. Does your **conclusion** fit with your prediction? If it does, you should say so. If it does not, then you may have found out something interesting. At this point, you may be able to make new predictions based on your conclusions.

My conclusion fits with my prediction, but I can't think of any new predictions to make.

Step 11: look at your data again

Evaluating your investigation is difficult. The place to start is your data. Are there any observations or measurements that do not fit into the overall pattern or trend? Point them out and try to explain why they do not fit.

Where do I start? The repeats are not repeats, because I could not get the temperature of the water exactly the same both times. I haven't plotted the result marked with a red ring, because it is so far out. I think I forgot to reset the stopwatch. The times for the higher temperatures are all over the place, so it was hard to decide where the line of best fit should go. This was because it was really difficult to tell exactly when the sugar dissolved, particularly at the higher temperatures, where a second made a big difference.

Step 12: how certain are you?

You need to make a **judgement** about the certainty of your conclusion. If you are not sure, you must say so. Your data may not show the pattern or trend you expected, or the trend may be unclear. Even if all your data fits into the pattern, you need to think whether your conclusion is generally true, or only true for your particular experiments.

I'm sure. The higher the temperature, the quicker sugar will dissolve.

I'm a scientist, so I'm never sure. Your conclusion is only correct for temperatures between 0 °C and 100 °C, when water is a liquid. Ice and steam will not dissolve sugar. Also, you haven't thought about different amounts of sugar. If the solution is saturated, then no more sugar will dissolve and raising the temperature may not help. Also, your conclusion may hold for liquid water, but it doesn't for other solvents. Sugar will not dissolve in dry cleaning fluid, or many other solvents.

OK. For liquid water, the higher the temperature, the quicker sugar dissolves, provided the solution does not get saturated.

Step 13: suggest improvements to the method

No experiment is ever perfect, so you should be able to think of ways to improve your method.

There are lots of improvements I would like to make. I would like to have a way of keeping the water at a set temperature, like the thermostat in my fish tank at home. Then the repeats would have been repeats and I could have taken an average. I also need a better method of deciding when all the sugar crystals have gone. Perhaps I could use some of the larger, coloured sugar crystals they sometimes serve in restaurants. They might be easier to see, particularly with white paper underneath. I would like to try every 5 °C from 5 °C to 95 °C, but this would only be possible if I had the apparatus for keeping the temperature constant. I would like to have repeated each temperature three times.

Investigations without experiments

Learn about

- Other types of investigation

Key to understanding these spreads:

black = main text

blue = 'Pippa the pupil'

green = some scientists

Working in the real world

I am a geologist. I study rocks because they tell me what happened to the Earth in the past.

I am an epidemiologist. I study the way in which diseases spread in a population.

I am a geneticist. I study genes and the way they are inherited.

I am an animal behaviourist. I study how animals in the wild live together in groups.

I am a cosmologist. I study the Universe.

Many scientists cannot test their ideas by designing and carrying out experiments in laboratories. Instead, they investigate their ideas by observing and measuring things in the real world.

I am going to investigate whether people with blond hair are more likely to have blue eyes than people without blond hair. My prediction is that people with blond hair are more likely to have blue eyes because both blond hair and blue eyes are due to lack of melanin.

Reducing the differences

When you are doing an investigation in the real world, you cannot control all the variables. For example, if you are studying people then every person is different from every other person. You have to try your best to reduce the differences. You may choose to work on people of a certain age, or a certain gender, or who live in a certain place, or all three. Planets, rocks and stars are all different too.

I don't think reducing the differences is that important for me, because people inherit their eye colour and their hair colour. My main problem will be people who dye their hair. I'll have to leave those out.

Definitions

If you are working in the real world, you have to decide exactly what you are working on. Scientists have to make decisions about how the stars they are studying are different from all other stars, or what type of behaviour is aggressive behaviour in chimps, or which symptoms indicate a particular disease.

I've been to a hairdresser. He gave me these samples of hair. I have made a card with ten hair colours on it. I'll put the whole card up to the person's hair and decide on the closest colour. If it is 1 to 4, then they are blond. The same with the eye colour, but I've made my own card. If the closest colour is 1 to 5, then they have blue eyes.

Sampling

*The larger your **sample**, the more likely it is to reflect the real situation. Your sample should be as large as possible. It is also important that you select your sample without bias. For example, if you are measuring fish then you need to make sure you are catching fish of all sizes. It ruins the investigation if some of the fish are small enough to get through the holes in the net, or large enough to swim away before the net can reach them.*

I've decided how to select my sample. I'll say to people: 'I am doing an investigation into hair colour and eye colour. Please may I look at the colour of your hair and your eyes? I hope you do not mind me asking, but do you dye your hair?' I am going to try to include everyone in the school who has Science lessons when I do. I've asked my teacher. She says that it will be about 400 people.

Analysing your data

Investigating using the real world can generate a lot of data. You need to include all the data in your report, but you need to present it in a way that makes it easy to understand. This can be different for each investigation, and you will have to ask for advice. You then have to decide whether your data supports your original idea or prediction.

I sampled 358 people. 43 were blond, which is 12%. 61 had blue eyes, which is 17%. However, of the 43 blond people, 36 had blue eyes (84%). I think this supports my prediction that having blond hair means you are more likely to have blue eyes.

How sure?

Drawing firm conclusions from real-world situations is difficult. Consider the work of John Snow on the disease cholera. In 1854, John Snow plotted the new cases of cholera on a map. He discovered that they were clustered about a certain public water pump. At that point, all John Snow could say was that the pattern made it likely that the cholera bacteria were in the water from that pump. He then removed the handle from the pump, and the outbreak of cholera stopped. This makes it even more likely that the water from that pump contained cholera bacteria. However, to be sure, he would need to find the cholera bacteria in the water.

I was careful to say that my data only supported my idea. I would need to collect data from other schools in other countries to be sure. Maybe I could do a survey using the Internet!

Secondary data

Often scientists do not collect their own data. Published data collected by other scientists, which can be used in an investigation, is called **secondary data**. One example of this is data collected by the Hubble space telescope. Any scientist can use the data the Hubble telescope collects. There are many sources of secondary data that you could use, for example, tables of data on the planets of the Solar System, height and weight charts and weather records.

I wonder if there is any secondary data I could use on hair colour and eye colour? I'll have to do some research.

Half-way house

Often scientists work on organisms in a laboratory rather than in the real world. Moving the organisms from the real world to the laboratory reduces the number of variables, for example, it can mean that all the organisms are in the same environment, or that all have grown up under the same conditions. However, it is still difficult to be sure that what you are measuring is happening because of the experiment. In this situation, scientists use **controls**. A control is a similar organism in similar conditions, which acts as a comparison. For example, if you want to show that light is necessary for photosynthesis, you put one plant in the dark and a similar plant in the light. The plant in the light is a control. If it does not make starch, then there is something wrong with the experimental conditions.

The story of Archimedes

Think about

- How scientists test their ideas

A new image

King Hiero reigned in Ancient Greece. One day, he decided that it was time for a new look. He was tired of his old robes. Everyone was getting ready to celebrate the feast day of one of the Greek gods. This was Hiero's chance to look good and be admired by everyone in his court. 'I know what I need – a brand new crown,' he thought. He sent for the court goldsmith and gave him a lump of gold to make the crown.

Crowning glory

Days later, the goldsmith delivered the crown. 'You look a real treat, your Highness, and I'll give you a 10% royalty discount,' he declared.

The next day, the King began to have doubts. Rumours were rife about the honesty of the goldsmith. The King had a nagging suspicion that the goldsmith had kept some of the gold and put cheap silver in the crown.

a What would you do if you had a suspicion like the King's?

Archimedes to the rescue

Hiero sent for his adviser, the brilliant young scientist Archimedes. 'I am sure you are the person to prove that the goldsmith is nothing but a common crook. Just be sure you don't damage the crown because I've got nothing else to wear for the celebration.'

Back home, Archimedes realised that solving this problem would be hard if he could not damage the crown. He decided to have a bath, and called a servant to fill a bathtub for him. Still lost in thought, he took off his clothes and climbed into the bath, not noticing that it was full to the brim! As he climbed in the water overflowed onto the floor.

That moment, he had a flash of inspiration. He leapt out of the bath and ran naked through the marketplace shouting 'Eureka!' which means 'I have found it!' in Greek.

b What do you think caused the water to overflow?

Archimedes burst into the throne room. (Luckily, a servant was able to throw him a towel on the way in.) 'Your Majesty, have you got a lump of gold the same as the one you gave to the goldsmith? I have worked out a way of testing your crown.'

Archimedes placed the crown on the left-hand side of a balance and then put the lump of gold on the right-hand side. The scales balanced.

'So, my crown is all gold,' the King said, somewhat surprised.

'Wait,' explained Archimedes as he filled a large washbasin with water. The wise men of the King's court watched, thinking 'What's he going to do now?'. Archimedes carefully lowered the crown into the basin and collected the water that overflowed in a larger basin. He then did the same thing with the lump of pure gold.

'It's pushed out less water than the crown!' cried the King.

c Did the crown and the lump of gold have the same volume?

'The crown is not made of pure gold,' went on Archimedes. 'If it was pure gold, it would have pushed out the same amount of water. The goldsmith has acted dishonestly. He has used some silver in the crown and kept some of the gold for himself.'

Archimedes explained that if you take a lump of gold and a lump of silver with the same volume, the silver is lighter than gold. So to make the crown the same mass, more silver was needed. The volume of the crown was greater than it should be if it was pure gold. It took up more space and displaced more water than the block of gold.

'Send for the goldsmith! He is not going to get away with this one,' shouted King Hiero. He shook Archimedes by the hand and thanked him, saying, 'Keep that other lump of gold, my friend.'

Mass, volume and density

Of course, Archimedes' test was based on **density**. The density of a lump of material depends on its **mass** and its **volume**.

$$\text{density} = \frac{\text{mass}}{\text{volume}}$$

Metal	Density in kg/m³
Gold	19 320
Silver	10 500

d Look at the table. The density of gold is roughly twice the density of silver. The goldsmith stole some of the gold and replaced it with silver to keep the mass the same. Roughly how much greater would the volume of silver need to be than the volume of gold he stole?

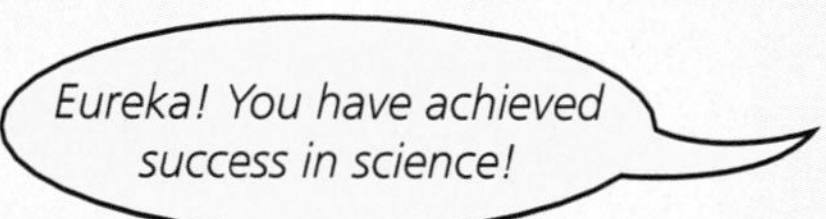

Questions

1. Why do you think that the King was surprised when the crown had the same mass as the lump of gold?
2. Do you think that Archimedes would have come up with the answer if his bath had not been full to the brim? Give a reason for your answer.
3. Explain to your partner why the crown displaced more water than the block of gold.
4. Which two variables do we have to take into account when we calculate the density of a material?
5. Imagine Archimedes weighed the new crown and found that it weighed more than the original lump of gold. The goldsmith insisted that he had put extra gold in the crown to perfect the design.
   - **a** What do you think Archimedes would have done next?
   - **b** How do you think it would be possible for Archimedes to prove that the crown has some lighter metal in it?
6. The King did not want Archimedes to damage the crown. How do you think Archimedes might have tested the crown if he could have damaged it?

Glossary

This glossary contains key words from only the first six units.

absolute zero the lowest possible temperature, at which the kinetic energy of the particles is zero. Absolute zero is about –273 °C.

active immunity someone with active immunity has been injected with a dead or inactive microbe. Their body makes antibodies which protect them from infection.

addiction the need to keep taking a drug. The user feels ill unless they can take more of the drug.

AIDS a disease that stops the immune system working. AIDS stands for acquired immune deficiency syndrome.

alcohol a legal drug found in beer, wine and spirits. It is produced by yeast during fermentation.

alveoli (singular alveolus) tiny air sacs in your lungs where gas exchange takes place

analogy a kind of comparison to help explain something

anatomy the study of the structure of the human body

antibiotic a medicine used to fight bacterial infections

antibodies chemicals produced by white blood cells to kill microbes. Each antibody kills only one type of microbe.

Archimedes screw a screw mechanism used to lift water from the ground

artificial insemination semen is put into the female's vagina through a long tube to make her pregnant without sexual intercourse

balanced equation a chemical equation that shows that the number of each type of atom is the same on both sides

balanced turning effect the effect of two turning forces of the same size acting in opposite directions around a pivot

breathing rate the number of times a person breathes in and out in one minute

bronchi (singular bronchus) two main tubes that carry air from the trachea. One bronchus leads to each lung.

bronchioles small tubes inside the lungs that carry air from the bronchi down to the alveoli

cancer a disease caused when cells divide out of control

carbon monoxide a poisonous gas found in cigarette smoke and produced in incomplete combustion

cell division the process in which one cell divides to form two cells

Celsius scale a temperature scale in which 0° is the freezing point of water and 100° is the boiling point of water. Celsius temperatures have the unit °C.

centigrade scale another name for the Celsius scale

chemical bond forces of attraction between atoms in a molecule/compound

clones organisms that have the same genes. All their genetic information has come from one parent.

competing/competition trying to get the same food source or other resources as other organisms

conduction the transfer of thermal energy from one particle to other particles that are touching it

convection the transfer of thermal energy by moving particles

convection current the movement in a liquid or a gas caused by the hotter parts rising and the cooler parts falling

correlation a link between a treatment (such as a medicine) and an effect (such as getting better)

counterbalance a weight used to balance another force, that stops something falling over

cylinder part of hydraulic and pneumatic machines. Pistons move inside cylinders.

depressant a type of drug that slows down the body's reactions and makes the user drowsy and relaxed. Alcohol is a depressant.

desirable features features that are useful, that you would choose to pass on in selective breeding

diaphragm a sheet of muscle below the lungs which helps us to breathe in and out

displace an element is displaced when it is removed from its compound by a more reactive element

displacement reaction a chemical reaction in which an element is removed from its compound by a more reactive element

dissipated spread around. When energy has been spread about evenly, we say it has been dissipated.

DNA the substance that genes are made of

dormant 'sleeping'. A dormant organism is not active.

drug a substance that when taken into the body will affect the way that the user thinks or feels

ductile can be pulled into wires

efficiency the proportion (or fraction) that ends up where you wanted it. Energy efficiency is the percentage of energy that ended up where you wanted it.

electrical conductivity how well a material conducts electrical energy

emissions the waste gases from a car exhaust or power station

equilibrium when the forces on an object are balanced, it is in equilibrium

extinct a species that becomes extinct dies out altogether

Fahrenheit scale a temperature scale in which the freezing point of water is at –32° and the boiling point of water is at 212°. Fahrenheit temperatures have the unit °F.

formal model a model that scientists use to explain what is happening when they can't see it

fungi (singular fungus) a group of organisms, separate from animals, plants and bacteria. Some fungi are microorganisms, like yeast and mould. Some fungi are quite large, like mushrooms and toadstools.

galvanisation coating an iron object with a more reactive metal such as zinc, to protect it from rusting

gas exchange the movement of oxygen from the lungs into the blood, and of carbon dioxide from the blood into the lungs. Gas exchange happens across the walls of the alveoli.

gears a machine made from several cogs (wheels) with teeth that turn each other

genes instructions for features which are passed on from parents to offspring

genetic engineering taking a gene out of one species and putting it into another to give desirable features

genetically modified (GM) food food produced from crops or other organisms that have had their genes changed by genetic engineering

germination the start of growth of a seed. Germination happens when conditions are right.

gravitational potential energy energy stored in an object because the object has been lifted up

group I the elements in the far left-hand column of the periodic table

hallucination seeing things that are not really there. Hallucinations can be caused by drugs.

hallucinogen a type of drug that causes the user to see things that are not really there. LSD is a hallucinogen.

hibernation sleeping through winter to avoid harsh conditions

hydraulic machine a machine that works by transferring pressure through a liquid

hyphae long thread-like tubes that form the main body of many types of fungi such as mould

illegal against the law

immune system an organ system that protects the body from infection by microbes

immune a person who is immune to a disease-causing microbe does not become ill when they meet that microbe

inclined plane a simple machine consisting of a slope, used to make it easier to lift heavy objects

incomplete combustion combustion that is inefficient because not enough oxygen gets to the fuel. It produces poisonous carbon monoxide.

infection an infection is caused when a microbe gets inside the body and grows and multiplies

infrared radiation infrared radiation transfers thermal energy from a hotter object to a cooler object. It is like light but has too low a frequency for us to see it.

inherited passed on from one from generation to the next

Glossary continued

interdependent relying on each other. Different species in a habitat are interdependent – they rely on each other for food.

internal energy the sum of the kinetic energy of all the particles inside an object

kelvin scale a temperature scale in which absolute zero is 0 and each degree is the same size as 1 °C. Kelvin temperatures have the unit K.

lactation producing milk

larynx a part of the trachea which produces your voice. The larynx is also called the voicebox.

lava magma (molten rock) that pours out of a volcano

lever a simple machine for lifting objects, that turns around a pivot

lichen a living thing made up of an alga and a fungus living together

load a force that is moved by a machine. The load is often the weight of an object.

magma molten rock

malleable can be pushed (beaten) into sheets

medicine a drug that if used correctly can make the body work properly or get better

microbe a living thing that can only be seen clearly with a microscope. Microbe is another word for microorganism.

micrometre very small things are measured in micrometres. A micrometre is one-thousandth of a millimetre (a millionth of a metre).

migration moving long distances to another country. For example, some birds fly to warmer climates in the winter, where it is easier to find food.

milk yield the amount of milk a cow produces

moment the turning effect of a force around a pivot. The moment of a force depends on the size of the force and its distance from the pivot.

newton metre the moment of a force is measured in newton metres

newton per square metre pressure is measured in newtons per square metre

nicotine an addictive chemical, found in cigarette smoke

nocturnal describes animals that are active at night

offspring new organisms made by reproduction

ovum egg

ozone a toxic form of oxygen

pascal pressure is measured in pascals. One pascal is equal to one newton per square metre.

passive immunity someone with passive immunity has been injected with ready-made antibodies

passive smoking breathing in smoke from other people's cigarettes

pathogen an organism that causes disease

photochemical smog the haze formed when the sun shines on nitrogen oxides and hydrocarbons in the air. Ozone is produced in the smog by chemical reactions.

physiology the study of how the organs of the human body work

piston part of hydraulic and pneumatic machines that acts like a plunger, moving in and out of the cylinder

pivot the point around which a lever turns

placebo 'dummy' tablets or medicine used as a control when testing new medicines. A placebo contains no medicine at all.

pneumatic machine a machine that works by transferring pressure through a compressed gas

population the number of organisms of a particular species living in a habitat

potential energy stored energy. Potential energy usually means energy stored in an object because the object has been lifted up.

precipitate a solid mass that falls out of a solution

predation one animal (the predator) hunts and eats another animal (the prey)

pressure the effect of a force spread out over an area

principle of moments this states that when two moments are balanced, the sum of the anticlockwise moments equals the sum of the clockwise moments

probability the chance of an event happening

pulley a simple machine made from ropes and wheels, which can make it easier to lift something

pyramid of numbers a diagram that we can draw if we count the number of organisms at each level in a food chain

radiation the transfer of thermal energy by infrared radiation (which is similar to light but has too low a frequency for us to see it)

reactive a reactive substance takes part in chemical reactions, usually quickly and releasing lots of energy

reactivity how reactive a substance is, or how easily it takes part in chemical reactions

reactivity series a list of metals arranged in order of reactivity with the most reactive at the top

resistant bacteria may become resistant to an antibiotic. The antibiotic does not kill the resistant bacteria.

sankey diagram a diagram that shows the amount of energy being transferred. The widths of the lines show the amounts of energy.

selective breeding choosing parents with desirable features to produce new varieties of animals or plants that have their desirable features

sexually transmitted disease a disease that is spread from one person to another during sexual intercourse, for example AIDS

solvent abuse breathing in the fumes from some glues, paints and lighter fluids. Solvent abuse damages the brain, liver and kidneys.

stamina the ability to exercise for long time without getting tired

stimulant a type of drug that speeds up the body's reactions and makes the user feel they have lots of energy. Caffeine and cocaine are stimulants.

strength the ability of muscles to exert a force on bones

suppleness the ability to move the body and limbs easily

tar a sticky black substance found in cigarette smoke. It clogs the alveoli and stops the lungs working properly. It can cause cancer.

temperature this measures the average amount of kinetic energy of the particles in a material

thermal conductivity how well a material conducts thermal energy

trachea the tube that leads from the mouth to the lungs. The trachea is also called the windpipe.

transition metals the elements in the centre section of the periodic table

tumour a rapidly dividing ball of cells caused by cancer

turning effect when there is a force on an object and the force arrow is to one side of the pivot, the force has a turning effect on the object

unbalanced turning effect the effect of two turning forces of different sizes acting in opposite directions around a pivot

unit of alcohol the amount of alcohol found in half a pint of beer, a small glass of wine or a measure of spirits

unreactive an unreactive substance does not take part in chemical reactions, or does so only slowly

vaccinated injected with a vaccine so that you become immune to a disease

volcano a hole in the Earth's crust that magma comes out of

water pressure the pressure in water. It is caused because water pushes on objects from all sides as the water particles collide with the object.

wheel and axle a simple machine. The wheel turns in a bigger circle than the axle, which makes some jobs easier.

white blood cell part of the immune system. White blood cells fight infection by producing antibodies or by swallowing up microbes.

Index

Note: page numbers in **bold** show where a word is **explained** in the text.
There are also definitions in the Glossary on page 134-7.

D

E

Index continued

H

I

J

K

L

R

S

Index continued

Heinemann Educational Publishers
Halley Court, Jordan Hill, Oxford, OX2 8EJ
a division of Reed Educational & Professional Publishing Ltd
Heinemann is a registered trademark of Reed Educational & Professional Publishing Ltd

OXFORD MELBOURNE AUCKLAND
JOHANNESBURG BLANTYRE GABORONE
IBADAN PORTSMOUTH NH (USA) CHICAGO

First published 2001

ISBN 0 435 57645 3

05 04 03 02
10 9 8 7 6 5 4 3 2

Edited by Ruth Holmes

Index by Indexing specialists

Designed and typeset by Ken Vail Graphic Design, Cambridge

Original illustration © Heinemann Educational Publishers 2001

Illustrated by Graham-Cameron Illustration (Harriet Buckley), Nick Hawken, Margaret Jones, B L Kearley Ltd (Shirley Bellwood), David Lock, Richard Morris, John Plumb, Sylvie Poggio Artists Agency (Tim Davies, Rhiannon Powell).

Printed and bound in Spain by Edelvives

Picture research by Jennifer Johnson

Acknowledgments
The authors and publishers would like to thank the following for permission to use copyright material:
extract, p15, Orion Publishing Co. *The Double Helix*; **table p24**, Avoncroft Sires Ltd;
leaflet p 68, Health Education Authority

The publishers have made every effort to trace the copyright holders, but if they have inadvertently overlooked any, they will be pleased to make the necessary arrangements at the first opportunity.

The authors and publishers would like to thank the following for permission to use photographs:

Cover photos: Solar energy receiver array, Tony Stone Images. **Hippo under water,** Tony Stone Images. **Mushroom-shaped rock pedestal**, Science Photo Library/Allan Morgan, Peter Arnold Inc.

1.1c, d Mary Evans Picture Library. **1.2a** Peter Gould. **1.2d** Environmental Images. **1.3b** Holt/Nigel Cattlin. **1.3c** Andrew Lambert. **1.3e** Environmental Images/Robert Brook. **1.5a** Peter Gould. **1.6a** Science Photo Library. **2.1b** Mary Evans Picture Library. **2.1c** Wellcome Trust. **2.1d** (a), (b) Science Photo Library/Dr Yorgos Nikas, (c) Science Photo Library/Don Fawcett. **2.1f** Science Photo Library/Ken Eward. **2.1g** Science Photo Library. **2.2a** Sally and Richard Greenhill. **2.3c** Andrew Lambert. **2.3e** Bruce Coleman/Kim Taylor. **2.3f** Holt Studios. **2.3h** (a) Holt Studios, (b) Bruce Coleman/Hans Reinhard, (c) Bruce Coleman/Jane Burton. **2.4e** Oxford Scientific Films/Alistair Shay. **2.6a** Frank Lane/R. Bird (2 pictures). **2.6b** Avoncroft. **2.6e** (a) Holt Studios/John Velton, (b) Holt Studios/Nigel Cattlin. **2.6f** Still Pictures/Nick Cobbings. **2.7e** Panos Pictures/Sean Sprague. **3.2g** Bruce Coleman/Hans Ranhard. **3.2e, f** Gareth Boden (2 pictures). **3.4b** Robert Harding. **3.4d** Empics (3 pictures). **3.4e** Science Photo Library/John Daughter. **3.4f** Gareth Boden (2 pictures). **3.5c** Bruce Coleman/Pacific Stock. **3.6c** Robert Harding. **3.7c** Eye Ubiquitous/Corbis/R. Obert and Linda Mostyn. **4.1a** Science Photo Library. **4.2b** Geoscience Features/A. Fisher. **4.2d, 4.3a, b, c, d, e, 4.4a, c** Peter Gould. **4.4d** Beken of Cowes. **4.6a** Science Photo Library/John Mead. **4.6b** Peter Gould. **5.1a** Science Photo Library/Antonia Reeve. **5.1c** Mary Evans Picture Library. **5.1d** SmithKline Beecham. **5.1b** Mary Evans Picture Library. **5.1g** Science Photo Library/GSL/CRRI. **5.1h** Mary Evans Picture Library. **5.2e** Empics. **5.4a** Science Photo Library/A. Glauberman. **5.4c** DETR. **5.5c** Science Photo Library/Andrew Syred. **5.5e** Science Photo Library. **5.6a** (a) Science Photo Library/CNRI, (b) Science Photo Library/H. C. Robinson, (c) Science Photo Library/Dr P. Marazzi. **5.6c** Science Photo Library/Eye of Science. **5.7a** Gareth Boden. **5.7b** NHS. **5.7c** (a) Andrew Lambert, (b) Science Photo Library/BSI/P. Beranger, (c) Science Photo Library/Conor Caffrey, (d) Science Photo Library/TekImage. **5.8a** Science Photo Library/TekImage. **6.1c** Science Photo Library. **6.1j** Science Photo Library/US Navy. **6.2c** Gareth Boden. **6.2d** Science Photo Library/F. Chillmaid. **6.2e** Stock Market/Kunio Swaki. **6.2f** Gareth Boden. **6.2g** Science Photo Library/Simon Fraser. **6.2h** Science Photo Library/James Holmes. **6.3f** Science Photo Library/Dr Jeremy Burgess. **6.4e, f, 6.5b** Peter Gould. **6.5f** Science Photo Library. **6.5g** Empics/Ted Leicester. **6.7a** Peter Gould. **7.6d** Environmental Images/Daphne Christelis. **8.5c** Peter Gould.

Tel: 01865 888058 www.heinemann.co.uk